WRITING PRACTICE

The Practice Book also provides reinforcement for the lessons relat[ed to]
writing concepts and skills. Each writing chapter in the Practice Book
features two pages related to the specific genre of the Student Edition
lesson and three pages related to specific writing skills, word study,
and study skills.

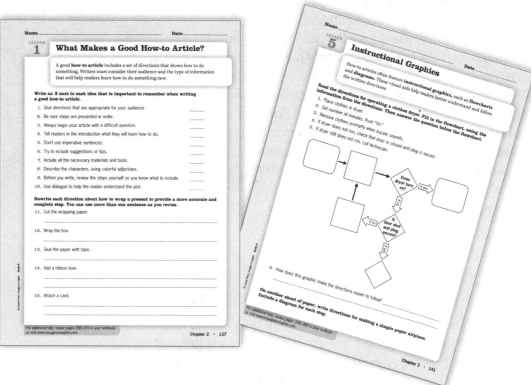

THROUGHOUT THE PRACTICE PAGES

Key concept boxes at the
top of every practice page
remind students of definitions
or important rules.

The *Voyages in English* **Web site**
and the corresponding Student Edition
lesson page numbers are listed to
assist parents or others who may
be helping students complete the
Practice Book page.

Plenty of meaningful,
challenging practice

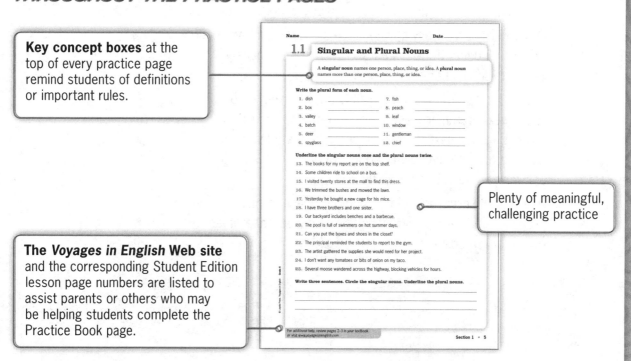

DAILY MAINTENANCE

A new feature of the Practice Book, Daily Maintenance, allows students to maintain grammar proficiency in concepts that have already been taught and mastered. This brief daily quiz and sentence diagramming exercise provides students with consistent reinforcement of previously taught grammar concepts for long-term understanding and application. Each lesson's Daily Maintenance exercise is designed to focus on grammar concepts to which students have already been introduced.

Teaching students how to approach this feature will increase its effectiveness. By establishing a routine, students will expect each grammar lesson to begin with Daily Maintenance and will automatically settle into the process. Allow students up to 15 minutes in the first two weeks of use; seven minutes should be the goal.

FOLLOW THESE STEPS TO BEGIN THE GRAMMAR LESSON

1. Direct students' attention to the day's Daily Maintenance section. Have partners discuss the items, using their notes or textbooks as reference tools.

2. Have students put away books and notes and complete the Daily Maintenance exercise independently. Allow five minutes.

3. Either correct the Daily Maintenance at a later time yourself or have students trade pages and correct immediately. Students should not mark their own papers.

4. Review incorrect items immediately after correction or prior to the next grammar lesson. Ask students to record the correct answer next to each error. To help students avoid future errors, model how to apply grammar concepts to answer each question correctly.

5. Use your observations and student feedback to plan whole-group or small-group mini-lessons for concepts that need review or remediation.

GRADING DAILY MAINTENANCE

Daily Maintenance exercises are not meant to be tests; they are designed to strengthen learning. Because this information is review and not being formally taught, it should not impact the progress report grade. It is recommended that Daily Maintenance exercises be averaged for the quarter or trimester and counted as one grade of many, or weighted as only five percent of the report card grade.

IMPORTANT POINTS TO REMEMBER

- Keep track of the time. Daily Maintenance exercises are meant to be completed quickly and should not become the lesson itself.

- Assign the Daily Maintenance exercise at the beginning of each grammar class, not as homework. Immediate teacher feedback and modeling ensures this feature's success.

- Have students complete the appropriate Daily Maintenance section, not the entire page of Daily Maintenance. Using Daily Maintenance pages as worksheets reduces the activity to "busywork" with no real learning outcome.

When used correctly, the consistent implementation of the Daily Maintenance feature can eliminate the need to remediate grammar concepts that students have already been taught and allow the much-needed time for instruction and mastery of grade-level grammar concepts.

SECTION 1 Daily Maintenance

1.1 Our friends will meet us at the mall.
1. What is the complete subject of the sentence?
2. What is the simple predicate?
3. What is the object of the verb?
4. What kind of word is *Our*?
5. Diagram the sentence here.

1.2 He is reading a book about Dolores Huerta.
1. What is the simple predicate of the sentence?
2. What tense is the verb?
3. Which word is an article?
4. Which word is a proper noun?
5. Diagram the sentence here.

1.3 The frightened mice quickly scurried under the brush.
1. What are the nouns in the sentence?
2. Which noun is an irregular plural?
3. Which word is an adjective?
4. What is the prepositional phrase?
5. Diagram the sentence here.

1.4 She will give us the keys to the cabin on Monday.
1. What is the tense of the verb?
2. What is the direct object?
3. What is the indirect object?
4. What is the singular pronoun?
5. Diagram the sentence here.

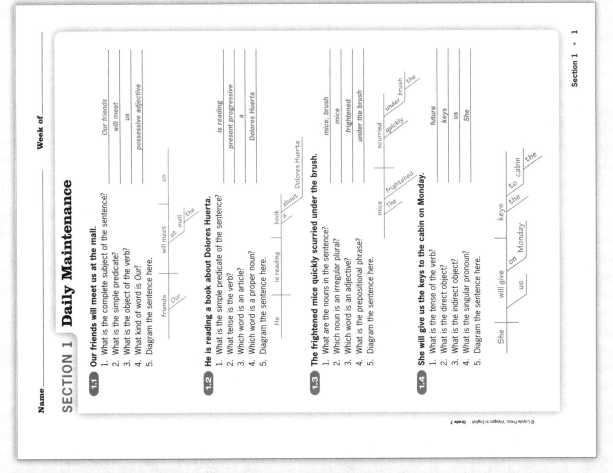

1.5 Eric and Mia saw Jim at the movies yesterday.
1. Is the verb regular or irregular?
2. Is the subject simple or compound?
3. What is the adverb?
4. Does the adverb show time, manner, or place?
5. Diagram the sentence here.

1.6 I cleared the table and washed the dirty dishes.
1. Is the subject or predicate compound?
2. What is the adjective?
3. Which word is a conjunction?
4. Is this sentence declarative or interrogative?
5. Diagram the sentence here.

1.1 Singular and Plural Nouns

Most **plural nouns** are formed by adding -s. Some plurals are formed by adding -es. Some plurals are not formed by adding -s or -es.

Write the plural form of each noun.

1. chair — *chairs*
2. variety — *varieties*
3. wheat — *wheat*
4. trout — *trout*
5. waltz — *waltzes*
6. dish — *dishes*
7. country — *countries*
8. tax — *taxes*

Underline each singular noun. Then write each singular noun's plural form.

9. The teams line up while each spectator fidgets on a bench. — *spectators, benches*
10. The mascots are a cougar and a fox. — *cougars, foxes*
11. I glance at my watch and the scoreboard. — *watches, scoreboards*
12. The quarterback catches the football and runs. — *quarterbacks, footballs*
13. The green team chases him while the crowd cheers. — *teams, crowds*
14. That small player is incredibly fast and agile. — *players*
15. He tackles our teammate and the pigskin disappears. — *teammates, pigskins*
16. Chaos ensues until a man screams "He's got it!" — *Chaos, men*
17. Our boys are running to the end zone. — *zones*
18. The running back does a victory dance. — *backs, dances*
19. It is a victory like this game that builds team spirit. — *victories, games, spirits*
20. The dentist checked my tooth for a cavity. — *dentists, teeth, cavities*
21. Can a louse bother a mouse or only bother a human? — *lice, mice, humans*
22. A lone deer stood still as a statue next to the tree. — *deer, statues, trees*

Choose four plural nouns from above, and write a sentence for each.

23. *Answers will vary, but each sentence should include at least one plural noun.*
24.
25.
26.

© Loyola Press, Voyages in English Grade 7
For additional help, review pages 2–3 in your textbook or visit www.voyagesinenglish.com.

1.2 More Singular and Plural Nouns

Most **plural nouns** are formed by adding -s. Some plurals are formed by adding -es. Some plurals have spelling changes but do not add -s or -es. Other plurals do not change from their singular forms.

Write the plural form of each noun. Use a dictionary to check your answers.

1. knife — *knives*
2. video — *videos*
3. hero — *heroes*
4. potato — *potatoes*
5. belief — *beliefs*
6. brother-in-law — *brothers-in-law*
7. passerby — *passersby*
8. sandbox — *sandboxes*
9. tomato — *tomatoes*
10. cliff — *cliffs*

Underline each singular noun once. Underline each plural noun twice.

11. My father's reasons for planting a garden are a mystery to us.
12. Every winter, he sits with seed catalogs piled by his chair.
13. He orders many different varieties of tomato plants, potatoes, and beans.
14. In the spring, the seeds and plants come in the mail.
15. After he plants them, he complains all evening about his back and his shoulders.
16. He spends long hours weeding the garden every weekend.
17. During harvest time, he picks bushels of red ripe tomatoes and succulent beans.
18. Then he eats tomato sandwiches, baked potatoes, and steamed beans at every meal!

Complete each sentence. Underline each singular noun once and each plural noun twice. *Answers will vary.*

19. I do not like
20. I really enjoy
21. In the fall, I like to see
22. My favorite book is about
23. Eventually I plan to
24. When I was younger, I
25. I want
26. Some of my favorite foods are

© Loyola Press, Voyages in English Grade 7
For additional help, review pages 4–5 in your textbook or visit www.voyagesinenglish.com.

1.3 Nouns as Subjects and Subject Complements

The **subject** tells what the sentence is about. A **subject complement** renames the subject; it refers to the same person, place, thing, or idea. A subject complement follows a linking verb.

Underline the subject of each sentence once. Underline each subject complement twice. Not all the sentences have subject complements.

1. My oldest brother is a pediatric doctor at County Hospital.
2. The wet newspaper lay at the end of the long, winding driveway.
3. The princess of that tiny country is a college student at the university.
4. Mrs. Green is my favorite math teacher at Seaside Middle School.
5. The fireworks lit up the night sky and filled the air with booms, whistles, and pops.
6. The campfire threw off sparks when John set another log on it.
7. Night crawlers are excellent bait for some freshwater fish, such as trout, carp, and walleye.
8. The seventh-grade class prepared for the trip to Washington, D.C.
9. The girls are members of the traveling soccer team.
10. The winners of the three-legged race were this pair of boys.
11. This former astronaut was also a professor at a nearby university.
12. The people in the newspaper story are heroes and should be recognized for their efforts.

Write whether each italicized noun is a _subject_ or _subject complement_. Then underline the noun each subject complement renames.

13. Natalie's necklace is made of gold and silver. _____ subject
14. The new rock band is _Seven Penguins_. _____ subject complement
15. The tart apple was a crisp surprise. _____ subject complement
16. A raisin was found on the windowsill. _____ subject
17. This quaint town is Four Corners. _____ subject

Write a subject complement to complete each sentence. *Possible responses are given.*

18. The bus is _an alternate form of transportation_.
19. His movie was _an eye-opening experience_.
20. The music was _a screeching horror_.
21. Our class is _a well-oiled machine_.
22. Many students are _community volunteers_.

For additional help, review pages 6–7 in your textbook or visit www.voyagesinenglish.com.

6 • Section 1

© Loyola Press. Voyages in English Grade 7

1.2 More Singular and Plural Nouns

Most **plural** nouns are formed by adding -s. Some plurals are formed by adding -es. Some plurals have spelling changes but do not add -s or -es. Other plurals do not change from their singular forms.

Underline each singular noun once. Underline each plural noun twice.

1. Did you untangle your hair with the green comb?
2. I will make your copies after I finish printing these.
3. Raul prefers plain water, but Gabriel's drink is orange juice.
4. Check these problems because these numbers do not make sense.
5. The green apple in the basket will last the longest.

Complete each sentence with the plural form of the noun in parenthesis.

6. Amy Tan was born in Oakland, California, to Chinese-born _parents_ (parent).
7. She is the author of many _stories_ (story) and _novels_ (novel).
8. Ms. Tan's books appeal to _men_ (man) and women across many _cultures_ (culture).
9. Her stories often highlight the _challenges_ (challenge) of cross-cultural living.
10. Amy Tan wrote her first book after meeting her _half sisters_ (half sister) in China.
11. In _The Joy Luck Club_, the author explores the different _points of view_ (point of view) held by mothers and daughters.
12. _The Joy Luck Club_ is divided into 16 _chapters_ (chapter).
13. She has written many other _books_ (book).
14. They also explore the relationships among mothers, daughters, and _sisters_ (sister).
15. Amy Tan also plays in a band that raises money for various _charities_ (charity).

Write a sentence using the plural form of each noun. *Possible responses are given.*

16. radio, patio The patios each had two radios.
17. dish, shelf The clean dishes were stacked on the shelves.
18. thief, roof Thieves used the roofs as nighttime highways.
19. medium, video Videos are more popular than most media.
20. goose, mouse The story was about a gaggle of geese and a nest of mice.

For additional help, review pages 4–5 in your textbook or visit www.voyagesinenglish.com.

Section 1 • 5

© Loyola Press. Voyages in English Grade 7

1.4 Nouns as Objects and Object Complements

The **direct object** tells *whom* or *what* after the verb. An **indirect object** tells *to whom* or *for whom*, or *to what* or *for what* the action is done. A noun can also be the **object of a preposition** or an **object complement**.

Write whether each italicized noun is a direct object, an indirect object, an object of a preposition, or an object complement.

1. Music lovers consider Scott Joplin a popular composer. — *object complement*
2. Ragtime music started as African American dance music. — *object of a preposition*
3. Eventually it became popular with the general public. — *object of a preposition*
4. Ragtime played a part in the development of jazz. — *direct object*
5. Scott Joplin wrote and performed *ragtime*. — *direct object*
6. This music is a kind of march that depends on *syncopation*. — *object of a preposition*
7. Syncopation highlights unexpected beats. — *direct object*
8. This rhythm gave the *music* the name "ragged time." — *indirect object*
9. Later "ragged time" was shortened to *ragtime*. — *object of a preposition*
10. Ragtime became less popular after Scott Joplin died. — *object of a preposition*
11. Many people declare Joplin's music a great achievement. — *object complement*
12. He remains the best known ragtime figure in *history*. — *object of a preposition*
13. Ragtime music is still popular among many piano *players*. — *object of a preposition*

Write sentences using each of the following at least once: a direct object, an indirect object, an object of a preposition, and an object complement. *Answers will vary.*

14. _____
15. _____
16. _____
17. _____

For additional help, review pages 8–9 in your textbook or visit www.voyagesinenglish.com.

© Loyola Press, Voyages in English **Grade 7**

1.4 Nouns as Objects and Object Complements

The **direct object** tells *whom* or *what* after the verb. An **indirect object** tells *to whom* or *for whom*, or *to what* or *for what* the action is done. A noun can also be the **object of a preposition** or an **object complement**.

Write whether each italicized noun is a direct object or an indirect object.

1. I threw the ball for my dog. — *direct object*
2. She taught *Milo* to read simple books. — *direct object*
3. We sang funny *songs* as we strolled the halls. — *direct object*
4. Hank gave the *postmaster* five dollars for postage. — *indirect object*
5. Millie and Seymour baked a delicious cake. — *direct object*
6. Eva bought a box of chocolates for her aunt. — *direct object*
7. Josh sent his *uncle* a batch of brownies. — *indirect object*
8. Dr. Hawkins stitched the cut on her finger. — *direct object*
9. The giraffe chewed the *leaves* on the tallest branches. — *direct object*
10. Our team yelled a cheer for Leon after his amazing catch. — *direct object*

Write a noun to complete each object of a preposition. *Answers will vary.*
11. The embroidery on the _____ was done by _____.
12. The rain fell on the _____ and ruined it.
13. We will leave after the _____.
14. We sent a quart of soup to _____ in hopes it would help her get well.
15. We walked into _____ without any fear.
16. Several people travel over _____ every _____.
17. In _____, the leaves of _____ turn a variety of _____.

Write an object complement to rename each direct object. *Possible responses are given.*
18. The students elected Helena *the class representative*
19. The team selected Josh *our captain*
20. The teachers announced the concert *a success*
21. The entire group unanimously declared blue and gold *the official colors*
22. Katrina and Josie chose flowers *the best gift*

For additional help, review pages 8–9 in your textbook or visit www.voyagesinenglish.com.

© Loyola Press, Voyages in English **Grade 7**

1.5 Appositives

An **appositive** renames a noun. A **restrictive appositive** is necessary in order to understand the sentence. A **nonrestrictive appositive** is not necessary to understand the sentence and is set off with a comma or commas.

Underline each appositive. Circle the noun it explains. Write *R* if the appositive is restrictive and *N* if it is nonrestrictive.

1. (Jackie Robinson), the grandson of slaves, broke professional baseball's color barrier. N
2. The Dodgers retired Robinson's (number), 42, in 1972. N
3. Branch Rickey was manager of a baseball (team), the Brooklyn Dodgers. N
4. The great (right-hander) Cy Young was a legendary baseball pitcher. R
5. John learned the Boy Scout (slogan) "Do a Good Turn Daily." N
6. The famous (songwriter) Cole Porter was named after his mother's last name. R
7. Chris loves to eat (chorizo), a spicy sausage. N
8. The American (composer) Aaron Copland meant to develop a uniquely American form of classical music. R
9. The (national poet) Robert Frost recited one of his own works at the inauguration. R
10. (Ryan), my brother, loves to play hockey after school. N

Use each set of words to write a sentence using an appositive. *Possible responses are given.*

11. Albert Einstein (genius)
The genius Albert Einstein was a poor student in his youth.

12. African American Olympic champion (Jesse Owens)
Jesse Owens, the African American Olympic champion, befriended some of his competitors.

13. Pennsylvania (the Keystone State)
Pennsylvania, the Keystone State, is north of Virginia and West Virginia.

14. goal (to improve my soccer game)
My father respected my goal, to improve my soccer game.

15. our sponsor (Ed's Tires and Brakes)
We thanked our sponsor, Ed's Tires and Brakes.

For additional help, review pages 10–11 in your textbook or visit www.voyagesinenglish.com.

1.5 Appositives

An **appositive** renames a noun. A **restrictive appositive** is necessary in order to understand the sentence. A **nonrestrictive appositive** is not necessary to understand the sentence and is set off with a comma or commas.

Circle the appositives. Then underline the noun each appositive explains.

1. Sheila, my (cousin) works in that department store.
2. I love to visit Pine Acres, our (cabin) in the mountains.
3. Our neighbor (Paul) is away on vacation.
4. The black widow, a (spider) is poisonous.
5. Mr. James, the (principal) is in the cafeteria with his brother, the third-grade (teacher).
6. Our dog (Blue) likes to climb up and sit in my lap.
7. My friend (Bindi) comes from India.
8. The Nile, a (river), is located in Africa.
9. Albert Einstein, a (physicist), revolutionized the study of space.
10. Springfield, the (capital) of Illinois, is my hometown.
11. The actor (Katharine Hepburn) has won more Oscars than any other actor.
12. Portland, the largest (city) in Oregon, is wet and rainy most of the year.

Write a sentence using each phrase in parentheses as an appositive to explain the italicized noun. Add commas as needed.

13. Grandma likes to play *mah jongg*. (a Chinese board game)
Grandma likes to play mah jongg, a Chinese board game.

14. Pablo Picasso was an influential figure in the visual arts. (the cofounder of cubism)
Pablo Picasso, the cofounder of cubism, was an influential figure in the visual arts.

15. *Charlie Chaplin* lived from 1889 to 1977. (the legendary actor)
Charlie Chaplin, the legendary actor, lived from 1889 to 1977.

16. Irving Berlin wrote *"White Christmas."* (the best-selling song of all time)
Irving Berlin wrote "White Christmas," the best-selling song of all time.

17. *Jim Thorpe* excelled in baseball, football, and track and field. (the great American athlete)
Jim Thorpe, the great American athlete, excelled in baseball, football, and track and field.

For additional help, review pages 10–11 in your textbook or visit www.voyagesinenglish.com.

1.6 Possessive Nouns

When nouns are used together to show **separate possession**, -'s is added to each noun. If the nouns show **joint possession**, -'s is added after the last noun.

Write _S_ if the sentence shows separate possession. Write _J_ if the sentence shows joint possession.

1. Kara and Anthony's paper was about the Great Depression.   _J_
2. Jake's and Jill's rattles are in the crib.   _S_
3. Men's and boys' pants are sold in that department.   _S_
4. My cousin and aunt's house is in Texas.   _J_
5. Lakesha and Chelsea's poster won the contest.   _J_
6. Mr. Clark's and Mrs. Williams's classrooms are next to each other.   _S_
7. The admiral's and the general's orders were given to the troops.   _S_
8. Lucky and Pretty Boy's birdcage is in the kitchen.   _J_

Rewrite each sentence to indicate separate possession.

9. Katrina and Josie projects were completed before Michael project.
   Katrina's and Josie's projects were completed before Michael's project.

10. We will visit San Francisco and Oakland museums next spring.
    We will visit San Francisco's and Oakland's museums next spring.

11. Do you think we can borrow Arif and Jaden bikes for the camping trip?
    Do you think we can borrow Arif's and Jaden's bikes for the camping trip?

12. I thought Rivu and Bryce paintings showed incredible talent.
    I thought Rivu's and Bryce's paintings showed incredible talent.

13. Chris and Paige dogs were barking all night and kept us awake.
    Chris's and Paige's dogs were barking all night and kept us awake.

14. Tiko and Onose pencils are blue, but mine are yellow.
    Tiko's and Onose's pencils are blue, but mine are yellow.

15. The president and vice president goals were nearly identical on this issue.
    The president's and vice president's goals were nearly identical on this issue.

For additional help, review pages 12–13 in your textbook or visit www.voyagesinenglish.com.

© Loyola Press. Voyages in English **Grade 7**

1.6 Possessive Nouns

A **possessive noun** expresses possession or ownership. To form the singular possessive, add -'s to the singular form of the noun, even if the noun ends in s. To form the possessive of plural nouns ending in s, add the apostrophe only.

Write the singular possessive and the plural possessive forms of each noun.

1. tomato — _tomato's_ — _tomatoes'_
2. country — _country's_ — _countries'_
3. salmon — _salmon's_ — _salmon's_
4. cliff — _cliff's_ — _cliffs'_
5. loaf — _loaf's_ — _loaves'_
6. cross — _cross's_ — _crosses'_
7. key — _key's_ — _keys'_
8. attorney-at-law — _attorney-at-law's_ — _attorneys-at-law's_
9. Chris — _Chris's_ — _Chrises'_

Underline each possessive noun. Write _S_ if it is singular and _P_ if it is plural.

10. The new radios were stacked neatly on <u>Sandy's</u> shelf.   _S_
11. The scientist crawled into the <u>wolves'</u> den to study their habits.   _P_
12. <u>Eli's</u> science project was very well prepared and deserved a high grade.   _S_
13. We went from <u>Odette's</u> house to <u>Cayla's</u> pool where I borrowed the <u>twins'</u> towel.   _S_ _S_ _P_
14. The <u>plants'</u> gorgeous coloring was nearly hidden by the thick grasses.   _P_
15. The <u>Stevens's</u> yard was covered in the old <u>oak's</u> autumn leaves.   _S_ _S_
16. The <u>reindeer's</u> hooves thundered as they passed over the <u>tundra's</u> frozen ground.   _P_ _S_
17. Mrs. <u>Michael's</u> <u>dogs'</u> bones were scattered among the pebbles in the tiny yard.   _S_ _P_

For additional help, review pages 12–13 in your textbook or visit www.voyagesinenglish.com.

© Loyola Press. Voyages in English **Grade 7**

SECTION 2 Daily Maintenance

2.1 **The attorneys are presenting their arguments to the judge.**
1. What are the nouns in the sentence? _____ attorneys, arguments, judge
2. Which noun is singular? _____ judge
3. What tense is the verb? _____ present progressive
4. What kind of word is *their*? _____ possessive adjective
5. Diagram the sentence here.

attorneys | are presenting | arguments
The | | to | their
judge
the

2.2 **His sister is the best singer in the choir.**
1. Which noun is the subject of the sentence? _____ sister
2. Which noun is the subject complement? _____ singer
3. What is the simple predicate in the sentence? _____ is
4. What kind of verb is it? _____ linking
5. Diagram the sentence here.

sister | is | singer
His | best | the
in | choir
the

2.3 **The players chose Max captain of the football team.**
1. Which noun is a direct object? _____ Max
2. Which noun is an object complement? _____ captain
3. What is the prepositional phrase? _____ of the football team
4. What is the object of the preposition? _____ team
5. Diagram the sentence here.

players | chose | Max | captain
The | | of | team
the | football

2.4 **My friend Nicole is an accomplished violinist.**
1. What is the appositive in the sentence? _____ Nicole
2. What noun does it explain? _____ friend
3. Is the appositive restrictive or nonrestrictive? _____ restrictive
4. What part of speech is the word *an*? _____ article
5. Diagram the sentence here.

friend (Nicole) | is | violinist
My | an | accomplished

2.5 **The women's restroom is near the teachers' lounge.**
1. What are the possessive nouns in the sentence? _____ women's, teachers'
2. Are these nouns singular or plural? _____ plural
3. Which word is a preposition? _____ near
4. What is the object of the preposition? _____ lounge
5. Diagram the sentence here.

restroom | is | near | lounge
The | women's | | the | teachers'

2.1 Descriptive Adjectives, Position of Adjectives

A descriptive adjective gives information, such as color, number, or size, about a noun or pronoun. Adjectives may come before a noun, directly following a noun, as a subject complement, or as an object complement.

Underline the descriptive adjectives. Then circle the noun each adjective modifies.

1. Every wonderful (vista) gave me insight into why tourists choose to visit this area.
2. The quarrelsome (children) settled into an peaceful (slumber).
3. (Melanie) is so calm and thoughtful.
4. I decided nine (guests) were more than enough after I calculated the cost of each meal.
5. The young (man) is exceptionally skillful with this difficult (program).

Underline each adjective. Identify its position by writing _BN_ if the adjective comes before the noun it describes, _AN_ if it comes after the noun, _SC_ if it is a subject complement, or _OC_ if it is an object complement.

6. Elliot is talented and creative. _SC, SC_
7. The orange seed pod on that plant is delicate. _BN, BN, SC_
8. The ripe tomato is just the size for a delicious salad. _BN, BN_
9. My brother found the golf tournament difficult. _BN, OC_
10. In the spring the lush green hills invite us all to go for a hike. _BN, BN_
11. The persistent runner pushed through the crowd to the finish. _BN_
12. Mr. Lee was short-tempered, but he was also fair. _SC, SC_
13. I really love taffy, chewy and sweet. _AN, AN_

Write a descriptive adjective to complete each sentence. _Possible responses are given._

14. I decided to buy _seven_ watermelons.
15. My favorite food is _sweet_ and _salty_.
16. We all sat around the _long_ table.
17. Tenicia dyed the fabric _maroon_.
18. Kay writes _lyrical_ poetry and _fanciful_ short stories.
19. Every summer is too _brief_, and every winter is too _long_.
20. The _gray_ tabby cat stalked the _wary_ mouse.

For additional help, review pages 18–19 in your textbook
or visit www.voyagesinenglish.com.

© Loyola Press, Voyages in English **Grade 7**

2.2 Demonstrative, Interrogative, and Indefinite Adjectives

Demonstrative adjectives point out definite people, places, things, or ideas. **Interrogative adjectives** are used in questions. **Indefinite adjectives** refer to any or all of a group. Indefinite adjectives can be singular or plural.

Write whether each italicized adjective is _demonstrative, interrogative,_ or _indefinite._

1. _That_ necklace belongs to Sophia. _demonstrative_
2. _Some_ boys brought home the wallets they made at camp. _indefinite_
3. _What_ week are we going on vacation? _interrogative_
4. Have you made _this_ meal before? _demonstrative_
5. _Those_ flowers grow well in the sun. _demonstrative_
6. _Whose_ laundry is in the washing machine? _interrogative_

Underline the demonstrative, interrogative, or indefinite adjectives.

7. Which dessert did you choose?
8. Every child can submit a single entry into this contest.
9. We saw several kinds of kitchen wallpaper, but I only liked a few designs.
10. I know you didn't get these shoes at this store, so which store had them?
11. That teacher told us to choose any desk.
12. Mom asked, "Will you bring me another plate from that stack on the counter?"

Complete each sentence with a demonstrative, an interrogative, or an indefinite adjective. _Possible responses are given._

13. _Every_ days Kyle would ask his mother if he could get a dog.
14. Diego decided to invite _several_ of his friends over to play games on his birthday.
15. The police determined that _neither_ driver was responsible for the accident.
16. Mrs. Holbert decided that we needed _another_ day to complete the assignment.
17. _Which_ set of collectors' cards has Vlad acquired _this_ week?
18. I don't know _what_ decision to make about _either_ problem.
19. _These_ lockers still need to be cleaned out for the summer.
20. Will you bring me _those_ new notebooks?

For additional help, review pages 20–21 in your textbook
or visit www.voyagesinenglish.com.

© Loyola Press, Voyages in English **Grade 7**

Practice Book Answer Key • 13

2.2 Demonstrative, Interrogative, and Indefinite Adjectives

Demonstrative adjectives point out definite people, places, things, or ideas. **Interrogative adjectives** are used in questions. **Indefinite adjectives** refer to any or all of a group. Indefinite adjectives can be singular or plural.

Write whether each italicized adjective is demonstrative, interrogative, or indefinite.

1. *Which* class do you have first thing in the day? _____ interrogative
2. Few birds come to the feeder in the middle of the winter. _____ indefinite
3. Is there *another* solution to the problem that costs less? _____ indefinite
4. *Many* skiers now choose to wear helmets. _____ indefinite
5. *Whose* shoes are by the front door? _____ interrogative
6. Which person picked *that* color to paint the living room? _____ demonstrative

Underline the demonstrative, interrogative, and indefinite adjectives in the story.

7. Brian and I wanted to earn some money, so Mom suggested that we rake leaves. Nobody was home in the first few houses we visited. Several people politely declined. Then we came to a tiny house. The yard was covered in leaves. Most bushes were overgrown. "Whose yard is this?" we wondered. An elderly woman answered the door. We knew she couldn't afford to pay us. We thanked her and turned to leave, but then thought that someone needed to help her. We ran home for tools. "You rake these leaves," I said. "I'll trim those bushes." It took us many hours to get that yard cleaned up, but we felt proud of our accomplishment.

Complete each sentence with the type of adjective in parentheses. *Possible responses are given.*

8. _____ Which puppy should we adopt at the shelter? (interrogative)
9. We saw _____ some girls at the store yesterday. (indefinite)
10. We can go to the play on _____ this night or _____ that one. (demonstrative)
11. We took _____ another way to the old high school and got lost. (indefinite)
12. _____ What recipe do you have for your favorite dessert? (interrogative)
13. _____ Whose brother is in the band? (interrogative)
14. _____ Several volunteers brought more helpers with them. (indefinite)
15. _____ Every student is expected to help out in some way. (indefinite)

On another sheet of paper, write a paragraph about a topic of your choice. Use at least three of each kind of adjective: demonstrative, interrogative, and indefinite.

For additional help, review pages 20–21 in your textbook or visit www.voyagesinenglish.com.

Section 2 • 17

© Loyola Press. Voyages in English Grade 7

2.3 Comparative and Superlative Adjectives

The **positive degree** of an adjective shows a quality of a noun or pronoun. The **comparative degree** compares two items or two sets of items. The **superlative degree** is used to compare three or more items.

Write the comparative and superlative forms of each positive adjective.

1. strong	stronger	strongest
2. efficient	more/less efficient	most/least efficient
3. bad	worse	worst
4. slow	slower	slowest
5. legible	more/less legible	most/least legible
6. good	better	best
7. low	lower	lowest
8. international	more/less international	most/least international

Write P for positive, C for comparative, and S for superlative to identify the degree of comparison of each italicized adjective.

9. I truly adore the *biggest* poodles, the standard. _____ S
10. The little poodles are cute, but they do not seem like real dogs to me. _____ P
11. Our standard poodle, Toto, is *medium-sized*. _____ P
12. She is *most exuberant* when we first walk in the door. _____ S
13. In fact, Toto is *friendlier* than a lot of other dogs we meet. _____ C
14. When we take her to the dog park, she is *eager* to play. _____ P
15. It is not until I pull out a ball that you start to see her *true* nature. _____ P
16. I use a ball flinger to throw the ball *farther* than everyone else. _____ C
17. Of all the dogs, Toto is the *most determined* to get to the ball first. _____ S
18. She grabs the ball and runs *faster* than the other dogs to bring it back. _____ C
19. Toto is *more fun* than any other dog I have ever had. _____ C
20. She makes me feel like the best dog owner just because I throw a ball. _____ S
21. When it comes time to go, Toto is *less excited* to get back in the car. _____ C
22. She's the *smartest* dog ever; she knows that when we get home she'll get a treat. _____ S

On another sheet of paper, write a paragraph about a favorite thing. Use each kind of adjective at least three times.

18 • Section 2

For additional help, review pages 22–23 in your textbook or visit www.voyagesinenglish.com.

© Loyola Press. Voyages in English Grade 7

2.4 Few and Little

Concrete nouns name things that can be seen or touched. **Abstract nouns** name things that cannot be seen or touched. Use *few, fewer,* and *fewest* to compare concrete nouns. Use *little, less,* and *least* to compare abstract nouns.

Circle the abstract nouns. Underline the concrete nouns.

1. The (bravery) of the dog earned it the highest (honor) in the city.
2. Mr. Johnson was disappointed by the (deceit) his employee practiced.
3. Hadley showed (dedication) when she attended school every day.
4. I do not know if (curiosity) ever killed a cat, but it did cover mine in red paint once.
5. We decided to extend our (trust) to include Jacob and his little brother.

Use the correct form of *few* or *little* to complete each sentence.

6. There are a _few_ iguanas left in the tank.
7. Jan took _fewer_ tissues for her project than Maria did.
8. The company's president has _less_ wealth this year than last year.
9. That watering hole always has the _fewest_ antelopes of all.
10. Of all the chefs, Mark uses the _least_ amount of salt in his recipes.
11. There is _little_ time to play today.
12. We cleaned _fewer_ uniforms this week than last week.
13. This engine is _less_ trouble than the one it replaced.
14. The clerk placed a _few_ umbrellas by the door.
15. The third-floor apartment uses the _least_ heat of all the apartments.

Complete each sentence. *Possible responses are given.*

16. The team captain trusts few _members of the opposing teams_
17. The dog showed little _concern over meeting us_
18. This month there are fewer _donations than last month_
19. Of all of us, Jorge has the least _interest in sports_
20. That country has the fewest _crimes per year_
21. Since the start of the school year, we all have less _time to play soccer_

© Loyola Press. Voyages in English Grade 7

For additional help, review pages 24–25 in your textbook or visit www.voyagesinenglish.com.

2.3 Comparative and Superlative Adjectives

The **positive degree** of an adjective shows a quality of a noun or pronoun. The **comparative degree** compares two items or two sets of items. The **superlative degree** is used to compare three or more items.

Underline the positive, comparative, and superlative adjectives.

1. Grandmother is the best cook I have ever met; she's even better than my mom.
2. She is the happiest person in the world when she is in her warm kitchen.
3. In a more somber mood, Grandma told me about her worst disaster.
4. She had chosen the fanciest cut of meat for an important party she had planned.
5. When it was done, she placed the expensive meat on a high counter.
6. While she set the table, her bigger dog, Thor, ate the delicious meal.

7. **Write the words you underlined above into the correct column of the chart.**

POSITIVE	COMPARATIVE	SUPERLATIVE
warm	better	best
important	more somber	happiest
expensive	bigger	worst
high		fanciest
delicious		

Complete each sentence with the comparative or superlative form of the adjective in parentheses.

8. The hexagonal window is _more unusual_ (unusual) than the rectangular one.
9. It is a _better_ (good) idea to travel as a group than to travel alone.
10. The door finally opened when Brandon used a _more forceful_ (forceful) blow.
11. Out of all of us, Kara did the _best_ (good) job.
12. I thought Metin's performance was the _most professional_ (professional).
13. We saw _fewer_ (few) children at the park today than we did yesterday.
14. I think Harold seems even _crabbier_ (crabby) than the last time we saw him.
15. I wasn't feeling good this morning, and now I'm feeling _worse_ (bad).
16. The price of that jacket is _less expensive_ (expensive) than it was last month.

For additional help, review pages 22–23 in your textbook or visit www.voyagesinenglish.com.

© Loyola Press. Voyages in English Grade 7

2.5 Adjective Phrases and Clauses

A **prepositional phrase** is made up of a preposition, the object of the preposition, and any modifiers of the object. A **clause** is a group of words that has a subject and a predicate. It can be **restrictive or nonrestrictive.**

Underline each adjective phrase. Then circle the noun it modifies.

1. Have you read the (words) of our forefathers?
2. China wanted to protect itself from (barbarians) from the north.
3. (Women) in the United States have the (right) to vote.
4. Let's get together and give her a (gift) for her birthday.
5. Some (plants) in the Americas later became European imports.

Write whether the italicized words in each sentence are an *adjective clause* or an *adjective phrase.*

6. The teacher *with red hair* tells many funny stories. _adjective phrase_
7. The statue *of Paul Revere* is visited by millions each year. _adjective phrase_
8. The gift *that I received for my birthday* is precious to me. _adjective clause_
9. The plane ride, *which lasted two hours,* was far too bumpy. _adjective clause_

Underline each adjective clause. Then write whether it is *restrictive* or *nonrestrictive.*

10. Louisiana, which was once part of the French empire, is known for its Cajun food. _nonrestrictive_
11. Classes that include writing requirements are mandatory. _restrictive_
12. Mummies, which are found in many ancient cultures, are a way of preserving the dead. _nonrestrictive_
13. The sign that Megan posted read "Do not enter." _restrictive_

Rewrite the following sentence twice. First, add an adjective phrase to describe one of the nouns. Next, add an adjective clause. _Possible responses are given._

14. The letter was mailed from California.
The letter on the desk was mailed from California.
The letter, which Paul brought, was mailed from California.

For additional help, review pages 26–27 in your textbook or visit www.voyagesinenglish.com.

SECTION 3 Daily Maintenance

3.1 We asked them for directions to the nearest gas station.
1. What part of speech is the subject? _pronoun_
2. What is the person of this word? _first_
3. Which pronoun is the indirect object of the verb? _them_
4. Which word is a superlative adjective? _nearest_
5. Diagram the sentence on another sheet of paper.

[Sentence diagram: We | asked | them, with modifier phrase "for directions to the nearest gas station"]

3.2 Three tired puppies were sleeping on the brown rug.
1. What are the descriptive adjectives? _Three, tired, brown_
2. Are these common or proper adjectives? _common_
3. Are the nouns concrete or abstract? _concrete_
4. What tense is the verb? _past progressive_
5. Diagram the sentence on another sheet of paper.

[Sentence diagram: puppies | were sleeping, with "Three," "tired," "on the brown rug"]

3.3 The boy's new black shoes are shiny.
1. What are the descriptive adjectives? _new, black, shiny_
2. Which adjective acts as a subject complement? _shiny_
3. Which word is a possessive noun? _boy's_
4. Is this word singular or plural? _singular_
5. Diagram the sentence on another sheet of paper.

[Sentence diagram: shoes | are \ shiny, with "The," "boy's," "new," "black"]

3.4 These students will be studying Spanish literature in their next class.
1. What is the simple subject of the sentence? _students_
2. What tense is the verb? _future progressive_
3. Which word is a demonstrative adjective? _These_
4. Which word is a proper adjective? _Spanish_
5. Diagram the sentence on another sheet of paper.

[Sentence diagram: students | will be studying | literature, with "These," "Spanish," "in their next class"]

3.9 This bedroom has less space than that bedroom.

1. What are the demonstrative adjectives? — *This, that*
2. Which word is used as a comparative adjective? — *less*
3. Which word does this adjective modify? — *space*
4. What kind of noun does this adjective compare? — *abstract*
5. Diagram the sentence on another sheet of paper.

bedroom | has | space
This | less | than (has) bedroom | that

3.10 Each job applicant must submit these forms.

1. What kind of word is *Each*? — *indefinite adjective*
2. Is this word singular or plural? — *singular*
3. What kind of word is *these*? — *demonstrative adjective*
4. Is this word singular or plural? — *plural*
5. Diagram the sentence on another sheet of paper.

applicant | must submit | forms
Each | job | these

3.11 The proud parents applauded their children's achievements.

1. Which word is used as a descriptive adjective? — *proud*
2. Which word is a possessive noun? — *children's*
3. Is this word singular or plural? — *plural*
4. Which word is a possessive adjective? — *their*
5. Diagram the sentence on another sheet of paper.

parents | applauded | achievements
The | proud | their | children's

3.5 Several students in Ms. Ling's dance class entered the talent show.

1. Which word is an indefinite adjective? — *Several*
2. Is this word singular or plural? — *plural*
3. What are the other adjectives in the sentence? — *dance, talent*
4. Which word is used as a preposition? — *in*
5. Diagram the sentence on another sheet of paper.

students | entered | show
Several | in class | Ms. Ling's | dance | the talent

3.6 Which player is the tallest one on the volleyball team?

1. Which word is an interrogative adjective? — *Which*
2. What kind of adjective is the word *tallest*? — *superlative*
3. Which noun is used as a subject complement? — *one*
4. Which noun is the object of a preposition? — *team*
5. Diagram the sentence on another sheet of paper.

player | is | one
Which | the tallest | on team | the volleyball

3.7 Jim's and Bob's robots are good, but mine is better.

1. What are the adjectives in the sentence? — *good, better*
2. Which word is a comparative adjective? — *better*
3. Which nouns show possession? — *Jim's, Bob's*
4. Do they show separate or joint possession? — *separate possession*
5. Diagram the sentence on another sheet of paper.

robots | are | good ; Jim's / Bob's and ; but ; mine | is | better

3.8 Her report on global warming was very informative.

1. What is the compound noun in the sentence? — *global warming*
2. What does the adjective phrase modify? — *report*
3. What is the adjective *informative* used as? — *subject complement*
4. What part of speech is the word *very*? — *adverb*
5. Diagram the sentence on another sheet of paper.

report | was | informative
Her | on global warming | very

3.2 Subject Pronouns

A **subject pronoun** can be the subject or subject complement of a sentence. The subject pronouns are *I, we, you, he, she, it,* and *they.*

Circle the correct pronoun to complete each sentence. Then write subject or subject complement to indicate how the pronoun is used.

1. Kenny and (I) me) will write the report together. ___subject___
2. Is it (him) (he) at the gate? ___subject complement___
3. Was it (she) her) who went to London? ___subject complement___
4. Tomorrow Juan and (they) them) will go swimming. ___subject___
5. It was (he) him) who took the notebook. ___subject complement___
6. Ty thought it was Joy and (her) (she) who went running. ___subject complement___
7. The person who climbed the hill was (me (I)). ___subject complement___
8. (Me (I)) went looking for butterflies. ___subject___
9. (They) Them) took Carmen to the train station. ___subject___
10. Was it (he) him) who caught the largest fish? ___subject complement___

Complete each sentence with a subject pronoun that matches its antecedent.

11. My brother and I play trumpets, and ___we___ are both in the school band.
12. The Harrison twins play French horns, so ___they___ are in the band too.
13. Their father is the band director, and we all think ___he___ is pretty cool.
14. Our mother never misses a concert, and ___she___ always says we played well.
15. One day my brother broke my trumpet when ___he___ dropped it.
16. My parents took the instrument to the music store where ___it___ was fixed.

Write five sentences that describe a family member you admire. Use personal pronouns as the subjects and subject complements. *Answers will vary.*

17. _____
18. _____
19. _____
20. _____
21. _____

3.1 Person, Number, and Gender of Pronouns

A **pronoun** is a word used in place of a noun. The word that a pronoun refers to is called its **antecedent**. Pronouns change form depending on **person, number,** or **gender.**

Write the person and number of each italicized pronoun.

1. *They* went to the new water park. ___third person plural___
2. After lunch the tickets were divided among *us.* ___first person plural___
3. It must have been *she* who bought the card. ___third person singular___
4. *You* should wear this pair of sneakers. ___second person singular___
5. Beth gave *me* a lecture about cleaning up the kitchen. ___first person singular___
6. *We* do not want to wake up late tomorrow. ___first person plural___

Circle the pronouns. Write 1 above each first person pronoun, 2 above each second person pronoun, and 3 above each third person pronoun.

7. Have (you) heard of the great ballplayer Joe DiMaggio? Many people say (he) was one of the best players in baseball history. (They) point to that stellar ball-playing record attributed to (him). But Joltin' Joe, as (he) was called, also had a sense of grace and privacy about (him). (He) was married to actress Marilyn Monroe, and (I) don't think that marriage could have survived such a need for privacy. But (you) might be interested to know that after (she) died, (he) sent roses to that grave site for 20 years. (I) think (he) really loved (her).

Use the directions in parentheses to finish each sentence with the correct pronoun.

8. He is going to the shelter with ___me___ tomorrow afternoon. (first person singular)
9. ___We___ got the idea from a friend who lives there. (first person plural)
10. ___She or He___ says there are lots of families living at the shelter. (third person singular)
11. Parents need babysitters so ___they___ can go out for awhile. (third person plural)
12. We'll play games with the kids, and ___they___ will have fun. (third person plural)
13. We would like ___you___ to come too. (second person singular)
14. You could ride with ___us___ to the shelter. (first person plural)
15. If ___it___ goes well, we hope to go back next week too. (third person singular)

3.3 Object Pronouns

An **object pronoun** can be used as the object of a verb or a preposition. Write *D* if it is a direct object, *I* if it is an indirect object, or *O* if it is an object of a preposition. The object pronouns are *me, us, you, him, her, it,* and *them.*

Underline each personal pronoun. Write *D* if it is a direct object, *I* if it is an indirect object, or *O* if it is an object of a preposition.

1. Val told <u>me</u> the whole story on Monday afternoon. __I__

2. The senator from Alaska greeted <u>them</u> on the tour of the Capitol. __D__

3. Carlos and Miguel saw <u>her</u> at the library downtown. __D__

4. Pat heard that there is an expert on pioneer life among <u>us</u>. __O__

5. Samuel could not believe that Mr. Lopez loaned <u>him</u> the pliers. __I__

6. Can Teresa stand between Jane and <u>me</u>? __O__

7. Even the most familiar teachers did not recognize <u>you</u> in disguise. __D__

8. Peter spoke fluent Italian with <u>them</u>. __O__

Write the correct pronoun to complete each sentence.

9. I hoped the coach would pick ___me___ to demonstrate the kick. (I me)

10. I did not ask why he needed the pencil; I just gave it to ___him___ . (him he)

11. My dad is going camping with ___us___ next weekend. (we us)

12. Paulina gave the box to ___her___ after the piano recital. (she her)

13. All of ___us___ decided to get the teacher a present. (we us)

14. We saw ___them___ at the movie theater downtown. (them they)

15. Armando gave the bike to June and ___me___ . (I me)

Write the pronoun that correctly replaces the italicized antecedent.

16. Natalie went grocery shopping with each of *her brothers.* ___them___

17. My grandmother wants to see *my mom, my dad, my brother, and me.* ___us___

18. Our neighbor offered *Ava* money to mow the grass and trim the hedges. ___her___

19. The music teacher is married to *Coach Stevens.* ___him___

20. Carla sang *the song* as loudly as she could so everyone could hear. ___it___

21. The goal of *Carol and Sheila* was to win the softball game. ___her___

22. We liked Rover immediately and talked mom into keeping *the dog.* ___it___

23. Yesterday my math teacher called *my parents.* ___them___

For additional help, review pages 36–37 in your textbook or visit www.voyagesinenglish.com.

© Loyola Press. Voyages in English   Grade 7

Section 3 • 27

3.4 Pronouns After *Than* or *As*

The words *than* and *as* are used in comparisons. These **conjunctions** join two clauses, but remember that sometimes part of the second clause is omitted.

Circle the correct pronoun to complete each sentence. Then write the verb that has been omitted from the second clause.

1. Little Billy cries more than (he) him). ___cries___

2. Marie sings better than (she) her). ___sings___

3. Craig dances as well as (they) them). ___dance___

4. Does Brenda practice as much as (he) him)? ___practices___

5. Jamal ordered more food than (I) me). ___ordered___

6. The children were joyous, and the adults were as happy as (they) them). ___were joyous___

7. Samuel was more startled by the fireworks than (she) her). ___was startled___

8. Willis plays piano better than (he) him). ___plays___

9. Aisha ate more hot dogs than (I) me). ___ate___

10. Chuck took more time to finish than (I) me). ___took___

Use the chart to write sentences with *than* or *as* followed by pronouns.

	KEVIN	KATYA	MARIA
Games Won	5	5	7
Games Lost	2	3	0

11. Compared with Kevin: *Possible responses are given.*
Katya has won the same number of games as he.
Maria has won more games than he.

12. Compared with Katya:
Maria has won two more games than she.
Katya has played more games than they.

13. Compared with Maria:
Kevin has won fewer games than she.
Maria has lost far fewer games than they.

For additional help, review pages 38–39 in your textbook or visit www.voyagesinenglish.com.

© Loyola Press. Voyages in English   Grade 7

28 • Section 3

3.5 Possessive Pronouns and Adjectives

Possessive pronouns show possession or ownership. The possessive pronouns are *mine, ours, yours, his, hers, its,* and *theirs,* and the **possessive adjectives** *my, our, your, his, her, its,* and *their* always precede nouns.

Underline the possessive pronoun or the possessive adjective in each sentence. Circle the noun each possessive adjective modifies.

1. I would like to have an outfit like hers.
2. His (shirt) is the one with the striped pattern.
3. Mine is the house with the blue shutters.
4. I hope our (skit) is chosen for the school assembly.
5. You left your (backpack) in the gymnasium.
6. The black-and-white cat is theirs.
7. May I collect yours?

Complete each sentence with a possessive adjective. Use context clues.

8. The jacket is mine. I gave her ___my___ jacket because she looked so cold.
9. The house is theirs. We went to ___their___ house for lunch.
10. The collar belongs to the dog. Fido just loves ___his or its___ collar.
11. Layla made a dress. We all want one just like ___her___ dress.
12. Jacob built a table. He gave ___his___ table to the school for its charity auction.
13. Willem has five cards. He gave three of ___his___ cards to Tess.
14. Louis and Jaden did a great job. We think ___their___ project was the best.
15. Alaina won first place. Did you see ___her___ trophy?

Write a possessive that can replace the italicized words. Then write *A* if the word is a possessive adjective or *P* if it is a possessive pronoun.

16. The bikes are *my family's and mine*.   ___ours___   P
17. I think the dog is locked in *Collin's* room.   ___his___   A
18. Mom is cooking so she won't let us in *Mom's* kitchen.   ___her___   A
19. Don't throw away the old blankets; they are *my* blankets.   ___mine___   P
20. David took those photos in college. They are *David's* photos.   ___his___   P
21. The black-and-white cat is *Destiny and Eli's* cat.   ___theirs___   P
22. Josef's bag is the one laying in the hall.   ___his___   A

© Loyola Press. Voyages in English **Grade 7**

3.6 Intensive and Reflexive Pronouns

An **intensive pronoun** is used to emphasize a preceding noun or pronoun. A **reflexive pronoun** is used as the direct or indirect object of a verb or the object of a preposition.

Underline the intensive or reflexive pronouns in each sentence. Write whether the pronoun is *intensive* or *reflexive*.

1. You yourself must make this difficult decision.   ___intensive___
2. We taught ourselves the song they sing at all the football games.   ___reflexive___
3. I myself liked the idea, but it did not pass at the meeting.   ___intensive___
4. Can you really do all that work yourselves?   ___intensive___
5. Enrico himself ran to the store for butter.   ___intensive___
6. Kay laughed at herself and decided to give it another try.   ___reflexive___
7. I decided to take myself to the movies.   ___reflexive___
8. We ourselves preferred the pumpkin pie over the pecan pie.   ___intensive___
9. You deserve to congratulate yourselves on a job well done.   ___reflexive___
10. Quinn caught himself starting to yawn again and stifled it quickly.   ___reflexive___

Complete each sentence with an intensive or a reflexive pronoun. Then write *I* if the pronoun is intensive or *R* if it is reflexive.

11. We ___ourselves___ thought we would win the game.   I
12. You all must prepare ___yourselves___ for the test.   R
13. You ___yourself___ should try it.   I
14. I will finish the project ___myself___.   I
15. Dennis excused ___himself___ from the room.   R
16. The campers found ___themselves___ in a bad storm.   R
17. Kate taught ___herself___ to crochet a scarf.   R
18. The dog ___itself___ will star in a movie.   I
19. Jack decided to write a song for the school ___himself___.   I

On another sheet of paper, write about a time when, as a child, you attempted a difficult task on your own. Use at least three intensive or reflexive pronouns. Circle each intensive pronoun. Underline each reflexive pronoun.

© Loyola Press. Voyages in English **Grade 7**

3.7 Agreement of Pronouns and Antecedents

Pronouns must agree with their antecedents in person, number, and gender.

Underline the antecedent of each italicized pronoun. Write its person (1, 2, or 3), its number (S or P), and, if it applies, its gender (F, M, or N).

1. __3, S, N__ — Chess is a game of strategy. *It* does not take long to learn, but it can take a lifetime to master.
2. __3, S, M__ — Are you going to play the trivia game John brought? I like to play with *him* because he is fair.
3. __3, P, N__ — Players today can choose from many different kinds of games. *They* can choose from very high-tech games to simple word games.
4. __3, S, F__ — My friend Amy has a toy with much more ancient roots. *She* loves her game of mancala.
5. __1, P__ — My brother and I like to play a game in the car. Every time *we* see a certain kind of car, we yell "Bug!"
6. __2, P__ — Ann and Ron, have you ever played with jacks? *It* takes some concentration.
7. __3, S, N__ — A jump rope is good exercise, too, but it requires good coordination.
8. __3, P, N__ — John and Raul are playing with puzzle cubes. *They* are tricky to solve.

Complete each sentence with an appropriate pronoun. Make sure that each agrees in person, number, and gender with its antecedent. Underline the antecedent.

9. Will you and I be partners on the field trip? If so, __we__ can talk then.
10. Maggie and Paige have invited their mothers to come along with __them__.
11. Grandma adopts homeless animals, and five now live with __her__.
12. Mr. Barton gave us the key. After we lock up, we need to take it back to __him__.
13. Tenecia is a champion gymnast. We are going to watch __her__ compete today.
14. Where are Rivu and Walter? I have been looking everywhere for __them__.
15. Have Andy and Ayanna called? __They__ were going to call me this afternoon.
16. Do not jump on the couch, because __it__ might collapse.
17. Have you seen Thomas? This book belongs to __him__.
18. If you see Bryona, tell __her__ that Christy and Erica are looking for the book.
19. Max and I are leaving soon, and you can arrive with __us__.

On another sheet of paper, write three sentences that include clear antecedents and their related pronouns.

For additional help, review pages 44–45 in your textbook or visit www.voyagesinenglish.com.

© Loyola Press. Voyages in English   Grade 7

3.7 Agreement of Pronouns and Antecedents

Pronouns must agree with their antecedents in person, number, and gender.

Underline the antecedent for each italicized pronoun.

1. Julius Robert Oppenheimer did not use *his* first name.
2. Oppenheimer led the scientists of the Manhattan Project. *They* developed the atomic bomb.
3. Robert Oppenheimer was a theoretical physicist, and *he* taught physics.
4. He *himself* came from a wealthy family of businessmen and artists.
5. Robert Oppenheimer was brilliant. *He* spoke eight languages.
6. When Oppenheimer needed to present a lecture in Dutch, he learned *it* in only six weeks.
7. The U.S. government established the Manhattan Project in 1941. *It* put Oppenheimer in charge one year later.
8. The scientists successfully tested the first atomic bomb on July 16, 1945. Oppenheimer said, "*We* knew the world would not be the same."
9. Less than a month later, U.S. planes dropped two bombs on cities in Japan. *They* killed more than 140,000 people.
10. The bombs ended World War II, but Oppenheimer said, "The physicists have known sin; and this is a knowledge which *they* cannot lose."

Write the pronoun that goes with each underlined antecedent.

11. Oppenheimer had a brother, Frank, who was a physicist himself. __himself__
12. His wife was Katherine Oppenheimer. She was known as Kitty. __She__
13. Their daughter was Toni. She was born during the Manhattan Project. __She__
14. Their son was Peter. He was their firstborn child. __He__
15. Oppenheimer himself upset many powerful men of the time. __himself__
16. The men agreed among themselves that he was no longer helpful. __themselves__
17. All had security clearance, but Oppenheimer was stripped of his. __his__
18. But in 1963 the U.S. president himself gave Oppenheimer a prize. __himself__
19. The prize honored the man, and he clearly valued it. __it__

On another sheet of paper, write three sentences that each have a clear antecedent and a related pronoun.

For additional help, review pages 44–45 in your textbook or visit www.voyagesinenglish.com.

© Loyola Press. Voyages in English   Grade 7

3.9 Relative Pronouns

A **relative pronoun** is used to join a dependent clause to its antecedent in the independent clause. These pronouns are *who, whom, which, that,* and *whose.*

Underline each relative pronoun and circle its antecedent.

1. The (book) that I just finished was written in 1931.
2. The (woman) who was crying had hurt her knee.
3. A (scientist) who studies insects is called an entomologist.
4. I heard an aria by (Wolfgang Amadeus Mozart), about whom we had studied in class.
5. (Walker), which is my brother's middle name, goes well with our last name.
6. The (person) who has the best math score gets to skip tomorrow's test.
7. The (squirrel) that climbed the tree was throwing nuts at us.
8. We visited (Brussels), which is the capital of Belgium.

Rewrite the sentences to correct the use of relative pronouns. If the sentence is correct, circle the relative pronoun.

9. Abel, (who) likes to listen to that kind of music, might like the CD you bought.

_____

10. Evelyn Kuo, to who you hit the ball yesterday, thinks you are a great player.

Evelyn Kuo, to whom you hit the ball yesterday, thinks you are a great player.

11. Tanner, whom was division champ last season, is on my team this year.

Tanner, who was division champ last season, is on my team this year.

12. My brother, with who I share a birthday, is two years older than I am.

My brother, with whom I share a birthday, is two years older than I am.

13. Grace, (whom) I visited last week, says she might be able to come with us next year.

14. The Navajo Churro, (which) are raised for their coats, are America's oldest sheep breed.

My sister prefers cats that have dark stripes through their fur.

15. My sister prefers cats which have dark stripes through their fur.

For additional help, review pages 48–49 in your textbook or visit www.voyagesinenglish.com.

3.8 Interrogative and Demonstrative Pronouns

An **interrogative pronoun** is used to ask a question. A **demonstrative pronoun** points out a particular person, place, or thing.

Underline the interrogative pronouns and circle the demonstrative pronouns in each sentence.

1. Is (this) your backpack?
2. The waitress asked, "Who ordered (this)?"
3. Whom did you talk to about (that)?
4. What is making (that) loud noise?
5. Which of (these) is yours?
6. Who is your favorite singer?
7. Do you want to see (that) again?
8. Whose are (those) shoes?
9. To whom did you send the letter?
10. What does (this) say?

Complete each sentence with the correct interrogative pronoun.

11. _____Who_____ do you think will win the election?
12. _____What_____ was the score of last night's ball game?
13. _____What_____ will you do this summer on your vacation?
14. _____Which_____ of these costumes is your favorite?
15. To _____whom_____ should we address the invitation?
16. _____Which_____ recipe do you prefer for pancakes?
17. _____What_____ is the best way to get to Oakville from here?
18. _____Who_____ is going to read this book at the library tomorrow?
19. _____Which_____ of these are you going to buy, this one or that one?
20. With _____whom_____ will you share this delicious cake?
21. _____Whom_____ did you see traveling to the train station?

Use the the directions in parentheses to complete each sentence with the correct demonstrative pronoun.

22. Is _____that_____ the car you were telling me about? (far)
23. I think _____this_____ is the computer that I like best. (near)
24. Please get _____those_____ and bring them over here. (far)
25. I would like to hang several of _____these_____ on that wall. (near)
26. Where can we put _____that_____ so it will not get bumped? (far)
27. Is _____this_____ the one that belongs in the box? (near)
28. There are several, so let's put _____those_____ on the table for everyone to enjoy. (far)
29. How many of _____these_____ will you need to complete this project? (near)

For additional help, review pages 46–47 in your textbook or visit www.voyagesinenglish.com.

3.10 Indefinite Pronouns

An **indefinite pronoun** refers to any or all of a group of people, places, or things. Negative indefinite pronouns should not be combined with other negative words, such as *no*, *not*, and *never*.

Underline the indefinite pronouns in the sentences.

1. Did you remember to buy <u>any</u> when you were at the store?
2. <u>Both</u> rode their bicycles 50 miles yesterday.
3. Has <u>anyone</u> been able to get through on the phone?
4. We think you need <u>something</u> to do.
5. Jill ate <u>none</u> of her steak, so when she wasn't looking, the dog ate <u>all</u> of it.
6. <u>Several</u> tried to bid on the baseball tickets, but <u>none</u> won them.
7. <u>Some</u> were designed for hiking in the mountains, while <u>others</u> were for the beach.
8. <u>Everyone</u> was amused by the comedian's jokes, and <u>many</u> laughed out loud.
9. Homework? <u>Much</u> of my time was spent rocking the baby to sleep, but I did get <u>some</u> done.
10. <u>Nothing</u> is known about that author, so <u>another</u> might be a better choice.

Underline each indefinite pronoun. Write *subject, direct object, indirect object,* or *object of a preposition* to name its part of the sentence.

11. We are going to a chili cookoff. Have you been to <u>any</u>?   _object of a preposition_
12. <u>Most</u> offer a prize to the winner.   _subject_
13. <u>One</u> we entered specified that no beans could be used.   _subject_
14. The rules provided <u>some</u> a great deal of confusion.   _indirect object_
15. We tasted <u>several</u> and loved them all.   _direct object_
16. We were only disappointed that we couldn't have eaten <u>more</u>.   _direct object_
17. Mrs. Jackson's chili was preferred by <u>many</u>.   _object of a preposition_
18. <u>Nobody</u> had as popular an entry, so her chili won first prize.   _subject_

Rewrite each sentence so that the indefinite pronoun is used correctly. *Possible responses are given.*

19. Isn't nobody going to help me lift this?
 Isn't anybody going to help me lift this?

20. I have never seen nothing quite that expensive before.
 I have never seen anything quite that expensive before.

For additional help, review pages 50–51 in your textbook or visit www.voyagesinenglish.com.

3.9 Relative Pronouns

A **relative pronoun** is used to join a dependent clause to its antecedent in the independent clause. These pronouns are *who, whom, which, that,* and *whose.*

Underline the relative pronoun in each sentence. Circle the noun or noun phrase that is the antecedent of the relative pronoun.

1. e. e. cummings was a (poet) <u>who</u> eschewed capitalization and punctuation.
2. However, his (contribution) to American poetry, <u>which</u> was considerable, was about more than the mechanics of good writing.
3. The (poet) <u>who</u> was a Harvard student, first published poems while earning two degrees.
4. During World War I, cummings was sent to (France) <u>which</u> was an American ally.
5. After the war was over, he returned to (Paris) <u>which</u> is a city in France, to study art and to write.
6. e. e. cummings was greatly influenced by (Gertrude Stein) <u>whose</u> experimental use of language was unique.
7. A (style) <u>that</u> combined simple language with unusual grammatical structure changed little over the course of his career.
8. Much like (Emily Dickinson) <u>who</u> rarely titled her poems, e. e. cummings's poems are typically referred to by their entire first line.

Write a relative pronoun to complete each sentence.

9. Another New England poet, ___who___ died the same year as e. e. cummings but was born 20 years earlier, was Robert Frost.
10. Robert Frost's poems, ___which___ adhered to very strict structural rules, were popular during his life and earned him the moniker of national poet.
11. Many fans, ___who___ include everyday citizens and literary critics, find his work about simple rural life enjoyable.
12. The American public may never have known Frost's work if it weren't for the people of England, by ___whom___ his poems were first appreciated.
13. The American poet Amy Lowell, ___who___ discovered Frost's work in London, promoted it back in the United States.
14. Frost, ___who___ has been given many awards, became famous.
15. The many poems ___that___ were written by Frost are appreciated by audiences today.

On another sheet of paper, write sentences using each relative pronoun at least once: *who, whom, which, that, whose.*

For additional help, review pages 48–49 in your textbook or visit www.voyagesinenglish.com.

Practice Book Answer Key • 23

3.11 Agreement with Indefinite Pronouns

> An **indefinite pronoun** refers to any or all of a group of people, places, or things. When an indefinite pronoun acts as the subject of a sentence, the verb needs to agree with it in number.

Underline the indefinite pronoun once. Underline the verb or verb phrase twice.

1. Nothing was mentioned about the dance.
2. Has anything been decided about the transportation we will need?
3. Is something in the closet available for me?
4. Even after all the guests had arrived, no one was familiar.
5. As Henry claimed, all were invited earlier in the week.
6. In our family, everybody volunteers once a month.
7. Was anyone not interested in attending the play?
8. A few of the best writers always contribute poems to the contest.

Circle each indefinite pronoun. Then underline the correct verb choice.

9. (Everyone) at school (<u>is</u> are) excited about next week's visitors.
10. We are hosting a chamber orchestra of students, and (several) (is <u>are</u>) staying at our homes.
11. A (few) (has <u>have</u>) mastered the drums.
12. (Everybody) (want <u>wants</u>) to host a drum player.
13. A (few) (<u>play</u> plays) the horns, and (many) play the violin. (Others) (is <u>are</u>) cello players.
14. (Someone) (<u>strums</u> strum) the harp in the chamber orchestra.
15. I asked, "Does (anyone) (<u>strike</u> strikes) the xylophone?"
16. Some orchestra members are from other countries, but (all) (<u>speak</u> speaks) English.
17. I asked, "Will a (few) (<u>sleep</u> sleeps) on the floor?" Mom said, "No, there are enough beds."
18. Matthew and Onose are cellists, and (both) (is <u>are</u>) staying at our house.
19. (Neither) (like <u>likes</u>) scrambled eggs, but (both) (love <u>loves</u>) music.
20. (One) (<u>has</u> have) over 5,000 songs on his music player.
21. (Everyone) (dance <u>dances</u>) when he plugs it into speakers and turns up the sound.
22. Now that the orchestra has gone, (everyone) (miss <u>misses</u>) the talented and fun players.

On another sheet of paper, match each indefinite pronoun with a verb. Write an original sentence with each pair, using the pronoun as the subject. *Answers will vary.*

INDEFINITE PRONOUNS				VERBS			
nobody	both	few	each	wants	was	are	work
many	several	nothing	everyone	seems	were	helps	go

For additional help, review pages 52–53 in your textbook or visit www.voyagesinenglish.com.

SECTION 4 Daily Maintenance

4.1 Place the dirty laundry in the washer.
1. Is this an imperative or a declarative sentence?
2. What is the subject of the sentence?
3. Which word functions as the direct object?
4. Which word can be used as a noun and a verb?
5. Diagram the sentence on another sheet of paper.

imperative, (you), laundry, Place

4.2 The little black sheep ran behind the neighbor's barn.
1. Which word in the sentence shows possession?
2. Which noun is an irregular plural?
3. Is the verb regular or irregular?
4. Which words are descriptive adjectives?
5. Diagram the sentence on another sheet of paper.

neighbor's, sheep, irregular, little, black

4.3 The new president of the debate team is he.
1. Which word is a subject complement?
2. What are the person and number of this word?
3. What two words function as adjectives?
4. What is the adjective phrase?
5. Diagram the sentence on another sheet of paper.

he, third person, singular, new, debate, of the debate team

4.4 John and Jake like hamburgers, but they love pizza.
1. What is the pronoun in the sentence?
2. What is the antecedent of the pronoun?
3. Which words function as direct objects?
4. Which words are conjunctions?
5. Diagram the sentence on another sheet of paper.

they, John and Jake, hamburgers, pizza, and, but

4.9 Which of the used cars did they buy?
1. Is this sentence interrogative or imperative? — *interrogative*
2. Which word is an interrogative pronoun? — *Which*
3. Which word is a subject pronoun? — *they*
4. Which word functions as an adjective? — *used*
5. Diagram the sentence on another sheet of paper.

4.10 Everyone in the choir will perform at the holiday concert.
1. What is the verb phrase in the sentence? — *will perform*
2. Which word is an indefinite pronoun? — *Everyone*
3. Is this word singular or plural? — *singular*
4. What is the adjective phrase? — *in the choir*
5. Diagram the sentence on another sheet of paper.

4.11 Each student who participates in the marathon will receive a T-shirt.
1. Which word is a relative pronoun? — *who*
2. To which word does the relative pronoun refer? — *student*
3. Which word is an indefinite adjective? — *Each*
4. Is this word singular or plural? — *singular*
5. Diagram the sentence on another sheet of paper.

4.5 She invited them to her birthday party on Saturday.
1. What is the subject of the sentence? — *She*
2. Which word functions as a direct object? — *them*
3. Is this word singular or plural? — *plural*
4. Which word is a possessive adjective? — *her*
5. Diagram the sentence on another sheet of paper.

4.6 The beautiful portrait above the fireplace is hers.
1. What are the nouns in the sentence? — *portrait, fireplace*
2. Which word is a possessive pronoun? — *hers*
3. What is the adjective phrase? — *above the fireplace*
4. Which word is an adjective? — *beautiful*
5. Diagram the sentence on another sheet of paper.

4.7 We gave her a bouquet of flowers and eight pink balloons.
1. What are the adjectives in the sentence? — *eight, pink*
2. Which word is a subject pronoun? — *We*
3. Which word is an object pronoun? — *her*
4. Which nouns are used as direct objects? — *bouquet, balloons*
5. Diagram the sentence on another sheet of paper.

4.8 These are the photographs from my trip to Paris.
1. Which word is a demonstrative pronoun? — *These*
2. Does this word refer to something near or far? — *near*
3. What is the possessive adjective? — *my*
4. What are the common nouns in the sentence? — *photographs, trip*
5. Diagram the sentence on another sheet of paper.

Practice Book Answer Key • 25

4.1 Principal Parts of Verbs

The three **principal parts** of a verb are the **base form**, the **past**, and the **past participle**. The **present participle** is made by adding *-ing* to the base form. A **verb phrase** is two or more verbs that work together as a unit.

Underline each verb or verb phrase. Circle the auxiliary verb in each verb phrase.

1. We (have) chosen blue and yellow for the team's colors.
2. Henry and Vlad fixed Michael's bicycle this morning.
3. Dana, Katya, and Timothy flew to Texas last week.
4. I (had) called her yesterday, but she (did) not answer.
5. Neal and Abigail (could) hear the sound of rain on the tin roof of the front porch.
6. My sister and her husband drove me home tonight after play rehearsal.

Write the base, past, and past participle forms for each verb that you underlined in the sentences above.

	BASE	PAST	PAST PARTICIPLE
7.	choose	chose	chosen
8.	fix	fixed	fixed
9.	fly	flew	flown
10.	call	called	called
11.	answer	answered	answered
12.	hear	heard	heard
13.	drive	drove	driven

Complete each sentence with the past or past participle form of the verb in parentheses.

14. We _gave_ (give) the bell ringer two dollars for the charity.
15. Constance _sang_ (sing) beautifully at the service last week.
16. Hope and Kaylee _worked_ (work) on the assignment all day Saturday.
17. Did you know that plastic was _developed_ (develop) over a hundred years ago?
18. My dog was _picked_ (pick) to be on the fly ball team this year.
19. The neighbors have _gone_ (go) on vacation to Morocco this winter.
20. Chris and John have _eaten_ (eat) their breakfast already.

For additional help, review pages 58–59 in your textbook or visit www.voyagesinenglish.com.

Section 4 • 41

4.2 Transitive and Intransitive Verbs

A **transitive verb** expresses an action that passes from a doer to a receiver. A **phrasal verb** is a combination of the main verb and a preposition or an adverb. An **intransitive verb** does not have a receiver for its action.

Underline the verb, verb phrase, or phrasal verb in each sentence. Write whether it is transitive (T) or intransitive (I). If it is transitive, circle the direct object.

1. Aesop made up (fables), short moral stories with mostly animals as characters. **T**
2. The moral messages within these fables remain relevant today. **I**
3. One famous Aesop fable is called "The Fox and the Stork." **T**
4. One day Stork ran into (Fox). **T**
5. Fox invited (Stork) to his home for dinner. **T**
6. Fox served (soup) in a large, wide bowl. **T**
7. With her long beak, Stork could not sip the (soup). **T**
8. Stork left with a hungry belly. **I**
9. A few days later, Fox came to Stork's house for dinner. **I**
10. Fox found little (pieces) of food at the bottom of a jar with a long, narrow neck. **T**
11. Stork's long beak fit easily. **I**
12. Fox's nose did not fit in the jar. **I**
13. Stork just shrugged her (shoulders). **T**
14. After all, she had learned from Fox. **I**

Write two sentences for each verb. Use it as a transitive verb in the first sentence and as an intransitive verb in the second sentence. *Possible responses are given.*

15. **drive**
Transitive: *Today I will drive my car a hundred miles.*
Intransitive: *I will drive over the hills and through the woods.*

16. **teach**
Transitive: *She teaches English at the middle school.*
Intransitive: *Mrs. Simpson teaches at the middle school on Tuesdays and Thursdays.*

17. **help**
Transitive: *David and Kathy help each other with their homework.*
Intransitive: *Tony and I help after school at the homeless shelter.*

For additional help, review pages 60–61 in your textbook or visit www.voyagesinenglish.com.

42 • Section 4

Name ______________________ Date ____________

4.2 Transitive and Intransitive Verbs

A **transitive verb** expresses an action that passes from a doer to a receiver. A **phrasal verb** is a combination of the main verb and a preposition or an adverb. An **intransitive verb** does not have a receiver for its action.

Underline the transitive verbs. Circle the intransitive verbs.

1. The lifeguards gave safety lessons by the pool.
2. The little puppy shivered and then shook in the rain and snow.
3. John coughed loudly, but we all ignored him.
4. Every day at the lake, it rained or snowed.
5. Ken and James threw the ball for the dog.
6. Allison studied long into the night and aced her spelling exam.
7. The cats pounce and the kittens leap over each other at my house.
8. The Henderson's lush garden produces buckets of ripe vegetables every summer.
9. My younger brother sets up Civil War figurines and then reenacts epic battles.
10. I can concentrate only when I study at the library or in my room.

Underline the transitive verbs and circle the intransitive verbs. Then complete each sentence with an appropriate transitive or intransitive verb. *Students should choose verbs that fit the context of each sentence.*

11. The child closed his eyes and ____________ as he extinguished the candles.
12. Jorge usually walks, but today he ____________ in his father's new red car
13. Please tell me, did you ____________ the new movie this weekend?
14. Grandma Ethel ____________ and hugs us every time she visits.
15. Tina ____________ the dust out of her eyes, so she avoided a scratch to her cornea.
16. I ____________ the decrepit car as it backfired from three blocks away.
17. Ralph trembles because he will ____________ from the 10-meter platform.
18. John ____________ the song confidently because he knew all the words.
19. Uncle Albert always ____________, and he sleeps well a result.
20. She ____________ and the dogs ran to her immediately.

On another sheet of paper, write about some typical things you and your family do over a weekend. Then circle the transitive verbs and underline the intransitive verbs you used.

For additional help, review pages 60–61 in your textbook or visit www.voyagesinenglish.com.

Name ______________________ Date ____________

4.3 Troublesome Verbs

Troublesome verbs are those with similar pronunciations and spellings, but with different meanings and usage. These verb pairs are often confused.

Circle the verbs that correctly complete the sentences.

1. He (lied laid) the wood in the fireplace.
2. I think I will (sit set) here and rest for a while.
3. Please (let leave) your shoes by the door.
4. You can (set sit) that glass over there on the counter.
5. The sun (rose raised) at 6:30 this morning.
6. The waves (raised rose) above the dock during the storm.
7. (Let Leave) Satsu sit by the window.
8. Please do not (rise raise) your hands from the handlebars.
9. We watched the steam (raise rise) from the cup of coffee.
10. The dog decided to (lay lie) on the cold tile floor.
11. Did you (lend borrow) that rake from Mr. McCoy?
12. We like to (lie lay) on the sandy beach and soak up the summer sun.
13. The cat (sat set) on the windowsill and cleaned herself meticulously in the moonlight.
14. Mr. Hawthorne (learned taught) me the proper way to (rise raise) the flag.
15. (Let Leave) the video game alone, and please (sit set) down at the table.
16. The gray striped cat (lay laid) in the sun all afternoon.
17. Will you (sit set) the bowl on the table and help me (raise rise) the window?
18. My parents (let leave) me go to the community center, but when I am ready to (let leave), they will pick me up.
19. We should (lend borrow) Amy our extra jacket.
20. Joe and I (learned taught) how to tie knots and (sit set) tent pegs last weekend.

Rewrite the sentences to correct the use of troublesome verbs.

21. Natalie learned me how to do the algebra problems with which I was struggling.
    Natalie taught me how to do the algebra problems with which I was struggling.
22. Go set on the couch and let the poor dog alone.
    Go sit on the couch and leave the poor dog alone.
23. Please don't let your clothes laying all over the house.
    Please don't leave your clothes lying all over the house.
24. May Herb and Jake lend our lawn mower and return it tomorrow?
    May Herb and Jake borrow our lawn mower and return it tomorrow?

For additional help, review pages 62–63 in your textbook or visit www.voyagesinenglish.com.

4.5 Active and Passive Voices

Name _____   Date _____

When a transitive verb is in the **active voice**, the subject is the doer of the action. In the **passive voice**, the subject is the receiver of the action.

Underline the verb or verb phrase in each sentence. Then write whether that verb is in the active voice (A) or passive voice (P).

1. The overripe fruit <u>hit</u> the ground with a splat.   A
2. The story is read by the famous actor Melvin Belleville.   P
3. My brother reads quietly in the green chair every evening.   A
4. The bountiful harvest rewarded us all.   A
5. Only the cars were <u>damaged</u> in the three-car accident.   P
6. The stockings were <u>hung</u> by the youngest child in the family.   P
7. All night the watchdog carefully guarded the front gate.   A
8. The fire in the wood-burning stove is lit by me.   P
9. The dutiful mother cat follows her young kittens around the house.   A
10. Seventeen students participated in the trip to Washington, D.C.   A

Rewrite each sentence by changing the verb from passive to active voice.   *Possible responses are given.*

11. The trunk was lifted onto the bed by Charlie.
    Charlie lifted the trunk onto the bed.

12. The memo had been initialed by the chairperson.
    The chairperson had initialed the memo.

13. A new ambassador was nominated by the president.
    The president nominated a new ambassador.

14. The dough will be kneaded by Ryan in the morning.
    Ryan will knead the dough in the morning.

15. The team was invited to the awards banquet by Coach Evans.
    Coach Evans invited the team to the awards banquet.

16. The address numbers were nailed to the wall by a carpenter.
    A carpenter nailed the address numbers to the wall.

17. The items on the rack were neatly organized by the sales associate.
    The sales associate neatly organized the items on the rack.

46 • Section 4

For additional help, review pages 66–67 in your textbook or visit www.voyagesinenglish.com.

© Loyola Press. Voyages in English   Grade 7

4.4 Linking Verbs

Name _____   Date _____

A **linking verb** does not express action. Instead, it joins a subject with a subject complement.

Complete each sentence with the part of speech in parentheses. Underline the linking verb. Accept the parts of speech that match the context of the sentence.

1. The weather turned _____ last night. (adjective)
2. These sunflowers grow _____ in the garden. (adjective)
3. That person is an _____ . (noun)
4. Even though it was tired, the cat <u>remained</u> _____ . (adjective)
5. Hector and Jayden <u>are</u> _____ . (noun)
6. The fluffy buttermilk pancakes <u>tasted</u> _____ . (adjective)
7. The water <u>remained</u> _____ even after the storm. (adjective)
8. The caterpillar <u>became</u> a _____ . (noun)

Underline the linking verb in each sentence. Then write the subject complement for the linking verb.

9. The wasps <u>became</u> more active during the day.   active
10. Michael Jordan <u>was</u> an amazing basketball player.   player
11. Plymouth Drive <u>was</u> the street you should have taken.   street
12. The muffins from the bake sale <u>tasted</u> superb.   superb
13. The winning players <u>seem</u> terribly nervous.   nervous
14. The referee <u>remained</u> calm throughout the game.   calm
15. In the fairy tale, the lizard <u>is</u> actually a prince.   prince
16. Lindsey <u>feels</u> excited about her tryout.   excited

Underline the verb in each sentence. Then write whether that verb is transitive (T), intransitive (I), or linking (L).

17. Our family owns a set of dirt bikes.   T
18. My dad <u>taught</u> us the rules of the sport long ago.   T
19. My dirt bike <u>is</u> green with yellow flames.   L
20. Just about every weekend, we race in the desert.   I
21. My older sister <u>is</u> the best rider of us all.   L

For additional help, review pages 64–65 in your textbook or visit www.voyagesinenglish.com.

Section 4 • 45

© Loyola Press. Voyages in English   Grade 7

28 • Voyages in English

4.7 Indicative, Imperative, and Emphatic Moods

The **indicative mood** is used to state a fact or ask a question. The **imperative mood** is used to give commands. The **emphatic mood** gives emphasis to a simple present tense or past tense verb.

Underline the verb or verb phrase in each sentence. Then write whether the mood is *indicative, imperative, or emphatic*.

1. I can find the information for you. — *indicative*
2. Kate, hold your sister's hand. — *imperative*
3. When was Ronald Reagan president? — *indicative*
4. I did clean my room this morning. — *emphatic*
5. You should use more salt in that recipe. — *indicative*
6. Close the kitchen window. — *imperative*
7. Please do not tap your foot, Jack. — *imperative*
8. Juliet does love Romeo from the very first moment. — *emphatic*
9. He will read the new book to the children. — *indicative*
10. Emily did run for class president. — *emphatic*

Rewrite each sentence in the imperative mood. *Possible responses are given.*

11. It is very important to read all the instructions before you build the birdhouse.
Read all the instructions before you build the birdhouse.
12. The workers must be sure-footed and safety conscious.
Be sure-footed and safety conscious.

Rewrite each sentence in the indicative mood. *Possible responses are given.*

13. Learn to dance with rhythm and grace.
We will learn to dance with rhythm and grace.
14. Let's go to the beach today.
We can go to the beach today.

Write a sentence in the emphatic mood. *Possible response is given.*

15. *Maria and I do want to go to the concert with you.*

For additional help, review pages 70–71 in your textbook or visit www.voyagesinenglish.com.

4.6 Simple, Progressive, and Perfect Tenses

Simple tenses reflect the present, past, and future. **Progressive tenses** use a form of the auxiliary verb *be* and the main verb's present participle. **Perfect tenses** use a form of the auxiliary verb *have* and the main verb's past participle.

Underline each verb or verb phrase. Then write the letter that identifies its tense.

a. Simple tense b. Progressive tense c. Perfect tense

1. The tour bus will arrive at two o'clock this afternoon. — *a*
2. The icicles melt in the warm sun. — *a*
3. Her phone has been ringing all morning. — *c*
4. Kyle is learning about the history of France. — *b*
5. The pool will be opening the first week of June. — *b*
6. Martin's fate had been decided in April. — *c*
7. Sharon rode the roller coaster three times. — *a*
8. The costumes will have been constructed by opening night. — *c*
9. Jeremy was hiking on the Blue Mountain Trail. — *b*
10. I have been finished with the test for a long time. — *c*
11. Isaiah will apply to six schools in the area. — *a*
12. This dog has been trained in only six weeks. — *c*
13. The instructor will be giving each of us a schedule. — *b*

Complete each sentence using the verb and tense in parentheses. *Possible responses are given.*

14. Holly and Emma _____. (sing—future progressive)
Holly and Emma will be singing in the holiday concert.
15. My friends and I _____. (offer—past perfect active)
My friends and I had offered to help at the women's shelter this year.
16. The plants in the kitchen _____ (water—future perfect passive)
The plants in the kitchen will have been watered three times this week.
17. Amanda's father _____ (know—present perfect)
Amanda's father had known about the surprise party for some time.

For additional help, review pages 68–69 in your textbook or visit www.voyagesinenglish.com.

4.8 Subjunctive Mood

The **subjunctive mood** of a verb can express a wish, a desire, or a condition contrary to fact. It is also used to express a demand or a recommendation after *that* or to express an uncertainty after *if* or *whether*.

Underline each verb in the subjunctive mood. Then write whether it expresses a wish or desire (*W*), a condition contrary to fact (*C*), a recommendation or demand (*R*), or an uncertainty (*U*).

1. If I were looking for a new bike, I would have found one by now. — C
2. I wish I were a star on Broadway, nominated for a Tony award. — W
3. You could check out a library book if you were to arrive before closing. — R
4. Whether she be a pirate or not, that is a fine parrot on her shoulder. — U
5. My little brothers wish they were able to fly like Peter Pan. — W
6. We request that the club be responsible for the home game refreshments. — R
7. If I were sure of the way to go, I would not have looked at this map. — C
8. It's not important that he be at this meeting, as long as he attends the next one. — R
9. My teacher wishes we were more careful about our handwriting. — W
10. Mother asked that we be more considerate about one another's feelings. — R
11. Whether we be traveling to the beach or the mountains, it will be a good trip. — U
12. If I were you, I would take an umbrella just in case. — C

For each scenario, complete the sentence in the subjunctive mood. *Answers will vary.*

13. a student entering a contest
The student wished _____.

14. a teacher writing comments on a report card
The teacher asked that _____.

15. an athlete after losing a sporting event
If I were a better athlete, _____.

16. you make a suggestion to a friend about a purchase
I suggested that _____.

17. a police officer making an arrest
Whether the officer _____.

For additional help, review pages 72–73 in your textbook or visit www.voyagesinenglish.com.

Section 4 • 49

© Loyola Press. Voyages in English Grade 7

4.8 Subjunctive Mood

The **subjunctive mood** of a verb can express a wish, a desire, or a condition contrary to fact. It is also used to express a demand or a recommendation after *that* or to express an uncertainty after *if* or *whether*.

Circle the correct form of the verb that completes each sentence. Not all the verbs are in the subjunctive mood.

1. The rules require that each player (throws / **throw**) the ball to the person at the right.
2. Felicia couldn't decide whether this (**was** / were) the right sport for her.
3. Mom gave orders that she (**come** / comes) home right after each practice.
4. Mom also recommended that she (**take** / takes) the express bus from the stadium.
5. She insists that Felicia (**call** / calls) home if she's delayed.
6. If I (was / **were**) the team captain, I'd have fewer practice sessions.
7. I would make a good captain, if only I (wasn't / **weren't**) so busy with my other activities.
8. I'd insist that every player (**arrive** / arrives) promptly and in full uniform.
9. If a player (was / **were**) late, he or she would get a demerit.
10. I think it is essential that there (is / **be**) proper discipline on the team.

Write whether each underlined verb is *indicative*, *imperative*, or *subjunctive*.

11. Louis Armstrong <u>is</u> an important jazz figure. — indicative
12. Whether he <u>be</u> here or there, his influence is significant. — subjunctive
13. Let's <u>help</u> Mom clean up the mess in the kitchen. — imperative
14. John <u>is</u> considered a math wizard by most of us. — indicative
15. I wish you <u>were</u> able to meet my grandmother when she visits. — subjunctive
16. I <u>recommend</u> that we refrain from squabbling. — subjunctive
17. That dog <u>is</u> an impressive height. — indicative
18. <u>Read</u> the article about the new library as soon as you can. — imperative
19. What <u>is</u> being built at that construction site? — indicative
20. I <u>believed</u> him when he told me the truth. — indicative
21. She <u>would</u> be on time if she got up earlier. — subjunctive
22. I must <u>insist</u> that you be ready to leave at eight o'clock. — subjunctive

On another sheet of paper, write three sentences in the subjunctive mood.

50 • Section 4

For additional help, review pages 72–73 in your textbook or visit www.voyagesinenglish.com.

© Loyola Press. Voyages in English Grade 7

4.10 Agreement of Subject and Verb—Part I

A verb agrees with its subject in person and number. Watch for **intervening phrases** between the subject and verb.

Circle the verb that correctly completes each sentence.

1. The computer (is) are) on right now.
2. I (don't) doesn't) play chess.
3. That globe (were (was) made in the early 1900s.
4. Giraffes in the grassland (is (are) easy to spot.
5. My friend (doesn't) don't) understand the geometry problem.
6. You (were) was) my first choice for class president.
7. There (is (are) only two girls in my gym class.
8. A flock of Canada geese (are (is) flying overhead.

Complete each sentence with doesn't, don't, is, or are.

9. Arnold __doesn't__ want to play tennis this summer.
10. Lucille __is__ the best swimmer on our team.
11. Cayla and Paul __don't__ think they can come to the party on Friday.
12. Their parents __don't__ allow sleepovers, but they can stay until early evening.
13. We __are__ happy to be able to help in any way we can.
14. Who __is__ too tired to hike another five miles?
15. Main Street Hardware __doesn't__ carry trash cans anymore.
16. Casey and James __don't__ have a pet hamster now that Peanut is gone.

Circle the verb that correctly completes each sentence.

17. The boys and their mother, Mrs. Keppler, (is (are) were) going into the city.
18. The crabs, which come in bright, decorated shells, (does (don't) doesn't) cost much.
19. That map, which shows different climates, (were (is) are) Mrs. Hershoc's.
20. The feet of the arctic fox (is was (are) lined with fur to keep it warm.
21. This green plaid scarf (does don't (doesn't) match the shirt's red floral design.
22. Earlier I noticed that the sandy sneakers (were) is are) under the mudroom bench.

For additional help, review pages 76–77 in your textbook or visit www.voyagesinenglish.com.

4.9 Modal Auxiliaries

Modal auxiliaries are used to express permission, possibility, ability, necessity, obligation, and intention. Common modal auxiliaries are *may, might, can, could, must, should, will,* and *would.*

Underline each verb phrase with a modal auxiliary. Then write if the verb phrase expresses permission, possibility, ability, necessity, obligation, or intention.

1. All the guests might be offered some dessert. __possibility__
2. After the completion of her chores, Pam may go to the mall. __permission__
3. Sam should take his dog for a walk at least once a day. __obligation__
4. The students must clean the gym after the dance. __necessity__
5. You could take your test in the morning. __possibility__
6. Jason can make birdhouses out of milk cartons. __ability__
7. We might sing one more song in the winter concert. __possibility__
8. Helen and Emily will collect the donations this afternoon. __intention__
9. Emmanuel must go to the doctor because of his sore throat. __necessity__
10. With additional free time, we would volunteer more often. __possibility__

Complete each sentence with a verb phrase containing a modal auxiliary. Use the verb in parentheses with the meaning indicated after the sentence. *Possible responses are given.*

11. We __must plan__ (plan) the Middle School Fun Night for the spring. (necessity)
12. Irene __could make__ (make) the decorations for the party. (possibility)
13. Local businesses __might donate__ (donate) prizes for the games. (possibility)
14. Mr. Pearson __should be__ (be) a chaperone. (obligation)
15. Mrs. Li __can bring__ (bring) extra balls for the basketball court. (ability)
16. Anyone who helps __may attend__ (attend) without paying the entrance fee. (permission)
17. Degliomini's Deli says they __could provide__ (provide) the food. (possibility)
18. Everyone __must clean__ (clean) the multipurpose room thoroughly. (necessity)
19. We __could raise__ (raise) enough money for the eighth-grade field trip. (possibility)
20. We all __will be__ (be) there to make sure everything goes well. (intention)
21. Our cooperative group __can research__ (research) the topic after school. (ability)

Write a short paragraph about how students can improve your school. Use at least four different types of modal auxiliaries in your suggestions.

For additional help, review pages 74–75 in your textbook or visit www.voyagesinenglish.com.

4.11 Agreement of Subject and Verb—Part II

Compound subjects with *and* usually require a plural verb. If the subjects connected by *and* refer to the same person, place, or thing, or express a single idea, however, the verb is singular.

Underline the subject in each sentence. Circle the error in subject-verb agreement and write the correct verb.

1. Mathematics are my favorite subject. _____ *is*
2. The theater troupe are producing a play. _____ *is producing*
3. The scarf and gloves was on sale. _____ *were*
4. Every plant and animal need water. _____ *needs*
5. Ten dollars are what we paid for the movie. _____ *is*
6. The team have practiced all week. _____ *has practiced*
7. The cast are rehearsing tonight. _____ *is rehearsing*
8. Neither the cat nor the dogs is allowed in the house. _____ *are allowed*
9. The entire group are waiting outside. _____ *is waiting*
10. Every avenue and street were covered with snow. _____ *was covered*
11. An anxious crowd were gathering in front of the building. _____ *was gathering*
12. The jury are waiting to be seated. _____ *is waiting*

Complete each sentence with the present tense form of the verb in parentheses.

13. The track team _*travels*_ (travel) to distant competitions.
14. This team and its captain _*are*_ (be) going to Arizona.
15. Jones and Wong Accounting _*is*_ (be) in the office upstairs.
16. Cale and Merlin _*run*_ (run) up that hill every morning.
17. Everyone in the play _*comes*_ (come) to the postproduction party.
18. They _*say*_ (say) the instructions for the computer are clear.
19. This ham and cheese sandwich _*tastes*_ (taste) better than usual.
20. The stained-glass window _*diffuses*_ (diffuse) the light.
21. The football and baseball teams _*are*_ (be) using the weight room.
22. The moon _*seems*_ (seem) unusually bright tonight.

For additional help, review pages 78–79 in your textbook or visit www.voyagesinenglish.com.

SECTION 5   Daily Maintenance

5.1   **The plumber is fixing the sink in the kitchen.**
1. What is the complete subject of the sentence?
2. What is the verb phrase?
3. Is it a present participle or a past participle?
4. What is the adjective phrase?
5. Diagram the sentence on another sheet of paper.

The plumber | is fixing \ sink — The | the | in | the | kitchen — present participle — in the kitchen

5.2   **The Wongs have lived in that house for five years.**
1. What is the verb phrase in the sentence?
2. What is the past participle?
3. What is the auxiliary verb?
4. Which word is a demonstrative adjective?
5. Diagram the sentence on another sheet of paper.

The Wongs | have lived \ in | house — that — have lived — lived — that — for years — five

5.3   **The librarian found a book about Rome for us.**
1. What is the verb in the sentence?
2. What tense is the verb?
3. Is the verb transitive or intransitive?
4. Is *us* a subject or an object pronoun?
5. Diagram the sentence on another sheet of paper.

The librarian | found \ book — a | about Rome | for us — found — past — transitive — object pronoun

5.4   **Give me the outline for your research report on Monday.**
1. What is the verb in the sentence?
2. Is the verb form indicative or imperative?
3. Which word is the direct object?
4. Which word is the indirect object?
5. Diagram the sentence on another sheet of paper.

(you) | Give \ outline — the | for report | your | research — me | on Monday — Give — imperative — outline — me

5.5 This month they are volunteering at the animal shelter on Saturdays.
1. What is the verb phrase in the sentence? — *are volunteering*
2. Is the verb form indicative or imperative? — *indicative*
3. What tense is the verb phrase? — *present progressive*
4. Is the verb phrase transitive or intransitive? — *intransitive*
5. Diagram the sentence on another sheet of paper.

Diagram: they | are volunteering — at / shelter / the / animal — on / Saturdays — This / month

5.6 Our cat Oscar was lying on my bed last night.
1. What is the verb phrase in the sentence? — *was lying*
2. Is it past tense or a past participle? — *past participle*
3. Which word is an appositive? — *Oscar*
4. Which word does it rename? — *cat*
5. Diagram the sentence on another sheet of paper.

Diagram: cat (Oscar) | was lying — on / bed / my — night / last — Our

5.7 The first astronauts were very courageous people.
1. Which word is a linking verb? — *were*
2. Which words does it link? — *astronauts, people*
3. Which word is the subject complement? — *people*
4. Is very an adjective or an adverb? — *adverb*
5. Diagram the sentence on another sheet of paper.

Diagram: astronauts | were \ people — The / first — courageous / very

5.8 These Fuji apples taste sweet and juicy, but I prefer McIntosh apples.
1. Which word is used as a linking verb? — *taste*
2. What are the subject complements? — *sweet, juicy*
3. What kind of pronoun is the word I? — *subject pronoun*
4. What are the person and number of this word? — *first person singular*
5. Diagram the sentence on another sheet of paper.

Diagram: apples | taste \ sweet / juicy — These / Fuji — but — I | prefer — apples / McIntosh

5.9 That beautiful mosaic was created by a local artist.
1. What is the verb phrase in the sentence? — *was created*
2. Is it transitive or intransitive? — *transitive*
3. Is the verb phrase in the active or passive voice? — *passive voice*
4. Which words are adjectives? — *beautiful, local*
5. Diagram the sentence on another sheet of paper.

Diagram: mosaic | was created — beautiful / That — by / artist / a / local

5.10 The school's band will be performing in the holiday parade.
1. What is the verb phrase in the sentence? — *will be performing*
2. What tense is this verb phrase? — *future progressive*
3. Is it transitive or intransitive? — *intransitive*
4. Which word is a possessive noun? — *school's*
5. Diagram the sentence on another sheet of paper.

Diagram: band | will be performing — The / school's — in / parade / the / holiday

5.11 Our friend John can play the trumpet and the drums quite well.
1. What is the verb phrase in the sentence? — *can play*
2. Which word is a modal auxiliary? — *can*
3. Does this word express ability or obligation? — *ability*
4. Which words are adverbs? — *quite, well*
5. Diagram the sentence on another sheet of paper.

Diagram: friend (John) | can play \ trumpet / the / and / drums / the — Our — well / quite

5.1 Participles

Verbals are words made from verbs to function as another part of speech. A **participle** is a verb form used as an adjective. A **participial phrase** includes the participle, an object or a complement, and any modifiers.

Underline the participle in each sentence. Circle the noun or pronoun the participle modifies. Then underline the main verb twice.

1. Having eaten dinner, Colonel Mansard walked leisurely to the study.
2. He, entering the study, discovered that the silver had been stolen.
3. Did Mrs. Blaine, known for her extravagant lifestyle, take the silver?
4. Mr. Green, stalling for time, suggested everyone sit down for dinner.
5. Humming to herself, Abby seemed unconcerned by any of the fuss.
6. Professor Davis, having arrived late, was flustered by the events.
7. Mrs. Farin was cleared when the written confession matched her alibi completely.
8. A letter copied by hand implicated Mrs. Blaine and her ample handbag.

Underline the participial phrase in each sentence. Circle the noun or pronoun it modifies.

9. Having found the missing homework, Luis was relieved.
10. Workers cut down the trees burned in the wildfires.
11. The man speaking to the teacher is my father.
12. The signs posted on the wall are for next week's election.
13. A cat wearing a blue collar followed me home.
14. Can you reach the books placed on the top shelf?
15. The soup boiling in the black pot splattered all over the ceiling.
16. My favorite contestant was the dog taught to bark "Happy Birthday to You."
17. The hot tea steaming in the blue mug was a welcome sight on a cold day.
18. That silk dress hanging at the top of the display is finally on sale.

On another sheet of paper, write a sentence for each participial phrase. Circle the noun or pronoun that each participial phrase describes. *Answers will vary.*

19. looking through her purse
20. holding the roll of tickets
21. wounded by the enemy
22. formed by stones and boulders
23. followed closely by the excited puppy
24. acknowledging their hard work

For additional help, review pages 84–85 in your textbook or visit www.voyagesinenglish.com.

© Loyola Press. Voyages in English **Grade 7**

Section 5 • 57

5.2 Placement of Participles

Do not confuse a **participial adjective** after a linking verb with a participle that is part of a verb phrase. **Dangling participles** occur when a sentence does not contain the noun or pronoun the participle modifies.

Underline the participial adjectives in these sentences.

1. We visited the bustling zoo over the holiday.
2. The pacing lion was popular with everyone.
3. A frazzled father was too busy chasing his young twin sons to see the polar bears.
4. The sleeping koalas were not disturbed by the screaming monkeys.
5. Everyone cheered when the elephants emerged from the darkened cave.
6. We noticed there were no buzzing insects near the bat exhibit.
7. The annoyed camel kept turning its back on the crowd.
8. The patient snake docent helped turn a frightened child into a smiling one.
9. We never leave the zoo without a glimpse of the flying squirrels.
10. This time we made sure to visit the traveling butterfly exhibit.

Write phrases using each participle as an adjective before a noun. *Answers will vary.*

11. scrubbed _____ 14. broken _____
12. screaming _____ 15. wasting _____
13. driven _____ 16. wounded _____

Rewrite each sentence to correct the dangling participle. Add words as needed. *Possible responses are given.*

17. Coming home early, the house was empty.
   Coming home early, the children found the house empty.

18. Running through the park, a thunderous cheer erupted from the baseball field.
   Running through the park, I heard a thunderous cheer erupt from the baseball field.

19. Studying the footprints, it was the reason for the missing money.
   Studying the footprints, he now knew the reason for the missing money.

20. Examining the damage, the book should be replaced.
   Examining the damage, my brother said that the book should be replaced.

For additional help, review pages 86–87 in your textbook or visit www.voyagesinenglish.com.

58 • Section 5

© Loyola Press. Voyages in English **Grade 7**

5.4 Gerunds as Objects and Appositives

A gerund can be used as a direct object or as the object of a preposition. It can also be used as an appositive—a word or group of words used immediately after a noun to rename it and give more information about it.

Underline the gerund in each sentence. Write whether the gerund is a direct object (D), an object of a preposition (P), or an appositive (A).

1. My grandmother enjoys cutting hair. — D
2. Malaya excels in baking bread. — P
3. Calligraphy, writing fancy letters, looks like an interesting hobby. — A
4. Her record of jumping rope is an amazing feat. — P
5. Jared's job, washing the car, is something he likes to do. — A
6. Almost immediately, Sarah regretted losing her purse. — D
7. Maya's new baby loves playing the peekaboo game. — D
8. We will celebrate all patriotic holidays by raising the flag. — P
9. The officer pulled the car over and avoided stopping traffic. — D
10. Ava's science project, making a volcano, took almost two hours. — A
11. With hard work the boys succeeded in raising their grades. — P
12. This recipe calls out kneading the dough for 10 minutes. — D
13. Some college students need more paper for taking notes. — P
14. Her schedule included visiting relatives. — D
15. This task, raking the fallen leaves, takes the most time. — A

Write a gerund phrase to complete each sentence. Write whether the gerund is a direct object (D), an object of a preposition (P), or an appositive (A). *Answers will vary.*

16. I dread _____. — D
17. Cats and dogs benefit from _____. — P
18. Circumnavigation, _____, is an arduous task. — A
19. His keen sense of smell is useful for _____. — P
20. Today we celebrate _____. — D
21. Kate and Henry decided to postpone _____. — D

For additional help, review pages 90–91 in your textbook or visit www.voyagesinenglish.com.

5.3 Gerunds as Subjects and Subject Complements

A **gerund** is a verb form ending in *-ing* that is used as a noun. The entire **gerund phrase**—made up of a gerund and any other parts—acts as a noun. A gerund can be used in a sentence as a subject or a subject complement.

Underline the gerund phrase in each sentence. Write S if the gerund is the subject or SC if the gerund is the subject complement.

1. Throwing footballs is the best way for a quarterback to practice. — S
2. Jim's specialty is painting with oils. — SC
3. Putting together puzzles helped quiet the young child. — S
4. Watching sports is one way that my brother passes his time. — S
5. The girl's favorite pastime is listening to music. — SC
6. The high point of my trip was searching in the caves. — SC
7. Collecting stamps was how I received my last merit badge. — S
8. Humming a familiar song helped the nervous actor stay calm. — S
9. My least favorite job is vacuuming the hallway. — SC
10. Meena's preferred exercise is jogging through her neighborhood. — SC

Write a gerund used as a subject or a subject complement to complete each sentence. *Possible responses are given.*

11. __Inspiring__ scientists to ask questions is what Jupiter does best.
12. An important part of the Juno project is __studying__ the largest gaseous planet in our solar system.
13. Juno's mission is __Peering__ into the swirling gases is a function of the spacecraft.
14. __Answering__ difficult questions has long been the goal of our space programs.
15. __Exploring__ distant planets has captured the imagination of humanity.
16. __absorbing__ all these facts about space exploration.
17. Many of us are __helping__ us understand the planets.

Write a gerund phrase to complete each sentence. Use the verb in parentheses. *Answers will vary.*

18. _____ was a great time. (visit)
19. _____ should be fun. (swim)
20. My aerobic exercise is _____. (run)

For additional help, review pages 88–89 in your textbook or visit www.voyagesinenglish.com.

Practice Book Answer Key • 35

5.6 Infinitives as Subjects and Subject Complements

An **infinitive** is a verb form, usually preceded by *to*, that is used as a noun, an adjective, or an adverb.

Underline each infinitive or infinitive phrase. Write whether the infinitive is used as a subject or subject complement.

1. To complain is a waste of time. — *subject*
2. Her wish is to travel throughout Europe. — *subject complement*
3. To tell the truth was the best choice. — *subject*
4. His primary goal is to do the best job he can. — *subject complement*
5. To express your emotions is healthy. — *subject*
6. Our first goal is to visit the Grand Canyon. — *subject complement*
7. My plan for getting the role is to practice my lines. — *subject complement*
8. To swim in a tropical lagoon would be a wonderful thing. — *subject*
9. To snowboard should be quite exciting. — *subject*
10. The purpose of the poster is to symbolize freedom. — *subject complement*

Write an infinitive or infinitive phrase to complete each sentence. Write if the infinitive is used as a subject (S), or a subject complement (SC). *Answers will vary.*

11. _____ was common in the Old West. **S**
12. The goal of many people is _____. **SC**
13. _____ is a challenge for many students. **S**
14. _____ is often a requirement for success. **S**
15. A precursor for victory in any race is _____. **SC**
16. _____ was needed for combustion to occur. **S**
17. Another useful character trait is _____. **SC**
18. Henderson's primary talent was _____. **SC**
19. _____ is key to traveling safely. **S**
20. One way to see the world would be _____. **SC**
21. _____ is a task for most motivated students. **S**
22. A wish I have had for a long time is _____. **SC**

For additional help, review pages 94–95 in your textbook or visit www.voyagesinenglish.com.
© Loyola Press. Voyages in English **Grade 7**

5.5 Possessives with Gerunds, Using -ing Verb Forms

Gerunds may be preceded by a possessive form—either a possessive noun or a possessive adjective. These possessives describe the doer of the action of the gerund.

Circle the word that correctly completes each sentence.

1. (Me / **My**) agreeing to the decision was a mistake.
2. (Dad / **Dad's**) cracking his knuckles made me wince.
3. (**Dana's** / Dana) slamming the door woke everyone up.
4. She did not understand her (friend / **friend's**) rejecting the ideas for the project.
5. (We / **Our**) finishing the hallway mural on time was a good idea.
6. (**Tim's** / Tim) winning the race made him the conference champion.

Write whether the italicized word in each sentence is used as a gerund (G), a participial adjective (A), or a participle in a verb phrase (P).

7. I hope I have the *winning* raffle ticket. **A**
8. *Winning* the raffle was a surprise. **G**
9. Carla practiced *sprinting* for the big race. **G**
10. She was *thanking* her family for their support and encouragement. **P**
11. *Sitting* on the edge of our seats, we waited to see what would happen next. **G**
12. The clown was *juggling* six basketballs at once. **P**

Write a sentence using each word as a gerund, a participle, or a verb in the progressive tense. Then write how you used the word. *Answers will vary.*

13. running: _____
   Word used as _____
14. shining: _____
   Word used as _____
15. making: _____
   Word used as _____
16. finishing: _____
   Word used as _____

For additional help, review pages 92–93 in your textbook or visit www.voyagesinenglish.com.
© Loyola Press. Voyages in English **Grade 7**

5.8 Infinitives as Appositives

An infinitive functioning as a noun can be used as an appositive. An appositive is a word or group of words used after a noun or pronoun to rename it and give more information about it.

Underline the infinitive phrase used as an appositive in each sentence. Then circle the word that each appositive explains.

1. It was the actor's (role), to make the audience laugh, that he accomplished best.
2. Her (endeavor), to climb the world's tallest mountain, will take much preparation.
3. Our (dream), to visit all the U.S. national parks, will come true someday.
4. Tia's (kindness), to help the small child, earned her respect from her parents.
5. Dillan's (assignment), to write a short story, is due in two weeks.
6. The country's (need), to conserve natural resources, requires everyone's commitment.
7. Miguel's (goal), to win the spelling championship, occupies a great deal of his time.
8. The (agreement), to share the money equally, pleased both sides.
9. The children's (reward), to visit the amusement park, was well deserved.
10. Our (objective), to improve school spirit, proved most difficult.
11. The president's (oath), to serve our country, is an essential part of the inauguration.
12. My primary (focus), to keep from getting seasick, did not last long.

Underline each infinitive or infinitive phrase. Write whether the infinitive is used as a subject, a subject complement, a direct object, or an appositive.

13. To allow sweets was more than the nanny would allow. _____ subject
14. Our hope, to walk the deck before night fell, was thwarted. _____ appositive
15. The king was permitted to rule the country. _____ direct object
16. To suggest cooperation seemed disloyal. _____ subject
17. Julie tried to prevent the captain's escape. _____ direct object
18. The cook's idea, to invite Karen for dinner, was a good one. _____ appositive
19. Eva's greatest fault, to argue every point, annoyed us all. _____ appositive
20. The purpose of the signs was to warn us of the danger. _____ subject complement
21. Javier strained to picture the next season. _____ direct object

On another sheet of paper, write three sentences that each use an infinitive as a noun.

For additional help, review pages 98–99 in your textbook or visit www.voyagesinenglish.com.

5.7 Infinitives as Objects

An infinitive functioning as a noun can be used as a direct object in a sentence. This direct object may be preceded by a noun or pronoun. The infinitive and its subject form an **infinitive clause.**

Underline the infinitives used as a direct object in each sentence.

1. The builders wanted to support the roof by reinforcing the walls.
2. The suspect wrote to confess to the crime.
3. John intended to propose to Mary on the transcontinental train trip.
4. The children were taught to tolerate different points of view.
5. Adelle continued to deny any involvement in the prank.

Underline the infinitive, infinitive phrase, or infinitive clause in each sentence. Circle the verb of which each is the direct object.

6. The old cat (loved) to abandon its toys in the middle of the carpet.
7. The club president (needs) to increase recognition for the club in the school.
8. Carrie (tried) to understand the complex construction of the sentence.
9. Rolph (wanted) to watch his favorite movie over and over.
10. We (regret) to inform you that your application to Upstart Academy has been denied.

Underline each infinitive used as a noun. Write whether the infinitive is used as a subject (S), a subject complement (SC), or a direct object (DO).

11. The missionaries wanted to build a school. _____ DO
12. My plan for vacation is to read several books. _____ SC
13. To study for two hours each night is my goal for this week. _____ S
14. We agreed that the best option was to postpone the trip. _____ SC
15. The politician promised to make the public aware of the issues. _____ DO
16. To cross the finish line was my goal. _____ S
17. When did you decide to administer the test? _____ DO
18. The guests are expected to return to their seats. _____ DO
19. The substitute teacher's first task was to take attendance. _____ SC
20. Roger's first task is to find an answer to all his questions. _____ SC

On another sheet of paper, write sentences using three infinitives. Use one infinitive as a subject, one as a subject complement, and one as a direct object.

For additional help, review pages 96–97 in your textbook or visit www.voyagesinenglish.com.

Practice Book Answer Key • 37

5.9 Infinitives as Adjectives

Infinitives can be used as adjectives to describe nouns and pronouns. These infinitives follow the words they describe.

Underline the infinitive phrase in each sentence. Then circle the noun it describes.

1. The (time) to check the list of ingredients is before you start baking.
2. The group chose this (book) to read for their report.
3. The company president stressed the (need) to advertise the new product.
4. Here's a list of the (rules) to follow.
5. I explained that the athletic director was the (man) to see.
6. That dog has the (talent) to track missing people.
7. Mr. Harper devised a (system) to organize all our homework assignments.
8. Before anyone else got home, Carl made an (effort) to clean up the mess.
9. At what point in history did women get the (right) to vote in elections?
10. It was Mother Teresa's (work) to feed and to clothe people who were poor.
11. The sign directed me to the (person) to see for the application.
12. The investigator knew this was the (case) to solve as quickly as possible.

Write an infinitive phrase that acts as an adjective to complete each sentence. Then circle the noun each describes. *Answers will vary.*

13. I know an easier (way) _____
14. Sheila is the (person) _____
15. The library is the (place) _____
16. Mother had a special (ability) _____
17. Two brothers made a (pledge) _____
18. The man invented a (machine) _____
19. We all made an (effort) _____
20. He thought of a more efficient (way) _____
21. Her creativity led to a (design) _____
22. Jack had an (idea) _____
23. We raised (money) _____
24. The children had a (chance) _____

For additional help, review pages 100–101 in your textbook or visit www.voyagesinenglish.com.

Section 5 • 65

© Loyola Press. Voyages in English   Grade 7

5.10 Infinitives as Adverbs

An infinitive can be used as an adverb—to describe a verb, an adjective, or another adverb.

Underline the infinitive phrase in each sentence. Write whether the italicized word each phrase modifies is an adjective (ADJ), an adverb (ADV), or a verb (V).

1. She was *nervous* to meet her grandparents. — ADJ
2. Cole *strained* to lift the weights. — V
3. Librarians *check* to see if books are returned in good condition. — V
4. We talked *quietly* to avoid waking the baby. — ADV
5. The farmer is *happy* to see the rain come down. — ADJ
6. Eli was *ecstatic* to ride on the team bus. — ADJ
7. Together we *worked* to clean the kitchen. — V
8. Nina had *arrived* to try a new recipe. — V
9. I reviewed my essay *carefully* to check for any errors. — ADV
10. The fitness test was too *easy* to give to the coach. — ADJ
11. We *struggled* to stand up in the wind. — V
12. Those children are old *enough* to know better. — ADV

Underline the infinitive phrase in each sentence. Write whether the infinitive phrase is used as a noun (N), an adjective (ADJ), or an adverb (ADV).

13. The year-end trip will be to camp by the lake. — N
14. The doctors were ready to handle any emergency. — ADV
15. The people to help right now are the ones waiting in line. — ADJ
16. Mom and Dad planned a party to celebrate their anniversary. — ADJ
17. Our goal was to help the victims as much as possible. — N
18. To raise money before the invoice was due is now our only hope. — N
19. Jacob and Julie worked together to produce a first-place project. — ADV
20. The band was so proud to win the competition. — ADV

On another sheet of paper, write three sentences. Use an infinitive phrase as a noun in the first sentence, as an adjective in the second sentence, and as an adverb in the third sentence.

For additional help, review pages 102–103 in your textbook or visit www.voyagesinenglish.com.

66 • Section 5

© Loyola Press. Voyages in English   Grade 7

5.11 Hidden and Split Infinitives

Sometimes infinitives appear in sentences without the *to*. Such infinitives are called **hidden infinitives**. An adverb placed between *to* and the verb results in a **split infinitive**. Good writers avoid split infinitives.

Underline the hidden infinitive in each sentence.

1. The runner felt his heart race as he listened for the starting gun.
2. The lost skier dared hope that the droning sound was a rescue plane.
3. When the scared boy saw his father slowly appear out of the fog, he sobbed with relief.
4. Our art teacher made us work slowly and carefully on the pencil sketches.
5. The cat let me help her out of the tight collar.
6. Emil watched the surgeon wipe the area clean.
7. The volunteers helped us learn our lines for the school play.
8. We did not dare take more than we needed.
9. Caleb heard the frogs croak right outside his window.
10. My mom let me go to the Middle School Fun Night, and I had a great time.

Underline the split infinitive in each sentence. Rewrite each sentence to eliminate the split infinitive. *Possible responses are given.*

11. I need to consistently keep memorizing these new vocabulary words.
I need to keep memorizing these new vocabulary words consistently.

12. The girls don't expect to quickly find their missing video game.
The girls don't expect to find their missing video game quickly.

13. Kate hopes to eventually write a best-selling novel.
Eventually, Kate hopes to write a best-selling novel.

14. I managed to efficiently use the soap so that it lasted the entire trip.
I managed to use the soap efficiently so that it lasted the entire trip.

15. The server learned to carefully handle the food to avoid cross-contamination.
The server learned to handle the food carefully to avoid cross-contamination.

16. The child wanted to effectively spin the swing so that all the water spun off.
The child wanted to spin the swing effectively so that all the water spun off.

For additional help, review pages 104–105 in your textbook or visit www.voyagesinenglish.com.

5.11 Hidden and Split Infinitives

Sometimes infinitives appear in sentences without the *to*. Such infinitives are called **hidden infinitives**. An adverb placed between *to* and the verb results in a **split infinitive**. Good writers avoid split infinitives.

Underline the hidden infinitive in each sentence.

1. The boy watched the toy boat sink slowly into the lake.
2. I did nothing but lay in the hammock all day.
3. Carl made me write thank-you notes to all my relatives.
4. I dared not forget Miss Delgado on the list of people to invite.
5. We watched the fireworks explode in the night sky.

Indicate with a caret (∧) where the adverb in parentheses belongs in each sentence. *Possible responses are given.*

6. We decided to continue to scoop water from the leaky boat. (rapidly)
7. The lion wanted to escape back into the jungle. (stealthily)
8. The librarian knew to handle the rare book with gloves. (not surprisingly)
9. I prefer to drive, but I don't mind being stuck in traffic if I'm in my car. (speedily)
10. Heber tried to study, but all he could think about was the party tomorrow. (intently)
11. Dad tried to start the car, but in the frigid temperatures, the battery had died. (doggedly)
12. Abigail started to apologize but then wondered if she was really wrong. (automatically)
13. Hutch and I didn't need to go home that way, but it did seem faster. (actually)
14. I hate to leave Mr. Peterson's class because it is so much fun. (genuinely)

Circle each hidden infinitive and underline each split infinitive in the paragraph. On another sheet of paper, rewrite the sentences to eliminate the split infinitives.

The last week of classes was a busy one. The students in Mr. Gray's class did nothing but (study) all day long. They wanted to fully understand the material for the final exam. Some students already felt well prepared. These students need not (take) all their textbooks home each night. Mr. Gray gave Jessica a special award. She had learned to confidently speak in front of the class. On Friday morning the class needed to attentively listen to the principal's announcements. The students hoped to quickly leave campus on their last day of school.

For additional help, review pages 104–105 in your textbook or visit www.voyagesinenglish.com.

SECTION 6 Daily Maintenance

6.1 **The frightened kittens hid inside the cardboard box.**
1. What is the complete subject of the sentence?
2. Is the verb regular or irregular?
3. Which words are adjectives?
4. Which word is a participial adjective?
5. Diagram the sentence on another sheet of paper.

6.2 **Drawing silly cartoons is Jake's favorite activity.**
1. What is the gerund phrase?
2. Is it used as a subject or a subject complement?
3. Which word is the object of the gerund?
4. How is the word activity used in the sentence?
5. Diagram the sentence on another sheet of paper.

6.3 **You can support our cause by donating school supplies.**
1. What is the verb or verb phrase?
2. What is the gerund?
3. How is the gerund phrase used in the sentence?
4. What is the direct object?
5. Diagram the sentence on another sheet of paper.

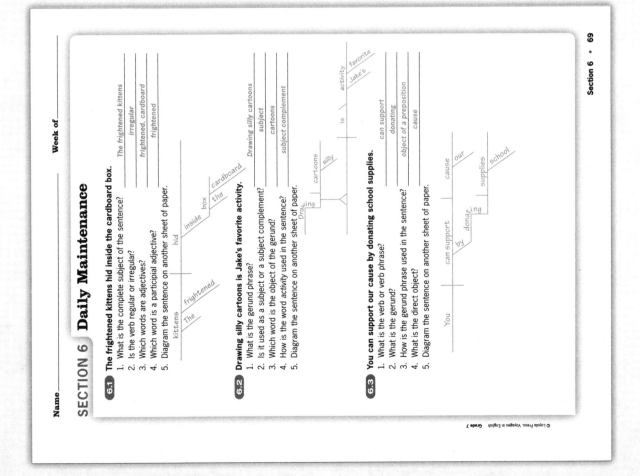

6.4 **An internship is a great way to learn about a career.**
1. What is the infinitive phrase?
2. Is it used as an adjective or an adverb?
3. Which word does the infinitive phrase describe?
4. How is the word way used in the sentence?
5. Diagram the sentence on another sheet of paper.

6.5 **The job of the proofreader is to find any mistakes.**
1. What is the infinitive phrase?
2. Is it used as a subject or a subject complement?
3. What is the adjective phrase?
4. What kind of adjective is the word any?
5. Diagram the sentence on another sheet of paper.

6.2 Interrogative Adverbs and Adverbial Nouns

An **interrogative adverb** is an adverb used to ask a question. An **adverbial noun** is a noun that acts as an adverb by describing a verb. Adverbial nouns usually express *time, distance, measure, value,* or *direction.*

Identify the italicized word in each sentence by writing IA (interrogative adverb) or AN (adverbial noun). Then write what each adverbial noun expresses.

1. *Where* was the first radar device used?   IA
2. *How* was the Panama Canal built?   IA
3. The church bells ring every *hour*.   AN   *time*
4. To get to the park, turn *east* on Main Street.   AN   *direction*
5. Alex runs many *miles* every day.   AN   *distance*
6. *Why* was the letter returned?   IA
7. The book I purchased dates back some 50 *years*.   AN   *time*
8. *When* did the first human walk on the moon?   IA
9. The puppy weighed four *pounds*.   AN   *measure*
10. The winning ticket cost only one *dollar*.   AN   *value*

Complete each sentence with an interrogative adverb. *Possible responses are given.*

11. _How_ can we fix this broken lamp?
12. _Where_ do you think I left my homework assignment?
13. _How_ are we going to fit all this stuff back in the box?
14. _When_ did you tell Dad we would be ready to be picked up?
15. _Why_ are we stopping at the store on the way home?

Complete each sentence with an adverbial noun that expresses the quality indicated in parentheses. *Possible responses are given.*

16. Our family traveled _west_ to go to the family reunion. (direction)
17. For the fund-raiser we walked 20 _miles_. (distance)
18. We must wait six more _days_ until the assignment is finished. (time)
19. He decided it was not worth it to spend 50 _dollars_ on the ticket. (value)
20. This tiny bird weighs only nine _ounces_. (measure)
21. The bookshelf is eight _feet_ tall, so it will fit in the room. (measure)
22. It took five _minutes_ for the runner to complete the mile run. (time)

For additional help, review pages 112–113 in your textbook or visit www.voyagesinenglish.com.

© Loyola Press. Voyages in English **Grade 7**

6.1 Types of Adverbs

An **adverb** is a word that describes a verb, an adjective, or another adverb.

Underline the adverbs and circle the word each adverb describes.

1. Cari has not (decided) where she will go to summer camp.
2. Scott and Julie (hopped) impatiently in the frigid air while waiting for the bus.
3. Sissy (ran) inside to escape the dog that was annoying her.
4. We were growing increasingly (concerned) about the weather.
5. The mail carrier (arrived) promptly every day at noon.
6. Kaitlyn and Zoe said the movie was rather (disappointing)
7. Hector carefully (replaced) the face of the broken watch.
8. Natalie did indeed (arrive) early for the first class.

Underline the adverb in each sentence. Write affirmation, degree, manner, negation, place, or time to identify the type of adverb.

9. Socrates was indeed a Greek philosopher and a teacher.   *affirmation*
10. He would usually teach a student through questions.   *time*
11. His questions were carefully presented to his students.   *manner*
12. Athenians cleverly nicknamed him "the Gadfly."   *manner*
13. Eventually his views became unpopular.   *time*
14. Socrates was fully condemned for his views.   *degree*
15. Plato diligently recorded much of what we know of Socrates.   *manner*

Complete each sentence with the type of adverb indicated in parentheses. *Possible responses are given.*

16. All the adults ran _outside_ when they heard the sirens. (place)
17. The detective walked _quickly_ down the dark street. (manner)
18. He had _not_ forgotten his wallet. (negation)
19. That necktie is _quite_ colorful. (degree)
20. Most of the wedding guests arrived at the church _early_. (time)
21. Charlie will do his homework _soon_. (time)
22. The get-well card _certainly_ made the patient smile. (affirmation)
23. The gymnast grasped the high bar _tightly_. (manner)
24. _No_, you do not need an umbrella. (negation)
25. Diane looked _up_ to see her mom waving from the window. (place)

For additional help, review pages 110–111 in your textbook or visit www.voyagesinenglish.com.

© Loyola Press. Voyages in English **Grade 7**

6.3 Comparative and Superlative Adverbs

Some adverbs can be compared. These adverbs have **comparative** and **superlative** forms.

Underline the adverb that correctly completes each sentence.

1. Josh (thoughtfully more thoughtfully) brought Helena some ice for her wounded knee.
2. My brother accepted the apology (graciously more graciously) than I had expected.
3. Our wood stove heats the house (more efficiently most efficiently) than the electric heater.
4. The (earlier earliest) showing of the movie is at 11:30 a.m.
5. Winter seemed to arrive (sooner soonest) than expected this year.

Complete the chart by writing the missing forms of each adverb.

POSITIVE	COMPARATIVE	SUPERLATIVE
6. late	later	latest
7. well	better	best
8. happily	more/less happily	most/least happily
9. badly	worse	worst
10. fluently	more/less fluently	most/least fluently
11. much	more	most
12. long	longer	longest
13. little	less	least

Complete each sentence with an adverb from the chart above and the form indicated in parentheses. Possible responses are given.

14. History is the subject I like _best/most/least_. (superlative)
15. Dana did _better/worse_ on this test than on the last one. (comparative)
16. Margie slept _latest/longest/worst/best_ of all the campers. (superlative)
17. He volunteered _more happily/more less/later_ than Pedro did. (comparative)
18. I _happily_ accepted the job of stage manager. (positive)
19. The new student reads this difficult text _less fluently/more fluently_ than I can. (comparative)

6.4 Troublesome Words

Troublesome adverbs are those adverbs that are commonly confused and often incorrectly used. When you use these adverbs in your writing, slow down and check that you are using the correct adverb.

Underline the correct adverb in parentheses to complete each sentence.

1. I found my name (further farther) down the list.
2. (There They're) ready to ship the packages tomorrow.
3. After so much training, Liz draws really (well good).
4. Her paintings are (well good).
5. I feel (bad badly) about not studying for the spelling test.
6. Will you be going to (there their) garage sale?
7. Alma gets along (well good) with her brother.
8. The old carpet was (bad badly) worn in several spots.
9. The family will go (they're there) at the end of the vacation.
10. If you want an apple, here is a (well good) one.
11. Do you have (they're their) CDs?
12. Both soccer teams played (well good).
13. We researched the issue (farther further) before voting on it.
14. Mom was upset that the baby behaved (bad badly) during the show.

Complete each sentence with there, their, or they're.

15. Max, Malachi, and Jacob are packing _their_ things for a camping trip.
16. _They're_ going to Seven Mountains with the scouts.
17. Max says he loves to go _there_ even though _there_ are bears.
18. _They're_ black bears that are searching for food.
19. The scouts are very careful not to leave food out _there_.
20. Malachi and Jacob are bringing _their_ compasses.
21. _They're_ hoping to earn an orienteering merit badge.
22. _Their_ enthusiasm is growing for the camping trip.
23. _There_ is always an adventure waiting for them at Seven Mountains.

6.4 Troublesome Words

Troublesome adverbs are those adverbs that are commonly confused and often incorrectly used. When you use these adverbs in your writing, slow down and check that you are using the correct adverb.

Complete each sentence with *farther* or *further*.

1. With the binoculars we could see ___*farther*___ than before.

2. We had to walk ___*farther*___ than we wanted.

3. We agreed there was nothing ___*further*___ to say on the subject.

4. Is it ___*farther*___ to the state of Washington or to Washington, D.C., from here?

5. This strange concept could not be ___*further*___ from the truth.

Complete each sentence with *good* or *well*.

6. We wanted to see ___*good*___ examples of modern art, so we went to the museum.

7. The twins behaved ___*well*___ at the dentist, so we all got to go to a movie.

8. Micah executes karate moves ___*well*___ because he has a black belt.

9. The entire class had ___*good*___ attendance, so we earned extra credit.

10. Eden explained ___*well*___ how to multiply fractions.

Complete each sentence with *bad* or *badly*.

11. The music was discordant and ___*badly*___ played.

12. I felt ___*bad*___ about losing Sara's car keys.

13. Fuzzy was not a ___*bad*___ dog; in fact, he was easy to train.

14. The food was ___*bad*___, but the conversation was excellent.

15. The planning was thorough, but it was ___*badly*___ executed.

Write a sentence using each word as an adverb. *Answers will vary.*

16. farther _____

17. further _____

18. well _____

19. badly _____

20. there _____

For additional help, review pages 116–117 in your textbook or visit www.voyagesinenglish.com.

© Loyola Press. Voyages in English • **Grade 7**

Section 6 • 75

6.5 Adverb Phrases and Clauses

Prepositional phrases used as adverbs to describe verbs, adjectives, or other adverbs are called **adverb phrases**. A dependent clause that acts as an adverb is called an **adverb clause**.

Underline each adverb phrase. Circle the word or words the phrase describes.

1. Many different ingredients (complement) each other in a recipe.

2. Holly (contributes) many ideas to the class.

3. Iron and carbon (are forged) together to form steel.

4. During the summer I (earn) money babysitting my younger brothers.

5. Julie (uses) nutmeg in casseroles, desserts, and even hot cocoa.

Underline each adverb clause. Circle the word or words the clause describes.

6. Until Henry needed to return home, he (helped) Mrs. McGillicuty.

7. The gyroscope (stabilizes) when it spins faster.

8. If there is a snowstorm tonight, school (will be canceled).

9. While the children sing for the program, the group (will perform) a simple dance.

10. The spinning tires (slip) when they pass over the thin layer of ice.

Write an adverb phrase to complete the first sentence in each pair. Then write an adverb clause to complete the second sentence. *Possible responses are given.*

11. It snowed ___*in the mountains*___

   It snowed ___*when we tried to leave*___

12. The knight fought the dragon ___*in the snow*___

   The knight fought the dragon ___*whenever it attacked the city*___

13. We slept ___*under the stars*___

   We slept ___*while our parents were fishing*___

14. Paulo will paint ___*in the morning*___

   Paulo will paint ___*if you help him*___

15. Jen can skate faster ___*on the pavement*___

   Jen can skate faster ___*because she has been practicing*___

16. We left for the airport ___*before noon*___

   We left for the airport ___*after we checked the arrival times*___

For additional help, review pages 118–119 in your textbook or visit www.voyagesinenglish.com.

© Loyola Press. Voyages in English • **Grade 7**

76 • Section 6

SECTION 7   Daily Maintenance

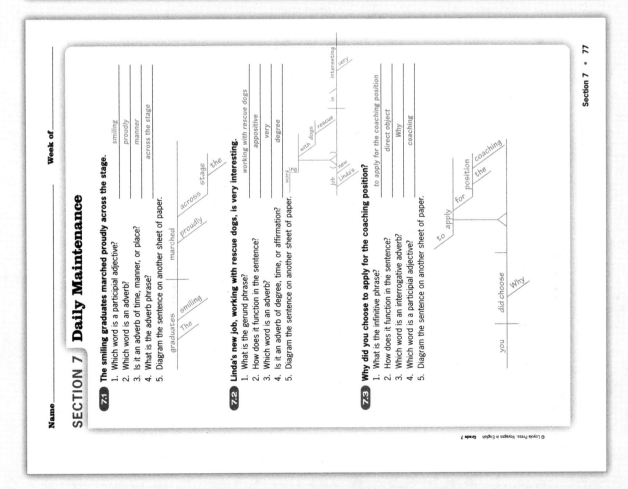

7.1 The smiling graduates marched proudly across the stage.
1. Which word is a participial adjective?
2. Which word is an adverb?
3. Is it an adverb of time, manner, or place?
4. What is the adverb phrase?
5. Diagram the sentence on another sheet of paper.

7.2 Linda's new job, working with rescue dogs, is very interesting.
1. What is the gerund phrase?
2. How does it function in the sentence?
3. Which word is an adverb?
4. Is it an adverb of degree, time, or affirmation?
5. Diagram the sentence on another sheet of paper.

7.3 Why did you choose to apply for the coaching position?
1. What is the infinitive phrase?
2. How does it function in the sentence?
3. Which word is an interrogative adverb?
4. Which word is a participial adjective?
5. Diagram the sentence on another sheet of paper.

7.4 My sister Laura sings more beautifully than I.
1. What is the adverb?
2. Is the adverb comparative or superlative?
3. How is the word *Laura* used in the sentence?
4. What is the person of the pronoun *I*?
5. Diagram the sentence on another sheet of paper.

7.5 Domingo plays best after he practices with his piano teacher.
1. Which word is an adverb?
2. What word does it describe?
3. Is the adverb comparative or superlative?
4. Which word is a proper noun?
5. Diagram the sentence on another sheet of paper.

7.6 When I feel sad, I write songs and poems.
1. What is the adverb clause?
2. Which word does it describe?
3. Which words are the direct objects?
4. Are the verbs regular or irregular?
5. Diagram the sentence on another sheet of paper.

7.2 Troublesome Prepositions

Troublesome prepositions are commonly misused. Carefully consider the meanings of troublesome prepositions to determine which one fits the context of your writing.

Underline the misused preposition in each sentence.

1. Mike did not want Julia to be angry <u>at</u> herself.

2. <u>Beside</u> Mike, Ernesto and I were also trying to cheer her up.

3. "Life is as if a race you can't ever win, but you can't stop running," said Julia.

4. "Forgive me if I differ <u>from</u> you," replied Ernie, "but I think life is full of hope."

5. "Sometimes <u>between</u> all those racers, nice guys finish first," submitted Mike.

6. "Some days are breezy and warm and the sun shines all day," I contributed, <u>"like the day was made just to touch your heart."</u>

7. "Choosing my best day from <u>between</u> those this month is not easy," Ernesto pointed out.

8. Mike sat besides me and said, "Sometimes you study hard for a test, and you ace it."

9. Julia smiled <u>like</u> she said, "OK, maybe you have a point. Sometimes the glass is half full."

10. "Even better," I said, pulling a water bottle <u>off</u> my backpack, "Sometimes the glass is full."

Circle the word or words in parentheses to complete each sentence.

11. The lions were (beside) besides) the giraffes at the zoo.

12. The editor divided the writing assignments (between (among) the five reporters.

13. I had enough money to buy this bicycle (off of (from) my uncle.

14. His parents (differ on) differ from) their approach to discipline.

15. Brittany was (angry with) angry at) her little brother.

16. Leon has his own business (beside (besides) his full-time job.

17. Choosing (among (between) the two desserts was very difficult.

18. Monique swam (like (as if) her life depended on it.

19. Who (beside (besides) the Hendersons are coming to dinner tomorrow night?

20. I kicked the ball (off of (from) where it rested on the grass.

21. The committee's job was to choose (among) between) the five nominees to pick a winner.

22. Lydia's ideas (differ on (differ from) mine when it comes to picking great movies.

23. I (differ from (differ with) my parents on how I should spend my savings.

For additional help, review pages 126–127 in your textbook or visit www.voyagesinenglish.com.

80 • Section 7

7.1 Single and Multiword Prepositions

A **preposition** is a word that shows the relationship between a noun or a pronoun and some other word in a sentence.

Underline each prepositional phrase. Circle each preposition.

1. Many species (of) jellyfish are found (throughout) the world's oceans.

2. (According to) one source, jellyfish are also known as medusa.

3. The jellyfish that are common (to) most coastal waters are the scyphozoan jellyfish.

4. (During) the spring, the number (of) jellyfish increases (in response to) an increase (in) food.

5. (Over) the course (of) the summer, jellyfish remain plentiful.

6. Because (of) the decline (in) food sources, jellyfish numbers decline (in) the fall and winter.

7. Jellyfish function (by means of) a web (of) nerves; they have no brain.

8. (Instead of) lungs, they simply absorb oxygen (from) the water (around) them.

9. Jellyfish may move (through) the water (with) contractions and stretches, but many simply float (with) the current.

10. Young jellyfish are tiny polyps that attach (to) the sea bottom.

11. When they reach a couple (of) millimeters, they float (off) (into) the water.

12. Most jellyfish aren't dangerous, but people avoid them (on account of) their painful sting.

Complete each sentence with a single or multiword preposition. *Possible responses are given.*

13. My mother and I walked ___around___ the garden, looking for her missing earring.

14. The train sped ___through___ the tunnel, illuminating the old stone walls.

15. I plan to study French ___in addition to___ Spanish, as long as they both fit in my schedule.

16. We packed the clothes ___in___ our new suitcases and hoped for the best.

17. The outdoor concert was canceled ___on account of___ the weather.

18. ___According to___ my brother, we are supposed to meet at Joseph's house tonight.

19. ___Because of___ the water main break, the entire student body was sent home.

20. I decided to wear my old jeans ___instead of___ a pair of shorts.

21. ___In spite of___ the brilliant sunshine, it was only 15 degrees that day.

On another sheet of paper, write three sentences that each use a preposition. Use at least one multiword preposition.

For additional help, review pages 124–125 in your textbook or visit www.voyagesinenglish.com.

Section 7 • 79

Practice Book Answer Key • 45

7.2 Troublesome Prepositions

Troublesome prepositions are commonly misused. Carefully consider the meanings of troublesome prepositions in order to determine which one fits the context of your writing.

Complete each sentence with the correct preposition. Use each preposition once.

| among | angry at | angry with | as | as if | beside | besides |
| between | differ with | differ on | differ from | from | like | off |

1. Many people ___differ on___ the topic of wolves and other similar predators.

2. ___Among___ wild animals, a great deal of research has been done on wolves.

3. If a wolf is ___angry at___ another wolf, it may arch its back and reveal its teeth.

4. ___Besides___ a heavy top coat, wolves have an undercoat of guard hairs.

5. There are common genetic traits ___between___ timber wolves and domestic dogs.

6. However, wolves ___differ from___ domesticated dogs in many important ways.

7. Wolves have large paws with webbing between the toes, and this trait gives wolves an advantage ___as___ predators.

8. Male and female wolves live together and do many activities ___beside___ each other.

9. They may separate ___from___ each other to hunt prey.

10. A playful wolf may wag its tail ___like___ a domesticated dog.

11. The pack will dine ___off___ a single animal carcass.

12. A tense wolf may crouch ___as if___ it is ready to pounce.

13. Some are ___angry with___ those who have improved the number of wolves in the wild.

14. Scientists may ___differ with___ ranchers on the importance of the wolf population.

Rewrite each sentence to correct errors in the use of prepositions.

15. We had to remove the trash off of the area around the stadium.

   We had to remove the trash from the area around the stadium.

16. The dog looked like no one had cared for it for months.

   The dog looked as if no one had cared for it for months.

7.3 Words Used as Adverbs and Prepositions

Some words can be either adverbs or prepositions. To distinguish between prepositions and adverbs, remember that a preposition must have an object.

Write whether each underlined word is used as an adverb (A) or a preposition (P).

1. Kioshi called out that he would see us <u>around</u>. ___A___

2. Can you see the clipper ship just <u>above</u> the horizon? ___P___

3. We walked <u>around</u> the block twice before finding the parakeet. ___P___

4. Jean fell <u>down</u> three times during the skating competition. ___A___

5. The ball went <u>through</u> the open window and landed on a couch. ___P___

6. The recovery crew is standing <u>by</u> for every football game. ___A___

7. Marcus and Caleb like to lead canoe trips <u>down</u> the river. ___P___

8. Please be home before supper to set the table. ___P___

9. <u>Below</u> the surface there is an abundance of minerals. ___P___

10. We needed to let the carpet dry <u>out</u> for a few days. ___A___

The first sentence in each pair uses the italicized word as an adverb. Add words to the second sentence to use the same word as a preposition. *Possible responses are given.*

11. Lift the box off. Lift the box off ___the kitchen table___.

12. The squirrel scurried along. The squirrel scurried along ___the fallen log___.

13. I read this book before. I read this book before ___my class___.

14. The wild mustang ran near. The wild mustang ran near ___the other horses___.

Write two sentences for each word. Use the word as an adverb in the first sentence and as a preposition in the second sentence. *Answer will vary.*

15. inside _____
_____

16. around _____
_____

17. since _____
_____

7.4 Prepositional Phrases as Adjectives

A prepositional phrase that describes a noun or a pronoun is called an **adjective phrase**.

Underline the adjective phrase in each sentence. Circle the noun it describes.

1. The (hometown) of Melinda and Paul's family is Plainview.
2. McKenzie likes to write (stories) about fanciful creatures that talk.
3. We all thought the best (plan) for the club was to meet on Tuesday nights.
4. During the boycott we all refused to buy (products) from that store.
5. We all gasped when the (sound) of breaking dishes filled the air.
6. (Several) of the players hit home runs in today's game.
7. Each week she hopes she has chosen the winning (numbers) on a lottery ticket.
8. The (balance) of his checkbook was appallingly low.
9. The mesmerizing (sound) of this classical music makes me feel so relaxed.
10. The loose (papers) on the student's desk will be corrected after school.
11. The air is crisp and clear that first (hour) after sunrise.
12. Our family's annual (trip) to the beach was rather eventful.

Complete each sentence with an adjective phrase. Then circle the word that the adjective phrase describes. *Answers will vary.*

13. The (kitten) *with the black paws* _____ is stuck in the tree.
14. A (person) *in the bleachers* _____ shouted frantically for help.
15. Anne's (photograph) *of her children* _____ won first prize in the contest.
16. Sarah enthusiastically enjoys reading (books) *about ancient Egypt* _____ are part of a class project.
17. The colorful (posters) *on the wall* _____
18. Her child likes the (ball) *with blue and white stripes* _____
19. The (bride) *with the long veil* _____ held a bouquet of white roses.

Write a sentence for each noun. Include an adjective phrase to describe the noun.

20. roller coaster *Answers will vary.* _____
21. basketball _____
22. passageway _____

7.5 Prepositional Phrases as Adverbs

Prepositional phrases that describe verbs, adjectives, or other adverbs are **adverb phrases**.

Underline the adverb phrases in these sentences. Circle the word each adverb phrase describes.

1. Her explanation seemed (contrary) to the facts.
2. The Board of Trustees meeting (started) at seven o'clock.
3. Our school (closed) during the summer, but some schools are open all year.
4. This spring's field (trip) was exciting for the students.
5. The pioneer family (settled) in Montana where its descendents are still found today.
6. We quietly watched the mouse (creep) farther into the hole.
7. Shane safely (drove) his new truck through the storm.
8. Stephen (studied) long hours about Egyptian pyramids.
9. The vehicle (passed) through the tollbooth and (drove) onto the bridge.
10. Chelsea (plunged) into the cold water but (was protected) by the special wet suit.
11. The raft (landed) on an island, and we were then disappointed that the ride was over.
12. The actors (rehearsed) on Saturday, but they (did not) (meet) on Sunday.

Complete each sentence with an adverb phrase. Then circle the word that the adverb phrase describes. *Answers will vary.*

13. After the drill the students (returned) _____
14. The president (spoke) late _____
15. Before the show I felt (nervous) _____
16. As they grow, tadpoles (develop) _____
17. The Mendozas (will begin) _____
18. Soon we (will travel) _____
19. All the students (emerge) _____
20. Our drama department (needs) props _____
21. That cloud (is shaped) _____
22. Those chickens (lay) eggs _____
23. My cousin (sets) the fork _____

7.6 Prepositional Phrases as Nouns

Occasionally, a prepositional phrase is used as a noun. The prepositional phrase may act as a subject or as a subject complement.

Underline the prepositional phrase used as a noun in each sentence. Write whether the prepositional phrase functions as a *subject* or a *subject complement*.

1. In a hammock is a good place to read a book. _____ subject

2. The worst time to travel is in the winter. _____ subject complement

3. Before dinner is the best time to visit. _____ subject

4. Between June and August can be the warmest time of year. _____ subject

5. The way we usually travel is by passenger train. _____ subject complement

6. After school is the only time I can rehearse my music. _____ subject

7. A great swimming hole is near the waterfall. _____ subject complement

8. In the Bahamas is where I want to be. _____ subject

9. On the dresser was the place where she put her wallet. _____ subject

10. The conference that Mark attends is usually in March. _____ subject complement

11. A bad place to sing is at the library. _____ subject complement

12. Beside the heater might be a grand place to sit. _____ subject

Complete each sentence with a prepositional phrase used as a noun. *Answers will vary.*

13. _____ was the best place to swim.

14. The young child was _____ .

15. My least favorite place is _____ .

16. _____ is where I keep a jar of change.

17. _____ will be considered out-of-bounds.

18. The usual place for the keys is _____ .

19. The dog's typical position can be _____ .

20. _____ is a method of transportation.

21. _____ was how she wore the necklace.

22. The lazy cat must be _____ .

23. _____ is a great time to do homework.

24. The missing book was not _____ .

For additional help, review pages 134–135 in your textbook or visit www.voyagesinenglish.com.

SECTION 8 Daily Maintenance

8.1 The photograph on this wall shows an image of Niagara Falls.
1. What are the prepositions in the sentence? _____ on, of
2. What are the prepositional phrases? _____ on this wall, of Niagara Falls
3. Do they function as adverbs or adjectives? _____ adjectives
4. Which words do they describe? _____ photograph, image
5. Diagram the sentence on another sheet of paper.

8.2 Because of her hard work, Lucy raised her grade in math.
1. What is the simple subject in the sentence? _____ Lucy
2. What is the single-word preposition? _____ in
3. What is the multiword preposition? _____ Because of
4. Which prepositional phrase describes *raised*? _____ Because of her hard work
5. Diagram the sentence on another sheet of paper.

8.3 Adrienne and I quietly walked past the sleeping baby.
1. What is the simple subject in the sentence? _____ Adrienne, I
2. Is *quietly* an adverb of degree, place, or manner? _____ manner
3. Is *past* used as an adverb or a preposition? _____ preposition
4. Which word is a participial adjective? _____ sleeping
5. Diagram the sentence on another sheet of paper.

8.4 The author of this novel also wrote a nonfiction book about Egypt.
1. What are the prepositions in the sentence? _____ of, about
2. What are the prepositional phrases? _____ of this novel, about Egypt
3. Which words do they describe? _____ author, book
4. Is the word *also* an adjective or an adverb? _____ adverb
5. Diagram the sentence on another sheet of paper.

8.5 **The mountain climbers watched in awe as an eagle flew above.**
1. What is the complete subject in the sentence? *The mountain climbers*
2. What is the dependent clause? *as an eagle flew above*
3. Is above used as a preposition or an adverb? *adverb*
4. Which word does above describe? *flew*
5. Diagram the sentence on another sheet of paper.

8.6 **Some of my friends have eaten at this restaurant before.**
1. What is the adjective phrase in the sentence? *of my friends*
2. Which word does the adjective phrase describe? *Some*
3. What is the tense of the verb? *past perfect*
4. Is before used as a preposition or an adverb? *adverb*
5. Diagram the sentence on another sheet of paper.

8.7 **We arrived at the hotel late in the evening.**
1. What is the simple subject and simple predicate? *We arrived*
2. Is at the hotel used as an adverb or adjective? *adverb*
3. What word does it describe? *arrived*
4. Is late used as an adjective or adverb? *adverb*
5. Diagram the sentence on another sheet of paper.

8.8 **The ski trail on the left is perfect for beginners.**
1. Which prepositional phrase acts as an adverb? *for beginners*
2. Which word does it describe? *perfect*
3. How is perfect used in the sentence? *subject complement*
4. Which prepositional phrase describes trail? *on the left*
5. Diagram the sentence on another sheet of paper.

8.9 **These red roses are beautiful, but I will buy those pink tulips.**
1. What are the demonstrative adjectives? *These, those*
2. What are the descriptive adjectives? *red, beautiful, pink*
3. Which word is a linking verb? *are*
4. Which noun and adjective does it link? *roses, beautiful*
5. Diagram the sentence on another sheet of paper.

8.10 **Chelsea will wrap the gift while I look for some ribbon.**
1. What is the adverb clause in the sentence? *while I look for some ribbon*
2. What is the subordinate conjunction? *while*
3. Which words does the adverb clause modify? *will wrap*
4. What type of adjective is the word some? *indefinite adjective*
5. Diagram the sentence on another sheet of paper.

8.11 **At the beach is my favorite place.**
1. What is the prepositional phrase? *At the beach*
2. What is the complete subject? *At the beach*
3. What is the subject complement? *place*
4. What type of adjective is the word my? *possessive adjective*
5. Diagram the sentence on another sheet of paper.

8.1 Kinds of Sentences

A **sentence** is a group of words that expresses a complete thought. A sentence consists of a complete subject and a complete predicate. Sentences can be declarative, interrogative, imperative, and exclamatory.

Underline each complete subject once and each complete predicate twice.

1. Alfred Sisley was a French painter in the Impressionist tradition.

2. His English parents supported him during the years of his youth.

3. After the war his family lost everything.

4. Did you know that Sisley's work did not immediately receive recognition?

5. You should see this artist's beautiful work.

6. Sisley's paintings are especially famous for their accurate portrayal of the French countryside.

7. The images of the intense blue skies help me imagine myself in France.

8. Who would not want to be able to paint like that?

Rewrite each declarative sentence as an imperative sentence, an interrogative sentence, and an exclamatory sentence. Add or delete words as needed. *Possible responses are given.*

9. The boys are going to plan a picnic.

Imperative: _Plan a picnic, boys._

Interrogative: _Are the boys going to plan a picnic?_

Exclamatory: _Wow, this is the best picnic you boys have ever planned!_

10. I want you to think about the opportunities.

Imperative: _Think about the opportunities._

Interrogative: _Will you think about the opportunities?_

Exclamatory: _Oh, these are unbelieveable opportunities!_

11. Our homeroom teacher will assign jobs to everyone.

Imperative: _Please assign a job to everyone._

Interrogative: _Will the homeroom teacher assign a job to everyone?_

Exclamatory: _Look, there are so many jobs!_

12. It is important to work together on this project.

Imperative: _Let's work together on this project._

Interrogative: _Are we going to work together on this project?_

Exclamatory: _What a team we will make for this project!_

For additional help, review pages 140–141 in your textbook or visit www.voyagesinenglish.com.

8.2 Adjective and Adverb Phrases

A **phrase** is a group of words that is used as a single part of speech. A phrase can be prepositional, participial, or infinitive. A phrase often functions as an adjective or an adverb.

Write *PREP* (prepositional), *PART* (participial), or *INF* (infinitive) to identify the italicized phrase in each sentence. Then write *ADV* (adverb) or *ADJ* (adjective) to identify how the phrase is used.

	TYPE OF PHRASE	USED AS
1. Weston remarked that he had never traveled *on a train.*	PREP	ADV
2. *Telling a happy story,* the speaker laughed.	PART	ADJ
3. Holt Skating Rink *in the park* was closed today.	PREP	ADJ
4. Allison's bouquet *of flowers* looked beautiful.	PREP	ADJ
5. People came *to see the movie star.*	INF	ADV
6. *Feeling tired,* the small child took a nap.	PART	ADJ
7. Lee looked *in the attic* to find the old trunk.	PREP	ADV
8. A good time *to get bread* is in the morning.	INF	ADJ
9. *Running in circles,* the children sang and laughed.	PART	ADJ
10. Each show ends *with a fireworks display.*	PREP	ADV

Underline each adjective phrase once and each adverb phrase twice. Write whether each phrase is prepositional (*PREP*), participial (*PART*), or infinitive (*INF*).

11. "Russian mountains" were frozen water over tall wood structures. __PREP__

12. The mountains were built during the 17th and 18th centuries. __PREP__

13. No one knows where the idea to build them originated. __INF__

14. Rising as high as 80 feet in the air, the mountains were a formidable sight. __PART__

15. People rode down the ice mountains on sleds. __PREP__

16. The mountains inspired rides in other parts of Europe. __PREP__

17. Using sleds on wheels, these rides predated the modern roller coaster. __PART__

18. Roller coasters are a special kind of rail system. __PREP__

19. The first roller coaster patent was issued on January 20, 1885. __PREP__

20. Roller coasters have tracks that rise and fall in elevation. __PREP__

21. Flipping the rider upside down, some designs have inversions. __PART__

22. Most modern roller coasters are found in amusement parks. __PREP__

23. Roller coaster designers want to produce an exciting sensation. __INF__

For additional help, review pages 142–143 in your textbook or visit www.voyagesinenglish.com.

8.3 Adjective Clauses

A **clause** is a group of words that has a subject and a predicate. An **independent clause** is one that expresses a complete thought and so can stand on its own. A **dependent clause** cannot stand on its own.

Underline the adjective clause in each sentence. Circle the noun that each adjective clause describes.

1. This (bus), which is at our stop, will be going downtown.
2. This is the (movie) that I told you about.
3. England is the (place) where the story begins.
4. My (sister,) whom I took ice-skating, enjoyed her day.
5. That (author,) whose books are popular with children, will be at our library.
6. (Mr. Vogel) who is my favorite teacher, is going on vacation.
7. Spring is the (time) when birds build their nests.
8. Dominique is the (reason) why I joined the photography club.
9. Canada is ruled by a constitutional (monarch) who is known as the Queen of Canada.
10. (Lincoln School) which usually holds its Sports Day in June, is moving the event to May.
11. (Carrots) which are easy to grow yourself, are rich in key vitamins.
12. The most surprising feature of the new (car) which runs on electricity, is its low cost.

Underline the adjective clause in each sentence. Circle the relative pronoun or subordinate conjunction in the adjective clause.

13. The praying mantis, (which) is primarily diurnal, relies heavily on its sense of sight.
14. Insects (that) the praying mantis eats include some agricultural pests.
15. The praying mantis's head, (which) can turn almost 300 degrees, is heart-shaped.
16. (When) it spies its victim, the praying mantis grabs and holds its live prey.

Write an adjective clause to complete each sentence. Answers will vary.

17. This morning, _____, I barely made it to school on time.
18. First, there was the incident with the peanut butter _____.
19. Then my brother, _____, couldn't find his trumpet.
20. Next, my mother couldn't find her keys _____.
21. My hope _____ was seeming pretty far-fetched.
22. We found the trumpet and keys and ran out to the car _____.

For additional help, review pages 144–145 in your textbook or visit www.voyagesinenglish.com.

Section 8 • 91

© Loyola Press. Voyages in English Grade 7

8.4 Restrictive and Nonrestrictive Clauses

Restrictive clauses are essential clauses without which a sentence will not make sense. An adjective clause that is not essential to the meaning of a sentence is a **nonrestrictive clause**.

Write if the italicized adjective clause is restrictive (R) or nonrestrictive (N).

1. Ancient Greek theater, *which was well-developed by 5th century BC,* was very different from attending a modern play. __N__
2. The three men *who were the actors played all the roles.* __R__
3. The venue, *which was always an outdoor theater,* was a large half-circle. __N__
4. The plays *that were produced were only performed once.* __R__
5. Every play, *which was part of a religious festival,* honored Dionysus. __N__
6. The polis, *who were the citizens of Greece,* paid for the production. __N__
7. The plays, *which were highly structured,* competed with other plays for first, second, or third prize. __N__

Underline each restrictive adjective clause once and each nonrestrictive adjective clause twice. Circle the noun to which each adjective clause refers.

8. (Kabuki) which is a highly stylized form of Japanese theater, began in the early 17th century.
9. The Kabuki (stage) which has special features and machinery, includes a hanamichi, or projection into the audience.
10. (Chunori) which adds dramatic effect, lifts an actor into the air.
11. The (wires) that lift an actor into the air have been in use since the mid-19th century.
12. Seri are a series of stage (traps) which raise and lower sets and actors on the stage.
13. The (sets) that rotate to make scene changes easier are called mawar-butai.
14. These special stage (features) which were developed to make sudden plot revelations or character transformations possible, give Kabuki sophistication.
15. A Kabuki (play) that retells famous moments in Japanese history might go on for a full day.
16. A full-length play is done in five (acts) which are each progressively faster in pace.
17. The final (act) which should provide a satisfying resolution, is almost always very short.
18. Kabuki actors wear (makeup) that tells the audience something about their characters.
19. Kabuki (actors) who are well-known by the audience may be rewarded by having members of the audience call out their names or those of their fathers.

For additional help, review pages 146–147 in your textbook or visit www.voyagesinenglish.com.

92 • Section 8

© Loyola Press. Voyages in English Grade 7

Practice Book Answer Key • 51

8.4 Restrictive and Nonrestrictive Clauses

Restrictive clauses are essential clauses without which a sentence will not make sense. An adjective clause that is not essential to the meaning of a sentence is a **nonrestrictive clause.**

Choose and write an adjective clause to complete each sentence. Add commas as needed. Write if the clause is restrictive (R) or nonrestrictive (NR).

> whose dog ran away which grow in ponds and lakes
> whose loom I bought that I just finished reading
> that was auctioned which is famous for cheese production

1. The ball _that was auctioned_ was signed by Michael Jordan. R
2. Water lilies, _which grow in ponds and lakes,_ live on the surface of water. NR
3. The weaver _whose loom I bought_ moved to Minnesota. R
4. Tyrone is the neighbor _whose dog ran away_ . R
5. Wisconsin, _which is famous for cheese production,_ is the country's largest producer of cranberries. NR
6. The biography _that I just finished reading_ is excellent. R

Write a restrictive or nonrestrictive adjective clause to complete each sentence. Add commas where necessary. *Answers will vary.*

7. The pond _____ was stocked with fish.
8. My best friend _____ helped me.
9. Before tomorrow's concert _____ we will be ready.
10. The next game _____ is Friday.
11. The lens _____ captures special memories.
12. The rain _____ canceled our plans.
13. We saw the rainbow _____ .
14. Our goal _____ was a worthy one.
15. We cleaned the table _____ .
16. The new puppy _____ made us laugh.

8.5 Adverb Clauses

An **adverb clause** is a dependent clause used as an adverb. An adverb clause describes or gives information about a verb, an adjective, or an adverb.

Underline the adverb clause in each sentence. Circle the subordinate conjunction.

1. When it is summer in the Northern Hemisphere, it is winter in the Southern Hemisphere.
2. After the time ran out on the clock, the students cheered wildly.
3. Eric will peel the potatoes while we make the salad.
4. Gina wrapped all the presents before she went to bed.
5. Jack cupped his hands around his ears because he couldn't hear the speech.
6. Don't start the test until I give the signal.
7. We smelled the peach cobbler as soon as we entered the restaurant.
8. When I heard the phone ring, I ran into the kitchen to answer it.
9. Although the children were tired, they didn't want to go to bed.

Underline the adverb clause in each sentence. Circle the word or words each adverb clause modifies.

10. As long as the dogs are trained, they can participate in agility competitions.
11. If you and I help, others will volunteer their time too.
12. Since the Parkers like board games so much, they made every Monday game night.
13. During the holiday celebrations, few people worked unless the job was really necessary.
14. When the beverages arrived, we added them to the buffet table.
15. After I clean my room, I plan to play soccer with my friends.
16. The class sang silly songs on the bus wherever we went on the field trip.
17. John wasn't interested in math until he was invited to compete in the contest.

Write an adverb clause to complete each sentence. *Possible responses are given.*

18. _After I have finished my chores_ , I plan to attend the party.
19. _When the swimmer has practiced rigorously_ , she usually swims well.
20. The batter has hit the ball harder _since he purchased that new wooden bat_ .
21. I often write best _if I can find a quiet and relaxing location_ .
22. _Until his chores are completed_ , Jake will not be able to join you.

8.6 Noun Clauses as Subjects

Dependent clauses can be used as nouns. These clauses, called **noun clauses,** typically begin with introductory words such as *how, that, what, whatever, when, where, whether, who, whoever, whom, whomever,* and *why.*

Underline the noun clause used as a subject in each sentence.

1. That my brother can climb the fence amazes me.
2. Whatever ate the apple is still in the yard.
3. Whoever arrived last left the door wide open.
4. Whomever we pick should already be a member of the club.
5. Why we keep losing the key to the back door is a mystery to me.
6. How this puzzle goes together is bewildering us.
7. What the principal had in mind was a celebration in the multipurpose room.
8. Whoever saw our dog in the field said he still had his collar on.
9. What Mr. Alexander did was teach us all a new way to do long division.
10. When we plan to go to the store determines whether there is time for one more game.
11. Whether Joe had wanted to quit the team was forgotten after his winning season.
12. Where the dog escaped the yard was a puzzle until we found the hole in the fence.

Choose an introductory word to complete each noun clause. Then underline the entire noun clause that is used as a subject. Possible responses are given.

13. __Where__ they are going is unknown.
14. __What__ the girls did with the treasure is a secret.
15. __Whatever__ you want for dessert is fine with me.
16. __That__ Joe should feel this way came as a surprise to all of us.
17. __Why__ no one remembered the homework assignment was hard to explain.
18. __How__ the magician made the tiger disappear was all we talked about.
19. __Whoever__ has worked at the pool will come back again.
20. __Whether__ they want to visit their parents will be decided later.
21. __Whomever__ we ask should already have experience with a hockey stick.
22. __Who__ owns this book is unclear, but there are ways to find out.
23. __When__ he will be arriving is written on the itinerary.

For additional help, review pages 150–151 in your textbook or visit www.voyagesinenglish.com.

8.7 Noun Clauses as Subject Complements

Like nouns, noun clauses can be used as subject complements.

Underline the noun clause used as a subject complement in each sentence. Circle the subject that the noun clause describes or renames.

1. Michael's greatest (achievement) was that he earned a scholarship at the technology fair.
2. The (question) is whether or not Mrs. Holcolmb can drive us all to the game tomorrow.
3. One (theory) explaining the disappearance of the cake is that the dog ate it.
4. Another (suggestion) has been that we all go together in one van to save on gas.
5. (Something) to think about is how we are going to get everyone to the competition.
6. A (reason) for concern is whether or not it might snow tonight.

Underline the noun clause in each sentence. Indicate if the noun clause is used as a subject (S) or as a subject complement (SC).

7. What I had for breakfast made me feel better. — S
8. Her wish was that all her friends could come to the party. — SC
9. The truth was that Mary was faster than Ted. — SC
10. Whatever the teacher said was inspiring. — S
11. Our main concern at the moment was how to get home before dark. — SC
12. The problem was that I forgot my homework. — SC
13. Jay's goal is that he can buy a new amplifier. — SC
14. What role he played is still a puzzle to the committee. — S
15. That he would win the contest was taken for granted. — S
16. The second house from the corner is where the Jacobs live. — SC
17. One of the school's mysteries is what is behind the locked red door. — SC
18. The fact is that February is a good month for ice-skating. — SC

Write a noun clause used as a subject complement to complete each sentence. Possible responses are given.

19. Randall's best character trait was _that he was a good sport_.
20. Mrs. Smith's favorite lesson is _how to classify types of beetles_.
21. The best prize is _whatever makes us happiest_.
22. My hope for the future is _that we learn to accept one another_.

For additional help, review pages 152–153 in your textbook or visit www.voyagesinenglish.com.

8.9 Noun Clauses as Direct Objects

A noun clause can act as a direct object. The introductory word *that* is often dropped from a noun clause used as a direct object, but omitting *that* after the verbs *feel, learn, say, see,* or *think* may change the meaning of a sentence.

Underline the direct object in each sentence. Identify whether it is a noun (N) or a noun clause (NC).

1. I'll choose whichever car gets the best gas mileage.   NC
2. She wondered what might be inside the box.   NC
3. Dad suggested that we help him set up the tent.   NC
4. The children sent letters to their pen pals.   N
5. We discussed how we wanted to spend the money.   NC
6. Joshua asked Sofia for help with dinner preparations.   N

Use the information about the speaker to write a noun clause used as a direct object to complete each sentence. *Possible responses are given.*

7. a young child
   "I hate _that I can't play outside right now_."

8. a college student
   "I must decide _which is the best course to take in the fall_."

9. a police officer
   "I explained _how children can help the police_."

10. a coach
    "I hope that this team works well together_."

11. a salesperson
    "I believe that this suit will look good on you_."

12. a ship's captain
    "I decided _that the seas were too rough to sail today_."

13. a teenager
    "I understand _why my parents want me home by a certain time at night_."

14. a teacher
    "I require _that all students submit their homework on time_."

For additional help, review pages 156–157 in your textbook or visit www.voyagesinenglish.com.

8.8 Noun Clauses as Appositives

A noun clause can be used as an appositive. An appositive follows a noun and renames it or gives more information about it.

Underline the noun clause used as an appositive in each sentence.

1. The fact that the store doesn't open until noon prevented us from going any earlier.
2. Many accepted the idea that the club could not function without a secretary.
3. Despite their belief that if they didn't wear their lucky shirts their team would lose, they opted to wear the new uniforms.
4. The understanding that the understudy would get to perform in one show encouraged Carol.
5. Mom wrote out her request that Mr. Oz should assign more math homework in a note.
6. Dad is a fan of the principle that the Super Bowl is an unofficial national holiday.

Underline the clause used as an appositive in each sentence. Then write whether it is a noun clause or an adjective clause.

7. Marie's hope that she would become a doctor came true.   noun clause
8. All the flowers that I planted last month are in bloom.   adjective clause
9. Jack asked the question whether the campers should leave in the morning.   noun clause
10. The report, whatever it was, caused the soldiers to celebrate.   noun clause
11. It is a fact that our club sold the most raffle tickets.   noun clause
12. The fact that exercise promotes good health is obvious.   noun clause
13. The Persian rugs that are in the storeroom will go in the hall.   adjective clause
14. She voiced her concern that it would be dark soon.   noun clause
15. The man's announcement that he had the winning lottery ticket thrilled his wife.   noun clause
16. Some of the pictures that I took during my trip are in this album.   adjective clause

Write a sentence that uses each noun clause as an appositive. *Possible responses are given.*

17. that animals act strangely before an earthquake
    The idea that animals act strangely before an earthquake has been studied by scientists.

18. whether we should cancel due to rain
    The question whether we should cancel due to rain was answered by a clap of thunder.

For additional help, review pages 154–155 in your textbook or visit www.voyagesinenglish.com.

8.11 Simple, Compound, and Complex Sentences

A **simple sentence** is an independent clause that stands alone. A **compound sentence** contains two or more independent clauses. A **complex sentence** has one independent clause and at least one dependent clause.

Write simple, compound, or complex to identify the sentences in each set.

1. a. My friend invited me to a dance. I do not want to go. — *simple*
   b. My friend invited me to a dance, but I do not want to go. — *compound*
   c. Although my friend invited me to a dance, I do not want to go. — *complex*

2. a. Paul, who studies history, knows Elaine, who studies math. — *complex*
   b. Paul studies history. Elaine studies math. — *simple*
   c. Paul studies history, and Elaine studies math. — *compound*

3. a. The explorers were ready. They entered the submarine. — *simple*
   b. When the explorers were ready, they entered the submarine. — *complex*
   c. The explorers were ready, so they entered the submarine. — *compound*

Underline each independent clause once and each dependent clause twice. Circle the relative pronouns and subordinate conjunctions.

4. Robin of Loxley, (who) was also known as Robin Hood, was a mythical character.

5. Robin Hood is said to have been a contemporary of King Richard II, (whom) Robin supported.

6. The name most often refers to an individual, (but) it was also a name for any outlaw.

7. Those written references, (which) are initially quite brief, refer to long-told oral tales.

8. Maid Marian and Friar Tuck appear in the stories, (which) were told through May Day plays, at the end of the 15th century.

9. Robin Hood was a yeoman, (so) he was neither royalty nor a peasant.

10. The truth of Robin's story, (which) is hotly debated, certainly is entertaining.

Use the information in parentheses to write a clause to complete each sentence. *Answers will vary.*

11. _____, who has been a great help to me.
    (independent clause)

12. I enjoy bicycling, _____.
    with a coordinating conjunction).

13. I sang a song _____.
    (dependent clause)

14. Even though I don't like astronomy, _____.
    (independent clause)

For additional help, review pages 160–161 in your textbook or visit www.voyagesinenglish.com.

8.10 Noun Clauses as Objects of Prepositions

A noun clause can function as the object of a preposition. An adjective clause is sometimes confused with a noun clause used as an object of a preposition. An adjective clause describes a noun or pronoun in the independent clause.

Underline the noun clause used as an object of a preposition.

1. The girls were thinking about what they could do to win Saturday's softball game.

2. I searched on the Internet for what other schools were doing to raise library funds.

3. This week we learned about how apple crisp is made.

4. What was the purpose of what those people were doing?

5. The principal must agree to whatever the clubs propose for activities.

Underline the noun clause in each sentence. Write whether each noun clause is the subject, the direct object, or the object of a preposition.

6. The doctor gives advice to whoever will listen. — *object of a preposition*

7. That I was angry must have been noticed by many people. — *subject*

8. Liz read about what should be planted here. — *object of a preposition*

9. I was amazed by what the baby could do. — *object of a preposition*

10. Whoever is chosen can participate in the event. — *subject*

11. Sam thinks that the horse is too young to ride. — *direct object*

12. We wondered whether our money would be refunded. — *direct object*

13. The host announced that the show would begin shortly. — *direct object*

14. Whatever we decide will be noted in the minutes. — *subject*

15. Mei Ling was interested in what she heard about the movie. — *object of a preposition*

Write a noun clause used as an object of a preposition to complete each sentence. *Answers will vary.*

16. The students learned about _____.

17. Our coach was astonished by _____.

18. Their next discussion focuses on _____.

19. Let's develop a plan for _____.

20. The reward will go to _____.

For additional help, review pages 158–159 in your textbook or visit www.voyagesinenglish.com.

SECTION 9 Daily Maintenance

9.1 **The dress with pink flowers is beautiful, but I want this red skirt.**
1. Is the sentence simple, compound, or complex?
2. Is the sentence declarative or interrogative?
3. What is the adjective phrase?
4. Which word is a subject complement?
5. Diagram the sentence on another sheet of paper.

9.2 **Martha is wearing a sweater that her grandmother knitted.**
1. Is the sentence declarative or imperative?
2. What is the adjective clause?
3. Which word does this clause describe?
4. What is the independent clause?
5. Diagram the sentence on another sheet of paper.

9.3 **Did you thank the man who found your purse?**
1. Is the sentence imperative or interrogative?
2. What is the adjective clause?
3. Is this clause restrictive or nonrestrictive?
4. Which words are used as direct objects?
5. Diagram the sentence on another sheet of paper.

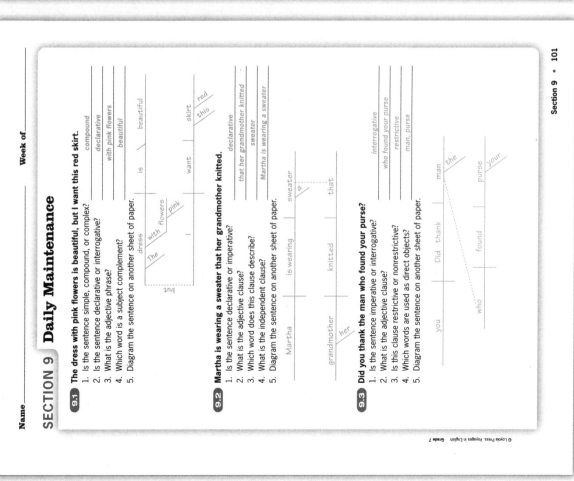

9.4 **If you need help in math, I can tutor you on weekends.**
1. Is the sentence simple, compound, or complex?
2. What is the subordinate conjunction?
3. What is the adverb clause?
4. Is this clause dependent or independent?
5. Diagram the sentence on another sheet of paper.

9.5 **That Meg is a talented artist is obvious.**
1. Is the sentence simple, compound, or complex?
2. What is the noun clause?
3. What is the introductory word of the clause?
4. What is the subject complement?
5. Diagram the sentence on another sheet of paper.

9.6 **We can only hope that he arrives before noon.**
1. What is the verb phrase in the sentence?
2. What is the noun clause?
3. What is the adverb phrase?
4. What does this phrase describe?
5. Diagram the sentence on another sheet of paper.

9.1 Coordinating Conjunctions

A **conjunction** is a word used to connect words or groups of words. A **coordinating conjunction** joins words or groups of words that are similar.

Underline the coordinating conjunction in each sentence.

1. Poodles _and_ Portuguese water dogs love physical activity.
2. These breeds originated in Asia, _but_ they were imported all over the world.
3. The Portuguese water dog would herd fish into nets _and_ carry items from boat to boat.
4. Today the dogs are primarily good companions, _yet_ they are still used in some professions.
5. The highly trainable _and_ playful nature of the poodle make it a good performer.
6. The athletic _and_ hard-working nature of the Portuguese water dog makes it a good water rescue dog.
7. Both dogs need careful grooming _and_ a lot of exercise.
8. The poodle _or_ the Portuguese water dog would make a great choice for a family pet.

Circle the coordinating conjunction in each sentence. Then write whether each conjunction joins words, phrases, or clauses.

9. Sam needs to practice every day, (or) he may not pass the test. _clauses_
10. Brittany decided to study physics (and) chemistry. _words_
11. The cat ran down the stairs (and) into the basement. _phrases_
12. Stephanie writes to her cousins (but) calls her friends. _phrases_
13. I will lend you money, (but) you must pay me back. _clauses_
14. Nancy takes cream (and) sugar in her coffee. _words_
15. She loves animals (yet) hesitates to keep a pet. _phrases_
16. The author did not speak long, (nor) did he sign any books. _clauses_
17. The police car raced down the street (and) into the alley. _phrases_
18. He is small (but) strong. _words_

Write three sentences with coordinating conjunctions. Connect two words in the first sentence, two phrases in the second, and two clauses in the third.

Answers will vary.

_____

For additional help, review pages 166–167 in your textbook or visit www.voyagesinenglish.com.

Section 9 • 103

9.2 Correlative Conjunctions

Correlative conjunctions are conjunctions that are used in pairs to connect words or groups of words that have equal importance in a sentence.

Circle the correlative conjunctions. Not all sentences have correlative conjunctions.

1. Our neighbor's garden has (both) flowers (and) shrubbery.
2. The team won (not only) the district championship (but also) the state championship.
3. (Neither) my mother (nor) my sister has red hair.
4. For dinner we had the choice of (either) chicken (or) steak.
5. Robyn and Joanna are both ordering spaghetti for lunch.
6. (Whether) he is winning (or) losing, Jim is always upbeat and optimistic.
7. Will you bring potato salad or deviled eggs to the picnic?
8. (Both) Carl (and) Leslie will enter the pie-eating contest.
9. My mom (not only) cooked all the food (but also) made the decorations.
10. We can spend the day at (either) the river (or) the lake.

Write correlative conjunctions from the box to complete each sentence.

| both . . . and | not only . . . but also | neither . . . nor |
| either . . . or | whether . . . or | |

Possible responses are given.

11. _Both_ squid _and_ eel are considered edible.
12. I don't know _whether_ rain _or_ snow is in the forecast.
13. _Either_ this chair _or_ that one would fit around the table.
14. Football is _both_ a game of strategy _and_ physical fitness.
15. _Not only_ can the seventh graders help, _but_ they can draw the posters to advertise the event.
16. _Neither_ the library _nor_ the post office is open today.
17. _Not only_ can Jake draw, _but_ he can _also_ sculpt.
18. I can't tell _whether_ I feel better _or_ not.
19. _Either_ tacos _or_ pizza would be a welcome treat for dinner.
20. _Neither_ this book _nor_ that one is written in English.

104 • Section 9

For additional help, review pages 168–169 in your textbook or visit www.voyagesinenglish.com.

9.3 Conjunctive Adverbs

Conjunctive adverbs connect independent clauses. A semicolon is used before the conjunctive adverb, and a comma is used after it. **Parenthetical expressions** are used in the same way as conjunctive adverbs.

Circle the correct conjunctive adverb or parenthetical expression to complete each sentence.

1. My brother plays golf at least once a week; (moreover) however, he often attends golfing classes on the weekend.

2. It was extremely foggy the day of the tour; (later (consequently), we were able to spot very few eagles.

3. I live in an area where groundhogs are common; (furthermore (nevertheless), the first time I saw one I thought it was a beaver.

4. There are many lakes in Minnesota; (in fact) nevertheless), the state's slogan is "Land of 10,000 Lakes."

5. Juanita isn't afraid of roller coasters; (otherwise (on the contrary), she was one of the first people to ride on the Cobra.

6. We have spent a long time on our homework; (finally (still), we can't solve the last two problems.

7. Gwen has always liked math and is very good at it; (however (therefore), she plans to become a math teacher.

8. Nate enjoys playing soccer and tennis; (besides (however), he has decided to try out for only one team.

9. Bob's Smoke Pit has great food; (indeed (therefore), it has the best ribs in town.

10. Our cabin is in the mountains; (however (therefore), we see many wild animals.

11. Danielle doesn't want to make a ceramic pot; (moreover (instead), she plans to make a large serving platter.

12. The waves are too high for surfing; (besides) consequently), the water is too cold.

Write a conjunctive adverb to complete each sentence. *Possible responses are given.*

13. Inventors are interested in things that make our lives easier; ___consequently___, many inventions are intended for use in the home.

14. Most dogs were working animals; ___therefore___, they were bred for specific jobs.

15. On the conductor's command, an orchestra may begin playing; ___moreover___, the musicians follow the conductor's signals for pace and volume.

16. Abby is getting good grades; ___nevertheless___, she wants to do even better.

For additional help, review pages 170–171 in your textbook or visit www.voyagesinenglish.com.

9.4 Subordinate Conjunctions

A **subordinate conjunction** is used to join an independent clause and a dependent clause.

Underline the subordinate conjunction in each sentence.

1. Because the understudy knew her lines, the show was saved.

2. We brought two balls so that we would have a spare if one was lost.

3. If anyone hosted a party, the neighbors were sure to show up.

4. Elliot's talent was in baseball, while Adam's talent was in football.

5. John jumped around the room, waving his arms as if he were playing a guitar.

Circle the subordinate conjunction in each sentence. Underline the dependent clause.

6. She acts as if nothing is wrong.

7. While they were in New York, it snowed 20 inches.

8. The basketball team forfeited the game because not enough players showed up.

9. We used bright colors so that our signs would stand out from the others.

10. Ellen has been driving to school since she turned 18.

11. I prefer tomatoes when they have ripened on the vine.

12. Trina skated better than she had ever skated before.

13. Why don't we wait here until it is time to leave?

14. After Chris heard about the accident, he rushed to the hospital.

15. When we visited Yosemite, we hiked to the top of Half Dome.

16. Although I like this dress, I cannot afford to buy it.

17. Kim will go to the concert even though she has not finished her homework.

Complete each sentence with an appropriate dependent clause beginning with a subordinate conjunction. *Possible responses are given.*

18. When the boys finished cleaning up ___, they were ready to go to the movies.___

19. So that their teeth stay in good health ___, many people see a dentist twice a year.___

20. Because she wanted to get good grades ___, Julie did her homework every night.___

21. As the week passed ___, Ty grew to enjoy the talks with his aunt.___

22. Unless you get an early start ___, you might be late for sports practice.___

23. Though more snow began to fall ___, the group decided to continue sledding.___

For additional help, review pages 172–173 in your textbook or visit www.voyagesinenglish.com.

9.6 Interjections

An **interjection** is a word that expresses a strong or sudden emotion.

Circle the interjection that is the best match for each sentence. *Possible responses are given.*

1. (Yikes) Yum), that had to hurt!
2. (Wow) No)! That last fireworks display was the best.
3. (Hello (Enough)! It's time to end the game and go inside.
4. (Sh) Oh, no)! The baby is finally asleep.
5. (Bravo)! Hush)! That was an excellent story for such a young author.
6. (Beware (Good grief), I really thought that she was going to steal second base!
7. (Gosh) Hooray)! I thought I had more money than this.
8. (Ha) Indeed)! That trick worked really well this time.
9. (Hush (Whew)! The bell will ring in just one more minute.

Write a sentence with an interjection to match each situation. *Answers will vary.*

10. a server in a restaurant who just dropped a tray of food

_____

11. a construction worker who hit his thumb with a hammer

_____

12. a librarian quieting children

_____

13. a scientist making an important discovery

_____

14. a child tasting her favorite food

_____

15. a person watching trapeze artists at a circus

_____

16. a student who discovers that she has forgotten her homework

_____

17. a customer politely seeking the attention of a salesclerk

_____

For additional help, review pages 176–177 in your textbook or visit www.voyagesinenglish.com.

9.5 Troublesome Conjunctions

Some conjunctions are frequently misused or confused.

Write without or unless to complete each sentence.

1. _Without_ proper storage, the lawn mower may rust over the winter.
2. Don't pick up that book _unless_ you have the time to read the entire thing.
3. _Unless_ we find a used part for the car, we won't be able to leave on our trip.
4. The animal will not thrive _without_ sufficient food and water.
5. Buy three tickets for the show _unless_ your sister says she doesn't want to go.
6. _Without_ my brothers in the house, it is very quiet around here.
7. _Unless_ more parents can attend, the field trip will have to be canceled.

Circle the correct item to complete each sentence.

8. (Unless (Without) his bus pass, he will not be able to ride the bus today.
9. I read through the magazine (as) like) I waited.
10. He acted (like (as if) he didn't get enough sleep.
11. Don't leave (unless) without) I call you first.
12. The huge snake looked (like) as if) a tree branch in the sand.
13. A computer won't work (unless) without) you plug it in.
14. (Unless (Without) the weather gets colder, we won't be able to go ice-skating.
15. I felt (like (as if) nothing could go wrong.
16. The climbers grew weary (like (as) the guide led them along the steep paths.
17. Our car looked (like (as if) no one had washed it in quite some time.
18. Gary ordered a sandwich (unless (without) onions or pickles.
19. The sound of the katydids in the trees was (like) as if) that of rain on the canopy.

Rewrite each sentence to correct the use of conjunctions and prepositions.

20. The dogs were barking like there was a stranger in the yard.
The dogs were barking as if there was a stranger in the yard.

21. The birds made their nest in the old wasps' nest, like my friend told me.
The birds made their nest in the old wasps' nest, as my friend told me.

22. You must see the new high school building it looks like a huge cement block.
You must see the new high school building as it looks like a huge cement block.

For additional help, review pages 174–175 in your textbook or visit www.voyagesinenglish.com.

Practice Book Answer Key • **59**

SECTION 10 · Daily Maintenance

10.1 A goldfish or a gerbil is a good pet for most children.
1. Is the sentence or the subject compound?
2. What is the correlative conjunction?
3. Which word is a subject complement?
4. What is the adjective phrase?
5. Diagram the sentence on another sheet of paper.

10.2 Silvia studied for the English test; however, she made several errors.
1. Is the sentence simple, compound, or complex?
2. What is the conjunctive adverb?
3. What is the adverb phrase?
4. Which word is an indefinite adjective?
5. Diagram the sentence on another sheet of paper.

10.3 When I lived in Canada, I often visited Lake Louise.
1. Is the sentence simple, compound, or complex?
2. What is the subordinate conjunction?
3. What is the adverb clause?
4. Which word is an adverb?
5. Diagram the sentence on another sheet of paper.

10.4 Liam cannot go unless his parents give their permission.
1. Is the sentence simple, compound, or complex?
2. What is the subordinate conjunction?
3. What is the independent clause?
4. Which words are possessive adjectives?
5. Diagram the sentence on another sheet of paper.

10.5 Wow! Lin's illustrations for this book look exquisite.
1. What is the adjective phrase in the sentence?
2. What is the linking verb?
3. What is the subject complement?
4. What is the interjection?
5. Diagram the sentence on another sheet of paper.

10.2 Exclamation Points, Question Marks, Semicolons, and Colons

Exclamation points are used after interjections and exclamatory sentences. **Question marks** are used to end interrogative sentences. **Semicolons** and **colons** are used in specific situations.

Add semicolons and colons where needed.

1. The singer used a microphone; nevertheless, we couldn't hear him.
2. Dear Dr. Greenbaum:
3. Sheila rides her bike to school; I prefer to walk.
4. There was a blizzard last night; hence, school was closed.
5. To Whom It May Concern:
6. Please call these people: Marvin, Jane, Anita, and Martha.
7. Joyce has three favorite hobbies; namely, knitting, dancing, and rock climbing.
8. I will visit three countries this summer: Greece, Spain, and Italy.

Add periods, question marks, or exclamation points where needed. *Possible responses are given.*

9. Hey, I can't believe you did that!
10. Oh, no! What kind of weather can we expect tomorrow?
11. What is that strange lump I see in the snow?
12. What interesting sights we can see through the Hubble Telescope!
13. I decided to call everyone in my class for a party next Friday.
14. Ah-ha! I believe we have found the culprit who raided the cookie jar.
15. Yikes! Is that how far we have to run for the physical fitness test?

Write a sentence for each topic. Use the correct punctuation. *Answers will vary.*

16. a question about a vacation you would like to take

17. an exclamation that shows happiness

18. a question about your favorite subject

19. an exclamation that is a warning

For additional help, review pages 184–185 in your textbook or visit www.voyagesinenglish.com.

10.1 Periods and Commas

A period is used at the end of a declarative or an imperative sentence, after an abbreviation, and after the initials in a name. **Commas** are used in a variety of ways to separate or set off words, phrases, and clauses.

Add commas where needed in these sentences. Then write the letter of the comma rule used in each sentence.

A. to separate words in a series
B. to set off nonrestrictive phrases and clauses
C. to set off words of direct address
D. to set off parenthetical expressions
E. to set off dates
F. to set off place names
G. to set off divided quotations

1. "After you finish your homework," said Maria, "I have a surprise for you." **G**
2. He was born in Fairbanks, Alaska, but he now lives in Seattle, Washington. **F**
3. The package will be there, I promise you, by next Tuesday. **D**
4. Myra, I can't make it to the play tonight. **C**
5. The Declaration of Independence was signed on July 4, 1776. **E**
6. Ronald Reagan, who had once been an actor, became our 40th president. **B**
7. Theresa went to the grocery store and bought bread, milk, and cheese. **A**

Rewrite the sentences to correct any errors in punctuation. *Possible responses are given.*

8. I e-mailed Ms Emily Rayward, with my decision on Sept, 15.
I e-mailed Ms. Emily Rayward with my decision on Sept. 15.
9. A local lawyer Mr Richard Kanton was quoted in the newspaper article yesterday
A local lawyer, Mr. Richard Kanton, was quoted in the newspaper article yesterday.
10. Emma made an appointment with Dr Richardson for May 4. 2010
Emma made an appointment with Dr. Richardson for May 4, 2010.
11. Tussey Mountain near State College Penn is home to a small ski resort
Tussey Mountain, near State College, Penn., is home to a small ski resort.
12. Yes Lilly, we do need to stop in Athens Georgia on the way home.
Yes, Lilly, we do need to stop in Athens, Georgia, on the way home.

For additional help, review pages 182–183 in your textbook or visit www.voyagesinenglish.com.

10.3 Quotation Marks and Italics

Quotation marks are used with direct quotations. **Italics** are used for titles of books, magazines, newspapers, movies, TV series, and works of art and for the names of ships and aircraft.

Add quotation marks and other punctuation where needed. Use underlining to indicate italics.

1. "Where can I park my bicycle?" asked Isaac.

2. Sylvia selected the short story called "The Year that We Disappeared."

3. I am reading an article titled "Budgeting for Teens" in Family and Home Magazine.

4. "No, I'm sorry," replied the clerk, "but Watership Down is not currently in stock."

5. "The boys left here just a half hour ago," said Mrs. Crosby.

6. "Wow! Look how high his paper airplane flew," yelled Marcus.

7. I cannot find the book A Tree Grows in Brooklyn anywhere.

8. Becky suggested, "We could all go to my house to practice for the play."

Write a sentence for each topic. Include a title in your sentence. Underline words to indicate italics where needed. *Possible responses are given.*

9. your favorite movie
   Last night we rented the movie Star Wars.

10. your favorite television show
    My family watched 60 Minutes last night.

11. your favorite book
    Have you ever read The Diary of Anne Frank?

12. your favorite magazine
    I get Sports Illustrated every week.

13. a song that you like
    My brother and I like to sing "Take Me Out to the Ball Game."

14. a poem you have read
    "Boa Constrictor" by Shel Silverstein is a funny poem.

15. a magazine article you would like to write
    I would like to write an article titled "How to Get Along with a Sister."

For additional help, review pages 186–187 in your textbook or visit www.voyagesinenglish.com.

10.4 Apostrophes, Hyphens, and Dashes

Apostrophes, hyphens, and **dashes** are used to clarify text for the reader.

Circle the letter that correctly explains the punctuation mark that is needed in each sentence. Then add the punctuation mark to the sentence.

1. I turned my head, it was only for a second, and missed the final shot of the game.
   a. A hyphen is used to separate parts of some compound words.
   b. A dash is used to set off words that indicate a change in thought.

2. The mansion has twenty-two rooms.
   a. A hyphen is used in compound numbers between twenty-one and ninety-nine.
   b. A dash is used to set off an appositive.

3. Sandy regularly borrows items from her sister's wardrobe.
   a. An apostrophe shows possession.
   b. An apostrophe is used to show the plurals of lowercase but not of capital letters, unless the plural could be mistaken for a word.

4. Call Raquel, she's on the prom committee, to get the directions.
   a. A dash is used to set off an appositive that contains commas.
   b. A dash is used to set off words that indicate a change in thought.

5. The i's were crossed, and the i's were dotted.
   a. An apostrophe is used to show the plurals of lowercase but not of capital letters, unless the plural could be mistaken for a word.
   b. An apostrophe shows possession.

Write a sentence for each description, using correct punctuation. *Possible responses are given.*

6. An apostrophe shows possession.
   Douglas's glasses were found broken on the ground.

7. A dash is used to set off words that indicate a change in thought.
   Let's talk to Carla—the girl we met last week at the fair—to see if she can help us.

8. A hyphen is used in compound numbers between twenty-one and ninety-nine.
   My brother has collected fifty-three books about bees.

9. A hyphen is used to form some temporary adjectives.
   We bought a container of steel-cut oats.

For additional help, review pages 188–189 in your textbook or visit www.voyagesinenglish.com.

10.5 Capitalization

Using **capital letters** correctly provides valuable clues for the reader that make your writing easier to understand.

Use the proofreading symbol (≡) to show which letters should be capitalized.

1. m̲y mother likes to watch old westerns.

2. u̲sually, i̲ won't watch them with her because i̲ prefer more modern movies.

3. l̲ast week a huge snowstorm hit my town, p̲lainview, m̲innesota.

4. a̲lice, x̲ander, and i̲ went sledding, and my dad took me out on his snowmobile.

5. p̲lainview isn't a very big town though, and everything was closed.

6. f̲inally, i̲ said, "i̲'ve been thinking, mom, that we should watch one of your movies."

7. s̲he introduced me to j̲ohn w̲ayne and j̲ack e̲ly.

8. t̲he towns all had names like d̲ry g̲ulch, d̲eadwood, and w̲indmill j̲unction.

9. a̲ll in all, it wasn't a bad way to spend a day with my mother.

Write a sentence that illustrates each rule for using a capital letter. *Possible responses are given.*

10. a title when it precedes a person's name

I asked Governor Halsey to read the memo.

11. the first word in a sentence

The photographer snapped several pictures.

12. a direction when it refers to a part of the country

Many of my relatives live in the East.

13. an abbreviation of a word that is capitalized

I have an appointment with Dr. Hernandez today.

14. a proper noun

My grandmother lives on Billings Road.

15. a proper adjective

We chose the Chinese restaurant for our party.

16. the principal words in the title of a book, play, or poem

She is the author of Weather Patterns of the World.

17. the first word of a direct quotation

Cheryl exclaimed, "That was the best day ever!"

For additional help, review pages 190–191 in your textbook or visit www.voyagesinenglish.com.

SECTION 11 Daily Maintenance

11.1 Brandy served her father the largest piece of steak.
1. How is the word *father* used in the sentence?
2. Is the verb regular or irregular?
3. What kind of adjective is the word *largest*?
4. How is the word *piece* used in the sentence?
5. Diagram the sentence on another sheet of paper.

11.2 Stephen King, an author of many novels, is my favorite writer.
1. What does the appositive rename?
2. Is the appositive restrictive or nonrestrictive?
3. Which noun is the object of a preposition?
4. How is the word *writer* used in the sentence?
5. Diagram the sentence on another sheet of paper.

11.3 The students have studied weather, and now they will make a rain gauge.
1. Is the sentence simple, compound, or complex?
2. Which word is a coordinating conjunction?
3. Which words are direct objects?
4. Which word is an adverb?
5. Diagram the sentence on another sheet of paper.

11.4 The small birds collect blades of grass and weave them into nests.
1. What is the complete subject?
2. Is the subject or the predicate compound?
3. What is the antecedent of the word *them*?
4. Which words are prepositions?
5. Diagram the sentence on another sheet of paper.

Practice Book Answer Key • 63

Name _____   **Week of** _____

11.5 **Blowing in the wind, the dandelions are floating like snowflakes.**
1. What is the simple subject?
2. What is the participial phrase?
3. Does it act as an adjective or an adverb?
4. What is the verb phrase?
5. Diagram the sentence on another sheet of paper.

11.6 **I improved my tennis skills by taking lessons from my friend's coach.**
1. What kind of pronoun is the word *I*?
2. Which word is a gerund?
3. How is the gerund phrase used in the sentence?
4. Is the possessive noun singular or plural?
5. Diagram the sentence on another sheet of paper.

11.7 **The raccoon is using its sharp claws to climb that tree.**
1. What is the infinitive phrase?
2. Is it used as a direct object or an adverb?
3. Is *its* a contraction or a possessive adjective?
4. What kind of adjective is the word *that*?
5. Diagram the sentence on another sheet of paper.

11.8 **A nocturnal animal is one that is active at night.**
1. What is the simple subject?
2. Which words are adjectives?
3. What is the adjective clause?
4. What word does this clause describe?
5. Diagram the sentence on another sheet of paper.

Name _____   **Week of** _____

11.9 **Laura is excited because everyone is coming to her violin recital.**
1. How is the word *excited* used in the sentence?
2. Is the adverb clause dependent or independent?
3. What is the adverb phrase?
4. What kind of pronoun is the word *everyone*?
5. Diagram the sentence on another sheet of paper.

11.10 **On rainy days we always hope that Mom will give us a ride to school.**
1. How is *On rainy days* used in the sentence?
2. How is the noun clause used in the sentence?
3. What part of speech is the word *always*?
4. What is the antecedent of the pronoun *us*?
5. Diagram the sentence on another sheet of paper.

11.11 **During the summer my brother Gary plans to work as a lifeguard on weekends.**
1. What is the appositive?
2. Is the appositive restrictive or nonrestrictive?
3. How is the infinitive used in the sentence?
4. Which words are prepositions?
5. Diagram the sentence on another sheet of paper.

11.2 Appositives

An **appositive** is a word or a group of words that follows a noun or a pronoun and further identifies it or adds information. An appositive names the same person, place, thing, or idea as the word it explains.

Diagram the sentences.

1. The mythical hall of the dead, Valhalla, has many doors.

2. This is my brilliant math teacher, Mr. Gomez.

3. In the play the main character is transported to Oz, a fantastic land.

4. Ben enthusiastically read J.K. Rowling's novel *Harry Potter and the Goblet of Fire.*

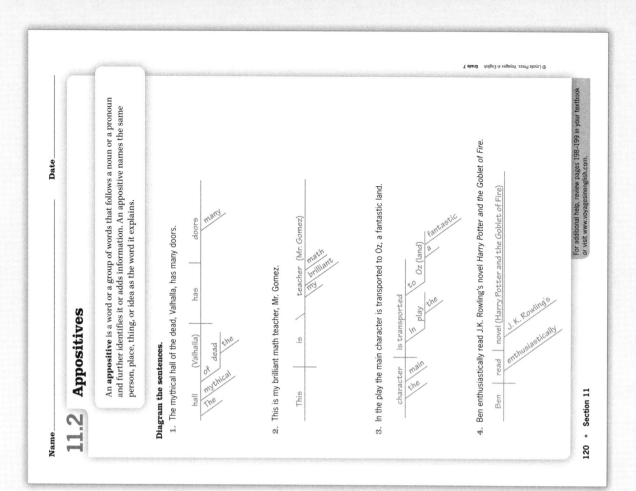

For additional help, review pages 198–199 in your textbook or visit www.voyagesinenglish.com.

120 • Section 11

11.1 Simple Sentences

A **diagram** is a visual outline of a sentence. It shows the relationships among words in a sentence. Diagramming shows how a sentence is put together. It identifies errors in a sentence and makes clear why they are errors.

Diagram the sentences.

1. A violet is a small purple flower.

2. My grandma sent me some new clothes.

3. We recently named the frisky brown colt Smarty.

4. A cat with a striped tail ran very quickly under the bushes.

For additional help, review pages 196–197 in your textbook or visit www.voyagesinenglish.com.

Section 11 • 119

Practice Book Answer Key • 65

11.4 Compound Sentence Elements

The subject and the predicate in a sentence may be compound. They may consist of two or more words connected by a coordinating conjunction.

Diagram the sentences.

1. This old silk pillow is smooth and soft.

2. Molly and Grace make their own beds and fold their own laundry.

3. The club president called or visited each member of the committee.

4. Craig and Joe wrote the music and the lyrics for this song.

© Loyola Press. Voyages in English **Grade 7**

For additional help, review pages 202–203 in your textbook or visit www.voyagesinenglish.com.

11.3 Compound Sentences

A **compound sentence** contains two or more independent clauses. An independent clause has a subject and a predicate and can stand on its own as a sentence.

Diagram the sentences.

1. The tourists visited Washington, D.C., and they toured the Lincoln Memorial.

2. Megan ordered a new computer, but it was delivered to her previous address.

3. Emanuel's stories are creative; however, they are often based on real events.

4. Maria prefers autobiographies, yet she frequently reads adventure stories.

For additional help, review pages 200–201 in your textbook or visit www.voyagesinenglish.com.

© Loyola Press. Voyages in English **Grade 7**

11.5 Participles

A **participle** is a verb form that is used as an adjective. A participial phrase is made up of the participle, its objects or complements, and any modifiers. The entire phrase acts as an adjective.

Diagram the sentences.

1. A smiling woman opened the locked door.

2. Tripping over the exposed tree root, I fell backwards.

3. The Renoir painting, displayed in a room with an expensive security system, is priceless.

4. Walking through the garden, we saw blooming flowers in a wide range of colors.

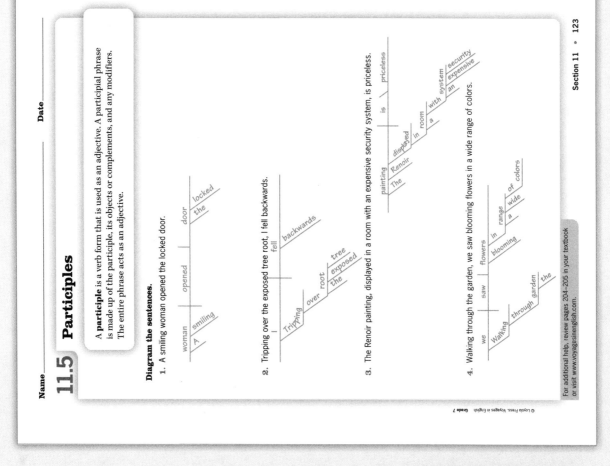

For additional help, review pages 204–205 in your textbook or visit www.voyagesinenglish.com.

11.6 Gerunds

A **gerund** is a verb form ending in *ing* that is used as a noun. A gerund can be used in a sentence as a subject, a subject complement, an object of a verb, an object of a preposition, or an appositive.

Diagram the sentences.

1. Diagramming sentences is a useful writing tool.

2. Gabe and T.J. enjoyed playing the game.

3. Miles easily won the competition by creating the best robot.

4. My goal, earning money for college, will require hard work.

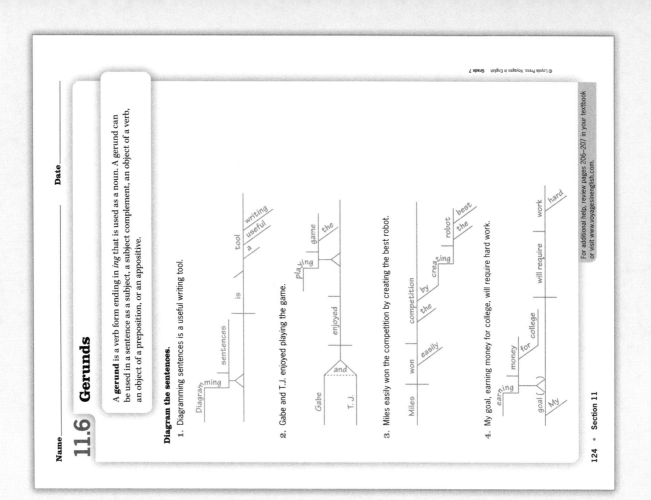

For additional help, review pages 206–207 in your textbook or visit www.voyagesinenglish.com.

11.8 Adjective Clauses

An **adjective clause** is a dependent clause that describes a noun or a pronoun. An adjective clause begins with a relative pronoun or with a subordinate conjunction.

Diagram the sentences.

1. Jim gave her the ring that he had brought from London.

2. This is the woman whose dog won the blue ribbon.

3. The artist who painted this lovely portrait lives in Mexico.

4. The department store where my brother currently works is having a sale.

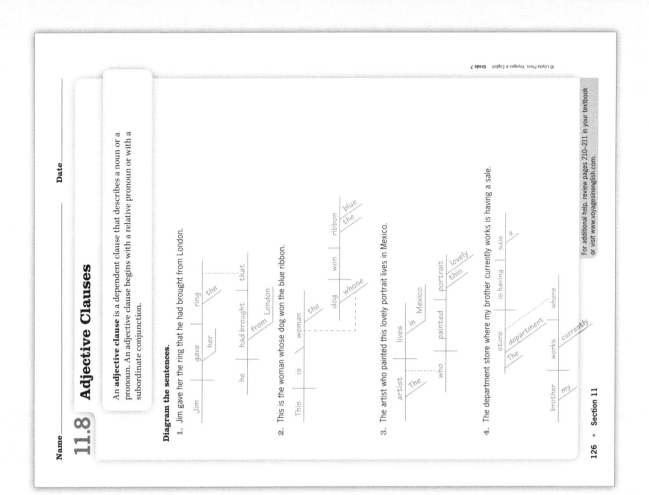

For additional help, review pages 210–211 in your textbook or visit www.voyagesinenglish.com.

11.7 Infinitives

An **infinitive** is a verb form, usually preceded by *to*, that is used as a noun, an adjective, or an adverb.

Diagram the sentences.

1. Our soccer team wants to score many points in this game.

2. Most students were anxious to see the final test results.

3. My idea, to hold a raffle, will raise money for charity.

4. To survive this powerful storm was their primary concern.

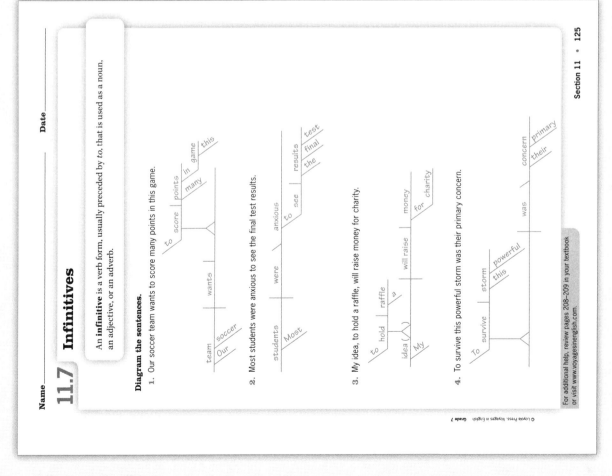

For additional help, review pages 208–209 in your textbook or visit www.voyagesinenglish.com.

11.10 Noun Clauses

Dependent clauses can be used as nouns. **Noun clauses** work in sentences in the same way that nouns do.

Diagram the sentences.

1. Billy now recalls why he kept his notebook from the previous school year.

2. That the animal is dangerous and unpredictable seems obvious.

3. The fact that she was intelligent could not be denied.

4. Whoever uses the new sports equipment should be appreciative.

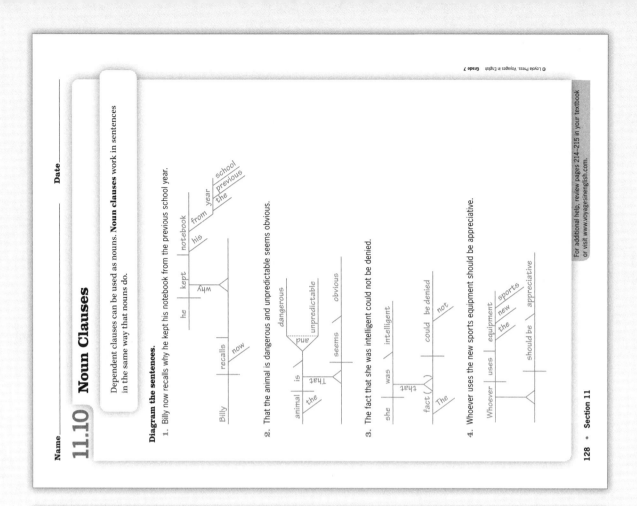

For additional help, review pages 214–215 in your textbook or visit www.voyagesinenglish.com.

11.9 Adverb Clauses

An **adverb clause** is a dependent clause that acts as an adverb; it describes a verb, an adjective, or another adverb. Adverb clauses begin with subordinate conjunctions.

Diagram the sentences.

1. Mrs. Hamaguchi canceled the birthday party because her daughter was sick.

2. Since Toby received the highest test score, he has new confidence in his math skills.

3. If Greg studies for another hour, he will finally finish his homework.

4. Maya's sister will call you whenever she needs a ride to school.

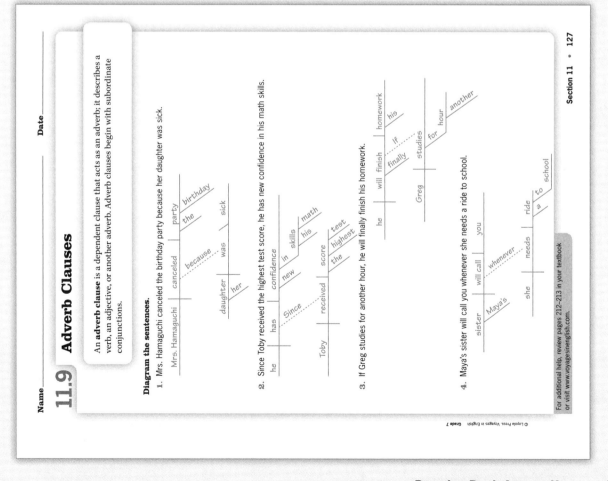

For additional help, review pages 212–213 in your textbook or visit www.voyagesinenglish.com.

LESSON **1**

What Makes a Good Personal Narrative?

A **personal narrative** is a true story about a particular event written by the person who experienced it.

Read each statement. Circle T if the statement is true or F if the statement is false. Then rewrite each false statement to make it true.

1. A personal narrative tells about events that really happened. **(T)** F

2. A personal narrative is written in the third person. T **(F)**
   A personal narrative is written in the first person.

3. The events of a personal narrative are written in a random order. T **(F)**
   The events of a personal narrative are usually written in the order in which they occurred.

4. A personal narrative should flow smoothly from beginning to end. **(T)** F

5. A good topic would be one that the writer thinks is a bit interesting. T **(F)**
   A good topic is one about which the writer feels strongly.

Write yes or no to show whether each idea would be an appropriate topic for a personal narrative.

6. instructions on how to build a bookshelf from wood — *no*

7. the morning I discovered that someone had stolen my bike — *yes*

8. my day volunteering at the hospital — *yes*

9. a tourist's favorite places to visit in Washington, D.C. — *no*

Write the tone of each passage.

10. "Stop!" I screamed, as I lunged to grab his jacket. — *excitement, fear*

11. "Look! Spring must be coming. The robin has returned!" — *excitement*

12. Swimming in the warm river, my cares floated away. — *tranquility, peace*

13. It was a clean snap! The quarterback made a break for it. — *excitement, anticipation*

14. Suddenly a wave of sorrow seemed to wash over me. — *sadness, grief*

15. I paused at that alley entrance, unable to see a thing. — *fear, anticipation*

For additional help, review pages 224–227 in your textbook or visit www.voyagesinenglish.com.

11.11 Diagramming Practice

Diagramming shows the relationships among words in a sentence. It shows how a sentence is put together.

Read the diagrams and write out the sentences.

1. *My favorite pastime is sewing patchwork quilts.*

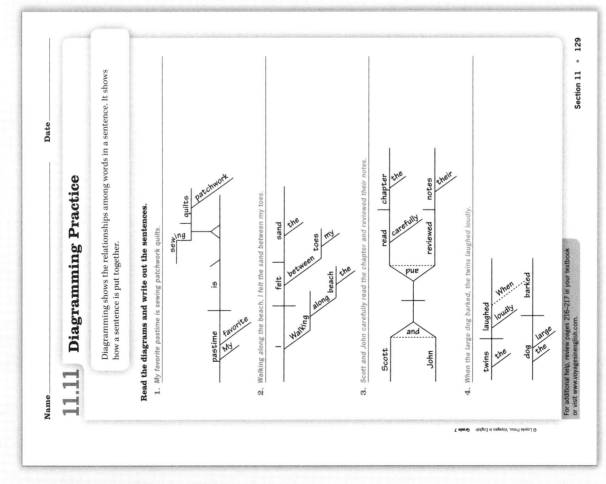

2. *Walking along the beach, I felt the sand between my toes.*

3. *Scott and John carefully read the chapter and reviewed their notes.*

4. *When the large dog barked, the twins laughed loudly.*

For additional help, review pages 216–217 in your textbook or visit www.voyagesinenglish.com.

LESSON 3

Revising Sentences

Revising sentences can help eliminate sentences that ramble or run on. Rambling sentences and **run-on sentences** make your writing harder to understand. You can avoid these kinds of sentences by being concise.

Each sentence pair has a rambling sentence and a run-on sentence. Circle the letter of the rambling sentence. Use proofreading marks to correct each sentence.

1. a. Larry walked onto the stage, his heart began to pound very fast.
   b. He could not speak, and he had a look of fear on his face, so Mrs. Burke began whispering his lines to him. ___ Consequently,

2. a. Fifteen students bought sweatshirts with the school logo, but the Pep Club still had dozens left to sell, and they had to be sold by the end of the day.
   b. Shaina had the idea that improved sales, each fan received a magnet for every sweatshirt sold.

3. a. With the team down by one point and two seconds to go, Jenna was fouled as she went up for the shot, and the ball went in and out of the basket.
   b. The referee handed her the ball at the free-throw line, she bounced it four times and then made her first free throw.

4. a. One of the first things the new teacher did was smile at each student, she wanted each child to feel comfortable.
   b. Little Jamie waited until the bell rang, and ran up and gave Miss Cross a picture that he had drawn in class, and Miss Cross taped the picture to her desk.

5. a. The women spent the day shopping at the mall, and they spotted many bargains, but they did not buy anything.
   b. Ursula looked at the glossy, polished diamond ring in the window, the sign noted that the ring was on sale.

Delete the redundant words in each sentence.

6. She was intent on eliminating and purging the redundant words in her writing.

7. Abby stared into the empty, vacant den and wondered where the wild wolves had gone.

8. Their host was courteous and interesting, while also being polite and sympathetic.

9. The costume was outlandish and bizarre, but Josh wasn't sure what was wrong with that.

10. "Ordinarily," I stammered, "Usually we start with a math warm-up and begin the lesson."

11. I was startled and frightened to see that my path was blocked by an enormous, tall man.

For additional help, review pages 232–235 in your textbook or visit www.voyagesinenglish.com.

LESSON 2

Introduction, Body, and Conclusion

A good personal narrative has an **introduction**, a **body**, and a **conclusion**.

For each part of a personal narrative, write the letter of the matching description.

1. introduction _c_ a. leaves the reader feeling satisfied and prompts the reader to think
2. body _b_ b. tells what happened in chronological order
3. conclusion _a_ c. sets the scene for the narrative

Read these mixed-up sentences from a personal narrative. Number the events in the logical order. Then circle the introduction and underline the conclusion.

4. After I put on my boots and skis, I took a lesson. _2_
5. I started down the mountain balancing on one leg. _8_
6. I will never forget the first time I went skiing. _1_
7. After a two-hour lesson, I felt confident to approach the chairlift. _3_
8. As I attempted to get out of the chairlift, my left ski came off. _6_
9. After that experience, I can safely say that two skis are better than one! _10_
10. Luckily, my instructor retrieved my left ski and handed it to me on her way down. _9_
11. The ride up on the chairlift made me feel calm as I gazed at the mountain scenery. _4_
12. I reached for my left ski, but unfortunately my right ski did not want to stop. _7_
13. The mountain scenery remained, but that calm feeling suddenly changed. _5_

Write a new introductory sentence for the above personal narrative. Then compare your introduction to the original, and tell how each is alike and different. *Answers will vary. Accept sentences that engage the reader.*

Students should compare and contrast the two introductions.

_____

Rewrite each sentence to make it a better concluding sentence. *Answers will vary.*

14. I was pretty happy with the way the day turned out.

_____

15. I decided not to go back the next day.

_____

For additional help, review pages 228–231 in your textbook or visit www.voyagesinenglish.com.

Graphic Organizers

A **graphic organizer** can help writers map out their ideas. A graphic organizer can help arrange subtopics and details related to a chosen topic. It also keeps writers from introducing unnecessary details.

Complete the time line. Add only the dates and events you consider most important to your life. *Answers will vary, but ideas should be placed in chronological order.*

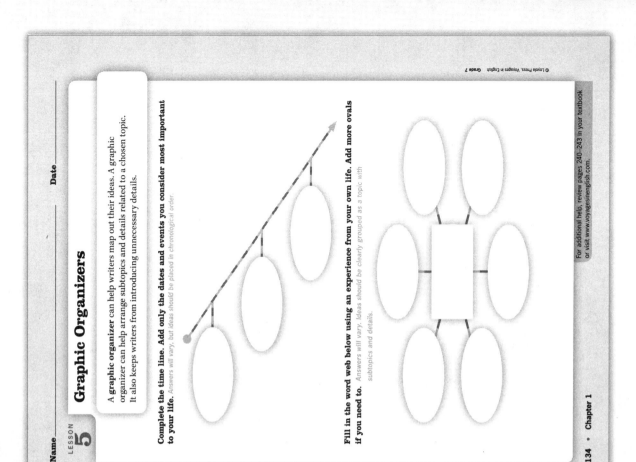

Fill in the word web below using an experience from your own life. Add more ovals if you need to. *Answers will vary. Ideas should be clearly grouped as a topic with subtopics and details.*

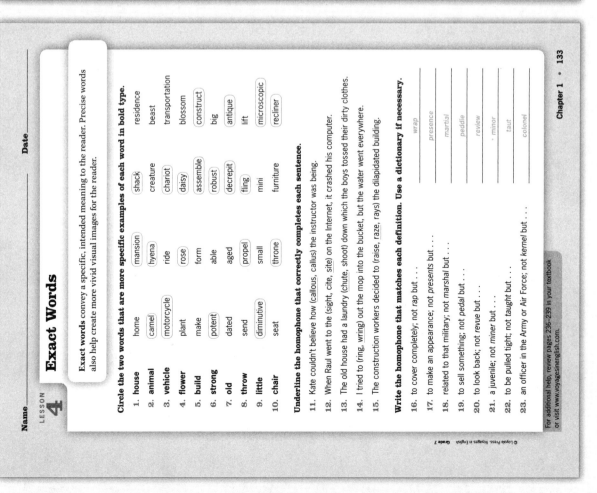

For additional help, review pages 240–243 in your textbook or visit www.voyagesinenglish.com.

Exact Words

Exact words convey a specific, intended meaning to the reader. Precise words also help create more vivid visual images for the reader.

Circle the two words that are more specific examples of each word in bold type.

1. **house**   home   mansion   shack   residence
2. **animal**   camel   hyena   creature   beast
3. **vehicle** motorcycle   ride   chariot   transportation
4. **flower**   plant   rose   daisy   blossom
5. **build**   make   form   assemble   construct
6. **strong**   potent   able   robust   big
7. **old**   dated   aged   decrepit   antique
8. **throw**   send   propel   fling   lift
9. **little**   diminutive   small   mini   microscopic
10. **chair**   seat   throne   furniture   recliner

Underline the homophone that correctly completes each sentence.

11. Kate couldn't believe how (callous, callus) the instructor was being.
12. When Raul went to the (sight, cite, <u>site</u>) on the Internet, it crashed his computer.
13. The old house had a laundry (<u>chute</u>, shoot) down which the boys tossed their dirty clothes.
14. I tried to (ring, <u>wring</u>) out the mop into the bucket, but the water went everywhere.
15. The construction workers decided to (raise, <u>raze</u>, rays) the dilapidated building.

Write the homophone that matches each definition. Use a dictionary if necessary.

16. to cover completely; not rap but . . .   *wrap*
17. to make an appearance; not presents but . . .   *presence*
18. related to that military; not marshal but . . .   *martial*
19. to sell something; not pedal but . . .   *peddle*
20. to look back; not revue but . . .   *review*
21. a juvenile; not miner but . . .   *minor*
22. to be pulled tight; not taught but . . .   *taut*
23. an officer in the Army or Air Force; not kernel but . . .   *colonel*

For additional help, review pages 236–239 in your textbook or visit www.voyagesinenglish.com.

Name _____ Date _____

LESSON 1

What Makes a Good Business Letter?

A **business letter** is a formal letter with a business-related purpose. It includes a heading, an inside address, a salutation, the body, and a closing.

Circle the words that correctly complete the sentences in this paragraph.

A letter of application is a type of (1. personal (business)) letter. It is (2. (a formal) an informal) letter that has a (3. general (specific)) purpose. The purpose of a letter of application is to apply for a (4. (job) license). This kind of letter should always be (5. long and rambling (short and to the point)).

Evaluate the sentences for appropriateness in a business letter. Cross out extraneous information. Then on another sheet of paper, rewrite the sentences that require a more professional tone. Answers will vary. Students should show an understanding of the appropriate tone for a business letter in their rewritten sentences.

6. I am sooo glad I picked your company from which to buy this little widget! rewrite

7. I am writing to express my displeasure with the service I received at store #103 on Tuesday, May 3. Of course, I write a lot of letters, but maybe you will actually answer this one.

8. Hi, I hope this letter finds you well. I am writing to thank you for your company's generous donation to our school fund-raiser. The family fun passes were very popular with bidders.

9. I received my order in the mail today. What were you thinking? This isn't a water dish; it's a swimming pool! I am returning the "dish." Please send me my refund. rewrite

10. We admire your company's dedication to the community and want to know how we can help. I really love to sing. Is there any way I can do something like that to help? rewrite

11. I am writing to explain my part in the events of last weekend. It is totally unfair that I am being blamed for the damage that was done. It's true I was there, but I was one of the people telling others that they should go find something else to do. rewrite

12. I want to work for your company. Could I come in and meet with someone to talk about that? Anytime would be cool with me. rewrite

13. Hey. We just want to say a big "Thank You!" for all the stuff you gave our club for the spring play. You guys totally rock! rewrite

14. Please accept this letter of recommendation for Raul Porras. He is one of my best friends. Raul is responsible. He can be counted on to stay positive under pressure. He is also a professional and friendly employee. In fact, we count on him to welcome newcomers.

15. I am writing to request a copy of my last bill. I seem to have lost mine. I'm sorry about that.

LESSON 2

Purpose, Audience, and Tone

A business letter should be written with the **purpose, audience,** and **tone** in mind. State your purpose early in the body and choose words appropriate for your audience and the tone you want to convey.

Write application, request, gratitude, or complaint to identify the purpose of each statement. Possible responses are given.

1. We would be grateful if you would consider visiting this fall. _request_

2. Unfortunately, the product does not meet our expectations. _complaint_

3. The gift you sent brought tears of joy to Mom's eyes. _gratitude_

4. My experience is uniquely suited to the demands of the job. _application_

5. I believe my dedication to assisting elderly people makes me an excellent match for this position. _application_

6. We found your simple gesture to be profoundly thoughtful. _gratitude_

7. Please think about donating a family pack of movie passes. _request_

8. This kind of customer service is simply not acceptable. _complaint_

Write an appropriate tone for each topic. Possible responses are given.

9. **Purpose:** You are applying to be a lifeguard at a pool. You summarize your swimming ability and safety training.
Audience: Bill Mueller, the head lifeguard at the pool
Tone: _polite and formal, confident_

10. **Purpose:** You are complaining to the manufacturer about a leaky hummingbird feeder. You describe when and where you bought the feeder and your experience in trying to use it.
Audience: a customer service representative
Tone: _firm and factual, but respectful_

11. **Purpose:** You are asking your uncle to send you a copy of the science-fiction novel he wrote. You describe science-fiction novels you've read and liked before.
Audience: your favorite uncle
Tone: _friendly and polite, slightly less formal_

LESSON 4 — Roots

A **root** is the base from which a word is built. Looking for a root inside a word can help you understand its meaning.

Underline the root in each italicized word. Write the letter of the matching root meaning. Use a dictionary if you need help. Then think about what your response would be to each sentence.

1. Name two things you *transport* to school.	_d_	a. life
2. Name two things a jeweler might *inscribe* on a ring.	_e_	b. listen
3. Name two *aquatic* animals.	_g_	c. people
4. Name two things you study in *biology*.	_a_	d. carry
5. Name two sounds you might hear in an *auditorium*.	_b_	e. write
6. Name two events you have attended as a *spectator*.	_f_	f. watch
7. Name two *epidemics* that have happened in the past.	_c_	g. water
8. Name two things you might see at a *graduation*.	_h_	h. step

Use each root to help you find the appropriate word to complete each sentence.

flect: meaning "bend."

9. Amber noticed how the light ___reflected___ off the clean glass.

10. Somehow Audrey managed to ___deflect___ all the criticism and stay positive.

gram: meaning "letter" or "written."

11. The teacher's focus on ___grammar___ helped the class improve its writing over the year.

12. Eduardo decided to draw a ___diagram___ to better communicate the idea in his report.

migr: meaning "change" or "move."

13. Every winter the birds ___migrate___ to a warmer climate.

14. Many ___immigrants___ to America work hard and hope to become productive citizens.

Study each word's root. Then write the meaning for each word on another sheet of paper. Use a dictionary as needed.

15. remiss
16. symphony
17. infinite
18. podium
19. photogenic
20. advocate
21. sanitation
22. query
23. appendix

For additional help, review pages 274–277 in your textbook or visit www.voyagesinenglish.com.

LESSON 3 — Adjective Clauses

Adjective clauses modify a noun or a pronoun and usually begin with a relative pronoun. Adjective clauses can improve your writing by shifting the emphasis, deepening the meaning, or increasing the variety of sentences.

Underline each adjective clause.

1. My brother, who is three years older than I, turned 13 last weekend.

2. My parents, who are normally strict, allowed him to get a pet of his own.

3. My brother was speechless, which is pretty unusual.

4. Carl, whom my brother called to tell about the gift, came running over to our house.

5. Dad turned onto the road that goes the past the school to get to the shelter.

6. The car wouldn't start, which is fairly typical.

7. We got in the van, which is in much better condition, and set off for the shelter.

8. It was lunchtime at the shelter, which is why all the dogs were barking, when we arrived.

9. We talked to the director who is in charge of adoptions and offered our help.

10. Pretty soon all the animals were quiet, which was a relief.

11. My brother, who had fallen silent, was staring at a group of cats.

12. The cats that were all in the first cage were mostly eating.

13. One cat that was gray and white was staring back at us.

14. It reached out a paw, which was the funniest gesture, as though it was waving at us.

15. My brother named the cat Tiger, which is a great name for a cat, and we brought it home.

Complete each sentence with an adjective clause that shifts the emphasis, deepens the meaning, or adds variety. *Answers will vary. Be sure those clauses not set off by commas add essential information to the sentence.*

16. Breakfast, _____, was a big meal.

17. His father, _____, was one of nine children.

18. I did not know you have a horse _____.

19. The team's mascot, _____, is called Clinky.

20. The man _____ is the one to ask.

On another sheet of paper, write three descriptive sentences. Use an adjective clause in each sentence.

For additional help, review pages 270–273 in your textbook or visit www.voyagesinenglish.com.

LESSON
1

What Makes a Good How-to Article?

How-to writing is a kind of expository writing. How-to writing provides information that explains how to do or make something.

Read the article. Then answer the questions. *Possible responses are given.*

Feeling bored on a windy day? Then go fly a kite. The first thing you need to do is get a kite and a large ball of string. Read the directions that came with your kite to find out how to put it together and how to attach the string. Next, take your kite to a large, open area with no tree branches or overhead power lines. Determine which way the wind is blowing. Then hold your kite as high as you can so the wind can lift it. As the wind catches the kite, begin to let out your string. Then start walking backward to keep the string tight. If your kite is stable, let out more string to make it fly higher. When you are ready to go home, slowly wind up the string and bring down your kite.

1. What is the purpose of this how-to paragraph?
   The purpose is to explain how to fly a kite.

2. Why are the sentences written as steps?
   The sentences are written as steps so the reader can understand the correct order
   in which to perform the actions.

3. What is the first step when you fly a kite?
   The first step is to get a kite and a ball of string.

4. What should you do after you find a large, open space?
   You should determine which way the wind is blowing.

5. Provide an example from the paragraph of a sentence in the imperative mood.
   Determine which way the wind is blowing.

6. What materials or tools has the author specified?
   The author says you will need a kite and string.

7. This article might be found in a book about kites. Where else might you find how-to articles?
   How-to articles can be found in how-to books, cookbooks, books related to certain games and
   hobbies, encyclopedias, and science textbooks.

For additional help, review pages 300–303 in your textbook or visit www.voyagesinenglish.com.

140 • Chapter 3

LESSON
5

Writing Tools

A **summary** is a condensed version of a text or other source, written in your own words. **Paraphrasing** is restating individual passages in a more detailed way than a summary. A **direct quotation** contains words identical to the original text.

Read each passage. Then identify the italicized text as a summary or a paraphrased piece and explain your answer. *Answers will vary, but students should be able to justify their responses.*

1. **Passage:** Superman was the original comic-book superhero. At his inception in 1938, he was faster than a speeding bullet, more powerful than a locomotive, and could leap tall buildings in a single bound. However, he could not fly until 1941.

   Superman was introduced in 1938 with all the powers he has today, except he could not fly.
   Summary. The text is short and condenses what the paragraph is about into a few words.

2. **Passage:** *The War of the Worlds* was a radio play based on a short story written by H.G. Wells. Many listeners who tuned into the show late missed the explanation that the radio show was fictional. They believed that the announcer and reporter in the show were real and that the events being reported, that Martians were invading Earth, were really happening.

   The War of the Worlds is a short story by H.G. Wells about Martians invading Earth. It was turned into a radio play. Even though it was announced that the show was fictional, some listeners missed this part. They believed that the events were actually occurring.
   Paraphrasing. The text restates the same ideas that are in the passage in a new way.

3. **Passage:** In 1945 Pennsylvania engineer Richard James was at home working with springs on a military invention. When he accidentally knocked one of the long, coiled springs off a bookshelf, he got the idea of marketing it as a toy instead. The inventor's wife, Betty, named the toy "Slinky." The Slinky has changed little since it was first introduced.

   A Pennsylvania engineer accidentally invented the Slinky in 1945 when he knocked a long, coiled spring off a bookshelf.
   Summary. The text tells the most important ideas from the passage.

4. What are some similarities and differences between a summary and paraphrasing?
   Answers will vary.

For additional help, review pages 278–281 in your textbook or visit www.voyagesinenglish.com.

Chapter 2 • 139

LESSON 3

Transition Words

Transition words connect ideas in a logical order. These words help the details in a how-to article flow smoothly.

Use the transition words in the box to complete the sentences. Use a variety of words, but repeat some words if they make the most sense. *Possible responses are given.*

above	after	because	before	behind	but	consequently	finally
first	however	instead	later	next	now	therefore	soon
still	then	so	yet	last	under	in conclusion	again

1. Cream the mixture ___*after*___ adding butter, eggs, and sugar to the bowl.

2. Use cotton if available; ___*however*___, this pattern will work for silk as well.

3. ___*In conclusion*___, I hope I have convinced you that anyone can cook a great quiche.

4. Tussah silk has a different texture ___*because*___ the silkworms eat real leaves.

5. Knead the dough ___*again*___, this time for only five minutes.

6. ___*Later*___, you can add a coat of clear varnish for durability.

7. ___*Finally*___, allow the bread to cool for 10 minutes before removing it from the pan.

8. ___*After*___ starting the engine, carefully adjust the choke.

9. Don't add the vanilla ___*yet*___; wait until after the fudge is boiling rapidly.

10. ___*First*___, lay out your materials on the table so each is easy to grab.

11. Place the second paper cutout ___*behind*___ the first one and glue together.

12. Pick up the second wrench ___*instead*___, and use it to secure the bolts.

13. ___*Now*___ congratulate yourself on assembling your very own laser pointer.

Choose one of the topics below. On another sheet of paper, write a how-to paragraph about your topic. Use at least five transition words in your paragraph.

A. You have developed a surefire strategy for earning high scores on a popular computer game. Write a paragraph that explains the first three steps in your strategy.

B. You want to make your favorite meal for dinner. Describe the first three steps you take to prepare the meal.

C. You are a guest instructor at a sports camp. It is your job to demonstrate how to perform a sports skill and teach a group of eight-year-olds how to perform it. Write a paragraph that explains the first three things you will do.

For additional help, review pages 308–311 in your textbook or visit www.voyagesinenglish.com.

LESSON 2

Relevant Details

Relevant details support the topic of a how-to article. A paragraph has unity when every detail relates to the topic sentence or main idea.

Choose a how-to topic from this list. Write the steps needed to complete the activity. If you have more than six steps, list them on another sheet of paper. Then answer the questions. *Answers will vary.*

How to multiply two-digit numbers   How to upload a document

How to make your favorite snack   How to fix a flat tire

1. STEP 1 _____

➤ STEP 2 _____

➤ STEP 3 _____

➤ STEP 4 _____

➤ STEP 5 _____

➤ STEP 6 _____

2. My most explicit details are _____.

3. The intended audience is _____.

4. The relevant details are arranged in _____ order.

5. My article would be clearer if I _____.

On another sheet of paper, use your steps to write a how-to paragraph. Exchange papers with a partner and look for any misfit sentences.

For additional help, review pages 304–307 in your textbook or visit www.voyagesinenglish.com.

LESSON 4 · Adverb Clauses

An **adverb clause** usually modifies a verb, though it can also modify an adjective or another adverb. Adverb clauses are used to add variety or change the meaning of a sentence and are introduced by subordinate conjunctions.

Underline the adverb clauses. Circle the word or words each clause modifies.

1. The alarm (went off) because the exit door was opened.
2. If you make Jan a card, maybe she (will help) you with your homework.
3. Kyle (has been arriving) at school on time since he started jogging in the morning.
4. The puppy (barked) until the bearded man held out his hand.
5. After the mulberry bush was damaged, the gardener (planted) a new bush.
6. Put on your shoes before you stub your toe on the sidewalk.
7. So that everyone gets a turn, each person (will speak) for only five minutes.
8. We all (can go) on the field trip, provided everyone turns in a permission slip.

Possible responses are given.

Revise each sentence pair by making one sentence an adverb clause.

9. My aunt introduced me to pickled okra. I don't know how I had lived without it.
After my aunt introduced me to pickled okra, I don't know how I had lived without it.

10. Check the pan carefully for cracks. Pour the batter into the pan.
Before you pour the batter into the pan, check it carefully for cracks.

11. Don't try to start the engine. Reconnect the throttle cable.
Don't try to start the engine until you have reconnected the throttle cable.

12. You are attending the drama club meeting. You can bring the box of costumes.
Since you are attending the drama club meeting, you can bring the box of costumes.

13. They will harden as they cool. The cookies may appear raw in the middle.
Although the cookies may appear raw in the middle, they will harden as they cool.

Complete each sentence with an appropriate adverb clause. *Answers will vary.*

14. While _____, the kitchen smelled like apples.
15. Her suitcase looked _____.
16. When _____, the dancers began their routine.
17. Call your parents if _____.
18. From the brush the lion watched the zebras until _____.

LESSON 5 · Dictionary

A **dictionary** contains an alphabetical list of words. For each word, the entry includes the definition, the syllabication, the part of speech, and the pronunciation.

Look up each italicized word in a dictionary. On another sheet of paper, write the definition that best fits the context of the sentence.

1. Michael *bristled* at the insinuation that he had cheated on the exam.
2. Suspecting a *bug*, the spy carefully dismantled the lamp to find the tiny wires.
3. We sorted the bills by their *denominations.*
4. They did everything to keep the flowers alive, but in the end the drought *prevailed.*
5. Our class staged a mock *summit* at the same time the world leaders were meeting.
6. The tone of the colors in the painting gave it a melancholy *mood.*
7. The president put Governor Rasband in charge of *affairs* of the state.
8. We were all encouraged to avoid *cheap* jokes in the talent show.
9. The family was a bit alarmed when Grandma decided to paint her bathroom a deep purple.
10. Don't *interfere* with the children's attempts to solve the problem on their own.

Find the meaning of each word. Write a sentence that illustrates its meaning.

11. feign _____

12. fiasco _____

Use the sample dictionary entry below to answer the questions that follow.

de • mean (di-mēn) *tr. v.* 1. To conduct or behave in a particular manner. [From Old French *demener*] 2. To lower, as in dignity or social standing. *The dog refused to demean herself by eating out of the trash.* [From English *mean*, to humble] **de • meaned, de • mean • ing, de • means**

13. What part of speech is *demean?* _____ verb _____

14. How many syllables does *demean* have? _____ two _____

15. How many meanings does *demean* have? _____ two _____

On another sheet of paper, write two sentences using *demean*. Each sentence should demonstrate a different meaning.

LESSON 1

What Makes a Good Description?

Descriptive writing uses vivid vocabulary to portray a person, a place, or a thing. A good **description** will capture a reader's senses and imagination.

Complete each sentence with information about descriptive writing. *Possible responses are given.*

1. Descriptive writing gives the reader *a vivid picture of a person, a place, or a thing*
2. A good thing to do before writing a description is to picture *the subject in your mind* and consider *the audience*
3. Writing a description is like painting *a picture* for the reader.
4. In descriptive writing, the author sets a mood or creates *a feeling*
5. *Immaculate* is a more vivid, exact word for clean.
6. *Generous* is a more vivid, exact word for nice.
7. *Squishy* is an example of a word that appeals to the sense of touch.
8. *Thwack* is an example of a word that appeals to the sense of sound.

Read each topic, picture the scene in your mind, and write three descriptive words you could use to describe the scene you visualized. *Answers will vary.*

9. rainy night

10. snowstorm

11. walk on a windy day

12. summer afternoon

13. late autumn day

Find an example of a descriptive paragraph. On another sheet of paper, answer the following questions about the paragraph. *Answers will vary.*

14. What is the topic of the paragraph?

15. How did the writer help you visualize what was being described?

16. What was the mood of the description? List three words or phrases the writer used to convey the mood.

17. List two examples of words the writer used to appeal to the senses.

For additional help, review pages 338–341 in your textbook or visit www.voyagesinenglish.com.

LESSON 2

Organization

Organize details so that one detail flows logically into the next. Depending on your topic, you may want to use different kinds of organization such as **spatial order, chronological order, and comparing and contrasting.**

Write whether you would organize each topic by spatial order, by chronological order, or by comparing and contrasting. *Possible responses are given.*

1. how my new game is better than my old one — *comparing and contrasting*
2. the interior of the International Space Station — *spatial order*
3. a visit to Ralph Waldo Emerson's home — *spatial or chronological order*
4. a trip to Japan and China — *comparing and contrasting*
5. the characters Voldemort and Uncle Olaf — *comparing and contrasting*
6. a birthday celebration — *chronological order*
7. a family vacation — *chronological order*
8. a sales brochure for a recreational vehicle — *spatial order*

Write details on this Venn diagram comparing and contrasting life in the city to life in the country. *Answers will vary.*

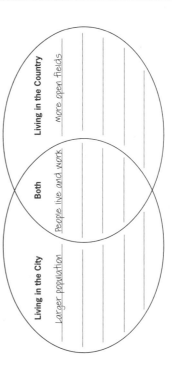

Living in the City — Larger population
Both — People live and work
Living in the Country — more open fields

On another sheet of paper, write five descriptive sentences comparing and contrasting life in the city to life in the country, using the ideas above.

For additional help, review pages 342–345 in your textbook or visit www.voyagesinenglish.com.

LESSON 3

Noun Clauses

A **noun clause** is a dependent clause used as a noun. A noun clause can be used as a subject, a subject complement, a direct object, an object of a preposition, and an appositive.

Underline the noun clause in each sentence. Write whether the noun clause is used as a subject, a subject complement, a direct object, an object of a preposition, or an appositive.

1. We do not know where the lost puppy lives. — direct object
2. Please tell her how to get to the library. — direct object
3. The best time is whenever you want it to be. — subject complement
4. Read the directions for what you should do next. — object of a preposition
5. What the baby needs is a warm blanket. — subject
6. Whoever swims the fastest will win the race. — subject
7. The idea that we can complete this in one night is ludicrous. — appositive
8. A coat of paint will restore the room to how it used to look. — object of a preposition
9. I love how my dog makes me feel when I get home. — direct object
10. The Baghetti brothers are who you should call for help. — subject complement
11. Whichever soap you choose will do the job as well. — subject
12. She will drive the horses that are white when she comes. — appositive

Use each set of words to write a sentence with a noun clause. Possible responses are given.

13. scientists believe, meteor may have caused climate changes
Many scientists believe that an ancient meteor may have caused climate changes.

14. everyone wondered, come through the door next
Everyone wondered who would come through the door next.

15. bank will give a reward, supplies them with information about the robbery
The bank will give a reward to whomever supplies them with information about the robbery.

16. children are well prepared, seems obvious
That the children are well prepared seems obvious.

17. a sign of fitness, heart rate responds to brisk activity
A sign of fitness is how your heart rate responds to brisk activity.

For additional help, review pages 346–349 in your textbook or visit www.voyagesinenglish.com.

LESSON 4

Adjective and Adverb Suffixes

A **suffix** can change the function, or use, of a word. Suffixes added to nouns or verbs can create adjectives, nouns, or adverbs. A suffix that creates an adjective is an **adjective suffix**. An **adverb suffix** creates an adverb.

Write a suffix to complete each sentence. Use a dictionary if needed.

1. We gasped, feeling the plan was exceptionally audiac_ious_.
2. The cat's maternal___ instincts were obvious when she moved to protect the kitten.
3. We thought Norford was being a little self_ish_ not to share his art supplies.
4. Helen is the most act_ive_ of the six children.
5. Albert thought_fully_ replaced the cap on the milk jug.
6. The scen_ic_ view from the cabin window enticed us to go outside.
7. The silk_en_ texture of the fabric gave the dress an elegant appearance.
8. My brother virtuous_ly_ did not to eat any of the leftover dessert.
9. We found the new computer program to be trouble_some_ and hard to use.
10. The barber careful_ly_ cleaned and stored the razors and scissors.

Write a new word made by adding an adjective suffix to each base word. Possible responses are given.

11. tact — tactful
12. vigil — vigilant
13. assist — assistant
14. hero — heroic
15. negate — negative
16. bother — bothersome
17. nature — natural
18. perish — perishable
19. grace — gracious
20. clear — clearly
21. differ — different
22. peril — perilous

Write a sentence using each base word and the suffix in parentheses. Answers will vary.

23. pleasant (-ly)
Sentence should include the word pleasantly.

24. rebel (-ous)
Sentence should include the word rebellious.

25. elude (-ive)
Sentence should include the word elusive.

For additional help, review pages 350–353 in your textbook or visit www.voyagesinenglish.com.

LESSON 5

Thesaurus

A **thesaurus** is a reference tool that gives synonyms for words.

Use a thesaurus to find synonyms for each word. Use the part of speech in parentheses to choose a synonym to complete each sentence. *Possible responses are given.*

flood

1. (verb) The water from the rain will _____saturate_____ the lawns.

2. (noun) The _____deluge_____ of water rushed over the bridge.

work

3. (noun) Moving the bed took a lot of _____effort_____.

4. (verb) Kenji will _____manipulate_____ the buttons on the control panel.

aid

5. (noun) The counselor's words will give the man the _____encouragement_____ he needs.

6. (verb) The vet will _____comfort_____ the wounded animal if she can.

space

7. (verb) _____Position_____ the text evenly on your poster.

8. (noun) Give Enrique some _____room_____ so he can catch his breath.

fair

9. (adjective) At the end of the story, the prince rescues the _____enchanting_____ maiden.

10. (noun) We can ride the Ferris wheel at the _____festival_____.

Underline the word in parentheses that best replaces the underlined word in each sentence.

11. John said, "Run! The kitchen is on fire!" (whispered bellowed sang enunciated)

12. I thought the book was very interesting. (curious absorbing boring appalling)

13. Honestly, I thought that the boy was quite rude. (unusually routinely completely much)

14. Today's hot lunch was good. (edible adequate delectable palatable)

15. Can you believe how big that cat is? (immense mature prominent insignificant)

16. Last night's show was simply amazing. (regular prodigious ominous mediocre)

17. Emily responded in a haughty tone of voice. (arrogant tranquil raucous dainty)

For additional help, review pages 354–357 in your textbook or visit www.voyagesinenglish.com.

Chapter 4 • 149

© Loyola Press. Voyages in English Grade 7

LESSON 1

What Makes a Good Book Review?

A **book review** gives information about a book and tells what the reviewer liked and disliked about it. A book review is more than a summary of a book; it is also an evaluation.

Read the book review. Then answer the questions. *Possible responses are given.*

At first when I read *The Giver*, I could not imagine a world like the one the main character, Jonas, lived in. Then I felt concern for Jonas as he had to make some extremely difficult choices.

In this utopian world, few people are given choices. Although he is young, Jonas is one of the people who is given the opportunity to explore creativity, to experience pain and love, and to make choices. Jonas wants to share what he experiences with everyone else.

The book is well written. Lois Lowry carefully creates an atmosphere in which the reader senses something is not quite right about this perfect world. Once it is clear exactly what is wrong, she keeps the reader in suspense. Lowry explores the theme of how feelings and emotions influence the choices we make. The ending is not perfectly clear because the reader chooses how to interpret it.

1. Underline the introduction. Why is this introduction effective, and how could it be improved?
   It explains that the book takes place in an alternate world that is hard to imagine and creates
   concern for the character. An improvement might be to use more attention-getting words or ideas.

2. Circle the section that summarizes the plot of the book.

3. How does the reviewer support his or her assertion that the book is well written?
   The reviewer details the uncertain and suspenseful atmosphere of the book.

4. What is the title, author, and genre of the book in the review?
   The title is The Giver by Lois Lowry, and it is a fantasy.

5. What do you learn about the characters, setting, and theme?
   The main character is Jonas, the setting is a utopian world, and the theme is about making
   choices.

6. What information do you think is missing from the review?
   Details of the setting are few, and there is little information about the main events.

For additional help, review pages 376–379 in your textbook or visit www.voyagesinenglish.com.

150 • Chapter 5

© Loyola Press. Voyages in English Grade 7

LESSON 3

Expanding and Combining Sentences

Good writers use a variety of sentences to keep the reader focused and interested. By **expanding and combining sentences**, writers vary sentence length and complexity and include more descriptive details.

Write additional details to expand these sentences to make them more interesting. Use the information in parentheses to help you add words. *Possible responses are given.*

1. Waves crashed. (adjective, adverb)

   Monstrous waves crashed loudly on the jagged rocks.

2. Kyra jumped. (adjective, prepositional phrase)

   Timid Kyra jumped out of her skin when she heard the loud bang.

3. The dog barked. (adjective, adverb, prepositional phrase)

   The yappy, little dog barked incessantly at the children playing outside.

4. The students gasped. (adjective, adverb, noun)

   The unaware students gasped audibly when the pop quiz was announced.

5. The bird flew. (adjective, adverb, prepositional phrase)

   The exotic bird flew gracefully from treetop to treetop.

Add words to complete the sentences in each pair. Then use a conjunction to combine the two sentences into a compound sentence. *Answers will vary.*

6. Tourists visit _____. Tourists also visit _____.

7. Many inhabitants are _____. Others are _____.

8. Sudden storms come. The weather in _____ is mostly _____.

9. Most teenagers eat _____. They drink _____.

10. Take a drive in _____. You will see _____.

For additional help, review pages 384–387 in your textbook or visit www.voyagesinenglish.com.

© Loyola Press. Voyages in English **Grade 7**

LESSON 2

Writing a Book Review

A good book review includes important information about the characters, setting, and plot; identifies the theme; and gives an evaluation of the book.

Write a word to complete each statement about book reviews. *Possible responses are given.*

1. A book review often begins by describing the ___characters___ and the setting.

2. Most of the body of a book review will ___summarize___ the plot of the book.

3. A ___theme___ is the overall idea that a book develops.

4. The ___evaluation___ gives the reviewer's opinions about the book and reasons to support those opinions.

Write what you learn about the main character and setting in each review.

Martin the Warrior, by Brian Jacques, is a classic tale of good versus evil. Bedrang the stoat, an ermine, is the bad guy whose captive mouse is the courageous Martin the Warrior. Martin is the most famous mouse in all of Redwall, an ancient stone abbey.

5. Main character: *Bedrang: an ermine, bad guy; Martin: a mouse, courageous warrior*

6. Setting: *Redwall, a stone abbey, probably set in medieval times*

Holes, by Louis Sachar, is an unusual story about unusual characters. The author describes a strange detention center where the teen inmates must dig holes for hours each day. In particular the tale follows the life of Stanley Yelnats and the story of his family, tracing the ancestors' lives as each endured the Yelnats curse.

7. Main character: *Stanley Yelnats; has a family curse, a teen in a detention center*

8. Setting: *a detention center where teens dig holes every day*

Circle the conclusion in the evaluation. Underline the reasons or examples that support the reviewer's conclusions. *Possible responses are given.*

9. Bill Bryson is an author of *A Really Short History of Nearly Everything*, a book for all ages. (This is a science book that is written like a great story.) In the first sentence of the book, he writes, "No matter how hard you try you will never be able to grasp just how tiny, how spatially unassuming, is a proton." That sentence makes me smile, but it also makes me want to learn more about protons—something I had never even heard of up until that point.

For additional help, review pages 380–383 in your textbook or visit www.voyagesinenglish.com.

© Loyola Press. Voyages in English **Grade 7**

Practice Book Answer Key • 81

LESSON 5

Prefixes

A **prefix** is a syllable or syllables added to the beginning of a word. A prefix changes the meaning of the word to which it is added.

Underline the prefix in each word and write its meaning.

1. extraordinary — _beyond_
2. immature — _not_
3. transcribe — _across_
4. misanthrope — _badly/wrongly_
5. superimpose — _more/over_
6. preamble — _earlier/before_
7. incorrect — _not_
8. postscript — _after_
9. antifreeze — _against_

Write the word from the box to match each definition.

| preclude | postdate | superhuman | incomplete | misspell |
| transpolar | antibody | interact | misfortune | indirect |

10. not finished — _incomplete_
11. something that acts against a virus — _antibody_
12. rule out in advance — _preclude_
13. write or say wrong letters — _misspell_
14. talk or act among one another — _interact_
15. more than average person — _superhuman_
16. bad luck — _misfortune_
17. not going straight to the point — _indirect_
18. across the North or South Pole — _transpolar_
19. to date something later than the real date — _postdate_

Add an appropriate prefix, using those found in the exercises above, to each word below. Then write a sentence using each new word. _Answers may vary._

20. cede
21. accurate
22. caution
23. merge
24. calculate

For additional help, review pages 392–395 in your textbook or visit www.voyagesinenglish.com.

LESSON 4

Outlines

An **outline** is a plan for a piece of writing that helps you organize your ideas. An outline helps you focus each paragraph on one idea and makes sure that every detail in the paragraph supports that idea.

Complete each sentence by circling all the choices that are correct.

1. An outline is
   a. a plan for writing that helps you organize ideas.
   b. a tool to ensure each paragraph focuses on one idea and the details support that idea.
   c. a division of ideas that follows a specific format.
   d. an organizer that helps you compare and contrast your opinions.

2. To create an outline,
   a. begin by deciding on a main idea.
   b. use only complete sentences with correct punctuation and capitalization.
   c. label each main idea with a Roman numeral followed by a period.
   d. list subtopics under each main idea and the details under each subtopic.

3. Once an outline is created,
   a. it should not be rewritten or modified.
   b. it can help you see what ideas need further revision.
   c. check for balance to make sure items show equal importance.
   d. look for details that are out of place or do not belong.

Read the section of an outline and answer the questions.

II. Body
  A. Percy learns the truth.
    1. Percy learns his father is the god Poseidon.
    2. His best friend turns out to be a satyr who was sent to protect him.
    3. He may be kicked out of school for fighting a monster.

4. What would you expect to come before this part of the outline? _an introduction to the book_
5. What is the subtopic? _Percy learns the truth._
6. What are the supporting details? _Percy learns the identity of his father and of his best friend, and he may be kicked out of school._

For additional help, review pages 388–391 in your textbook or visit www.voyagesinenglish.com.

LESSON 1

What Makes Good Fantasy Fiction?

Fantasy fiction takes readers to places they have never experienced. It has a beginning, a middle, and an end that provide an organized pattern of events and a clear line between good and evil.

Read each statement. Circle T if the statement is true or F if it is false.

1. Fantasy fiction is usually factual.   T   (F)
2. The setting of a fantasy story may be a different world.   (T)   F
3. The plot of a fantasy story is usually told out of sequence.   T   (F)
4. The problem or conflict is introduced toward the end.   T   (F)
5. The plot is usually developed in the middle of the fantasy story.   (T)   F
6. The series of spiraling events in fantasy fiction is called the climax.   T   (F)
7. The main character achieves his or her goal at the end of a fantasy story.   (T)   F

Write C if each passage introduces a character and S if it introduces the setting. Some passages may do both.

8. Hadley looked out at the rain-soaked scene from under the relative dryness of her home's doorway. The heavy mist that accompanied the rain this time of year meant she couldn't see far out over the sea, but she thought maybe those black dots might be something. Yes, she was sure they were moving. Her heart began to beat faster. Were those ships?   **S**

9. Chiara got unsteadily to her feet. What had happened? Where was everyone? She felt about to cry but took a deep breathe and then held it for a few seconds. Pull yourself together, she told herself. She was in a kind of underground cave. Light filtered in from above. Did I fall from up there? she wondered. The thought lifted her spirits a bit. She congratulated herself on being tough enough to survive that kind of fall. Then she began to look around for handholds. She knew she needed to get out of the cave.   **C, S**

10. Cascading down the rocky slope were thousands of waterfalls, weaving in and out of each other like an ever-changing dance of light. The setting sun gave the water a shimmering glow so that the young elf wondered for a moment if there might be gold under the surface.   **S**

11. Claude felt uneasy when he saw the castle walls. He was to go in through the main entrance and ask for Lord Phillipe, but he was overwhelmed by the feeling that this was a trap. Instinctively, he put his hand over the pocket sewn into his coat. The message wasn't for Lord Phillipe, but for his daughter. Claude jumped off his horse and rolled in the dusty road. He unbraided the horse's tail and removed the brass decorations from the saddle and bridle, working methodically until there were no signs left of his life as a prince.   **C**

LESSON 2

Plot Development

A good fantasy story includes a problem for the main character to face, obstacles to overcome, the dramatic moment toward which the story builds, and a satisfying resolution.

Write a word to complete each statement about the plot of a fantasy. *Possible responses are given.*

1. The _____resolution_____ comes after the problem is solved and ties up any loose ends.
2. After the hero rid the town of bothersome dragons, he discovered the real enemy was an evil wizard. This is a summary of the story's _____rising action_____.
3. The _____climax_____ is the most dramatic moment of the story when the main character finally solves or faces his or her problem.
4. The main character may face many problems, but one is a fundamental issue that thwarts the hero from accomplishing his or her goals. This is called the story's _____conflict_____.

Identify the conflict and resolution in each summary of a fantasy story.

Nima lives on a desert planet where widely scattered oases are the only support for a group of colonies. A new virus sweeps through her colony, so Nima and her friends set out to find help. One friend falls ill, but Nima finds the cure. Unfortunately, a sandstorm destroys the vehicle in which they were traveling, so Nima uses her wits to return in time to save lives.

5. Conflict: *Nima must persevere in the face of a harsh and unforgiving environment.*
6. Resolution: *Nima makes it back with the cure in time to save lives.*

Umi and Oni are royalty in an ancient African kingdom when they stumble across a way to travel forward in time. Umi searches desperately for a way to get home again, but Oni quickly adapts to modern life and doesn't want to return. Umi learns to make peace with the fact that this is her brother's decision, and Oni comes to see how his sister can take what she learned in the present and use it to improve the past. When they do find the way home, they return united and wiser.

7. Conflict: *Umi and Oni are stuck in the future, and only one of them wants to go home.*
8. Resolution: *Umi learns to trust Oni to make the right decision. Oni finds a reason to go home.*

LESSON 3

Dialogue

Dialogue adds interest to a scene by helping readers feel that they are right in the middle of the action. Dialogue is also an effective way of conveying emotion, humor, and subtle information about the characters.

Write nine words that can replace the word *said* and help describe the manner in which a character speaks. *Possible responses are given.*

1. _hissed_
2. _cooed_
3. _laughed_
4. _shouted_
5. _hollered_
6. _whispered_
7. _cried_
8. _gasped_
9. _joked_

Read the dialogue and answer the questions.

"Miguel and Tam, sitting in a tree," sang Elena in a singsong voice. "Stop!" Miguel yelled, and then more softly he continued, "That's not funny, Elena. Tam is my friend and she's very sick."
Elena looked surprised. "It's not—, I didn't mean—", she stammered, growing red-faced. Finally, she sighed, "I'm sorry, Miguel."

10. Which character is probably younger? Why? *Elena is probably younger. She is teasing Miguel and Miguel tries to be patient with her after initially being angry.*

11. How does the author use dialogue to show that the characters know each other well? *The characters use each other's name and squabble, but soon make up.*

Add punctuation to the dialogue for the first character. Then write a response of dialogue for the second character. *Answers will vary.*

12. Description: two children flying on an airplane for the first time
"Look at how small the houses seem," squealed Bridget
_____

13. Description: a paramedic helping a man in a car accident
"Do you think my leg is broken?" Jonathan cried
_____

14. Description: a comic-book hero confronting a villain
"So, hissed the evildoer, you think you can foil my diabolical plan, do you?"
_____

For additional help, review pages 422–425 in your textbook or visit www.voyagesinenglish.com.

© Loyola Press. Voyages in English **Grade 7**

Chapter 6 • 157

LESSON 4

Figurative Language

Figurative language compares one thing to another in a way that adds interest and insight to the comparison.

Complete each sentence with the figure of speech in parentheses. *Answers will vary.*

1. The tumbleweeds _____. (personification)
2. This pile of dirty clothes is _____. (hyperbole)
3. The baby's skin is _____. (simile)
4. Our new house is _____. (metaphor)
5. The flowers _____ in the breeze. (personification)
6. During the summer, the gym is _____. (simile)
7. That final exam was _____. (metaphor)
8. The chair _____ under the man's weight. (personification)
9. It's so cold today that _____. (hyperbole)
10. After the triathlon, my body _____.
11. My brother's old clunker of a car was _____. (simile) (metaphor)

Rewrite each sentence by replacing the underlined cliché with more effective figurative language. *Answers will vary.*

12. We tried to eat the bread rolls, but they were <u>hard as rocks</u>.
_____

13. The interior of the apple was as <u>white as snow</u>.
_____

14. The look in her eyes was as <u>cold as ice</u>.
_____

15. The mighty castle was as <u>old as the earth itself</u>.
_____

16. Hurrying here and there, the stonemason was as <u>busy as a beaver</u>.
_____

For additional help, review pages 426–429 in your textbook or visit www.voyagesinenglish.com.

158 • Chapter 6

© Loyola Press. Voyages in English **Grade 7**

LESSON 1

What Makes Good Expository Writing?

Expository writing provides factual information. Its purpose is to inform, explain, or define something to its audience. One kind of expository writing is the expository article.

Answer the questions. *Possible responses are given.*

1. What should a reader expect to learn from an expository article?

   The reader should expect to learn facts and details to support the main idea.

2. What should be included in the introduction of an expository article?

   The introduction tells what the article is about. It should include a topic sentence that states the main idea of the article.

3. How are the subtopics often organized in the body of an expository article?

   Subtopics are organized in a logical way that is appropriate for the topic of the article.

4. Should the writer include mostly facts or opinions in an expository article? Why?

   The writer should include mostly facts because he or she is informing, explaining, or defining information for the reader.

5. What is the purpose of the conclusion of an expository article?

   The purpose of the conclusion is to summarize the article.

6. How do the details for an expository article differ from its main idea?

   The main idea is what the expository article is generally about, while the details are specific information and examples that give substance to the expository article.

7. How might a writer gather details to support the main idea?

   The writer can note details that he or she already knows, list personal experiences, use reference sources, or ask experts to provide more details.

8. What may cause a writer's main idea to change as he or she gathers details?

   The writer may find more interesting details that support a different main idea. The details may contradict a writer's original main idea.

For additional help, review pages 452–455 in your textbook or visit www.voyagesinenglish.com.

LESSON 5

Limericks

The structure of a **limerick** follows exact rules, but the result is fun and easy to remember.

Circle the letter of the choice that correctly completes each statement.

1. Limericks are best described as
   a. poems that tell sad stories.
   b. poems about nature.
   c. silly rhymes that tell stories.
   d. real-life narratives.

2. Limericks usually feature all the following except
   a. fantastic characters.
   b. real people.
   c. surprising situations.
   d. humorous conclusions.

3. Limericks are probably a commonly used poetic form because they are
   a. easy to write.
   b. short, fun, and easy to remember.
   c. based on true stories.
   d. stories with a moral.

4. To find rhymes for a limerick, a poet might use
   a. an atlas.
   b. an encyclopedia.
   c. a dictionary.
   d. a rhyming dictionary.

Use syllable stress marks to identify the stressed and unstressed syllables in each line. Circle the line if it contains an example of anapestic rhythm.

5. There was an odd, damp odor.
6. She liked to collect ants.
7. "Won't you live in my shoe?"
8. Everyday they bought oranges.
9. Each morning at dawn.
10. He robbed the young man of defeat.

Underline the word that does not rhyme in each set and replace it with a word that does. *Possible responses are given.*

11. screwdriver, conniver, survivor, quiver _____ skydiver
12. bombastic, postmaster, gymnastic, elastic _____ fantastic
13. brother, our, power, shower _____ scour
14. chore, order, floor, oar _____ more
15. quicker, heretic, lunatic, dirty trick _____ candlestick

For additional help, review pages 430–433 in your textbook or visit www.voyagesinenglish.com.

LESSON 2 — Fact and Opinion

Facts are statements that can be proved true or false. **Opinions** are statements that tell what someone believes. In an expository article, opinions should be avoided unless they are those of experts.

Write *fact* or *opinion* to identify each statement. Circle the opinion signal words.

1. The American tree sparrow is common to Alaska and northern Canada.   *fact*
2. The amazing physicist Gwyn Jones used motorcycle parts in her work.   *opinion*
3. In 1794 Eli Whitney patented the cotton gin.   *fact*
4. Women give chocolate to men on Valentine's Day in Japan.   *fact*
5. In a charming return, men give women gifts a month later on White Day.   *opinion*
6. A tractor-drawn aerial is a fascinating type of fire truck that has a separate steering mechanism for the rear wheels.   *opinion*
7. Concerns over security have triggered proposed legislation requiring online sites with photographic maps to blur out public buildings.   *fact*
8. The Akashi-Kaikyo Bridge is the world's longest suspension bridge.   *fact*

Write one fact and one opinion about each topic. *Answers will vary.*

9. an occupation
   Fact: _____
   Opinion: _____

10. a recent school event
    Fact: _____
    Opinion: _____

11. an animal kept as a pet
    Fact: _____
    Opinion: _____

Cross out the statement that is least relevant to an essay about a mosquito control program.

12. There are approximately 3,500 species of mosquitoes.
13. Mosquitoes are the most deadly disease carriers known, killing millions of people each year.
14. Mosquitoes go through four stages in their life cycle: egg, larva, pupa, and adult.
15. Mosquitoes lay their eggs near open sources of water.

LESSON 3 — Noun and Verb Suffixes

A **suffix** is a syllable or syllables added to the end of a word to change its meaning. Suffixes may create nouns or verbs when added to other words.

Complete each sentence by adding a noun suffix to the word in parentheses.

1. The boxes in the ___basement___ need to be labeled and stacked. (base)
2. For your own ___safety___, please be sure your seatbelt is securely fastened. (safe)
3. After living in Iowa for most of her life, Liz is now a ___resident___ of Arizona. (reside)
4. The enthusiastic audience gave a standing ovation to the ___pianist___. (piano)
5. Because the hotel had no ___vacancy___, we had to keep driving. (vacant)
6. Their ___friendship___ has endured over the years. (friend)
7. The woman peered through the ___darkness___ as she tried to locate the light switch. (dark)
8. Joan valued her job as the ___assistant___ to the foundation's president. (assist)
9. By claiming an ___exemption___, Randolph received a substantial tax refund. (exempt)
10. Miles suddenly became aware of the ___reality___ of his situation. (real)

Write a new word by adding a verb suffix to each word. Then write a sentence for the new word. *Possible responses are given.*

11. soft   *soften*
    This new lotion seems to soften my skin.

12. active   *activate*
    Natasha can activate the credit card by calling the toll-free number on the back.

13. computer   *computerize*
    The purchase of new software will help the library computerize its checkout system.

14. terror   *terrorize*
    I know you don't like spiders, but there's no reason to let them terrorize you.

15. less   *lessen*
    Mrs. Taylor hopes that a good rest will lessen her cold symptoms.

16. real   *realize*
    The good grade on my test helped me realize how important it is to study.

LESSON 5 — Library and Internet Sources

When researching information, two of the most efficient ways of finding information are to use references from the **library and Internet sources.**

Write the letter to match each library reference or Internet source to its description.

a. a Web site developed by an organization
b. something published at regular intervals
c. articles on specific topics arranged alphabetically
d. maps and other geographic information
e. listings of magazine articles
f. a military Web site
g. a government Web site
h. a commercial Web site
i. a Web site developed by a school
j. annual facts, statistics, and news items

1. _b_ a periodical
2. _e_ Reader's Guide
3. _a_ a .org site
4. _d_ an atlas
5. _h_ a .com site
6. _c_ an encyclopedia
7. _i_ a .edu site
8. _j_ an almanac or a yearbook
9. _f_ a .mil site
10. _g_ a .gov site

Circle the letters of the two Web sites that would likely provide the most reliable information for each topic.

11. the number of Congressional state representatives for Massachusetts
    a. a .gov site for the U.S. Congress
    b. a .com site with educational games
    c. a .org site of nonprofit lobbyists
    d. a .org site for Massachusetts history

12. the meaning and etymology of a word
    a. a .edu site from a prominent university
    b. a .com site of a respected print dictionary
    c. a .com dictionary with numerous ads
    d. a .com site to which anyone can contribute articles or information

13. the life of President Lincoln
    a. a .gov site about Illinois history
    b. a .com site selling books about Lincoln
    c. a .gov site about former U.S. presidents
    d. a .org site about American presidents

List three library resources you could use to research the topic. Then list three keywords you might use to find information on the Internet. *Possible responses are given.*
Topic: the history of the Alamo
Resources: _encyclopedia, nonfiction book, Internet_
Keywords: _Alamo, Texas history, Texas Revolution_

For additional help, review pages 468–471 in your textbook or visit www.voyagesinenglish.com.

LESSON 4 — Quotations

Direct quotations are a person's exact words, either spoken or in print, that are incorporated into your own writing.

Circle the number of each sentence that is correct. Add the correct punctuation and capitalization to the sentences that are incorrect.

1. "I regret that I have but one life to give for my country," wrote Nathan Hale.
2. Socrates believed that "wisdom begins in wonder."
3. The teacher said, "Explain the proverb 'the road to a friend's house is never long.' "
4. "Where there is love there is life," said Mahatma Gandhi.
5. Ralph Waldo Emerson said, "People only see what they are prepared to see."
6. Quinn asked me what Francis Bacon meant when he said, "Knowledge is power."
7. "If you judge people, you have no time to love them," Mother Teresa proclaimed.
8. My father likes this quotation by Mark Twain: "You cannot depend on your eyes when your imagination is out of focus."
9. "You're happiest while you're making the greatest contribution," said Robert F. Kennedy.
10. "The future," declared Eleanor Roosevelt, "belongs to those who believe in the beauty of their dreams."
11. My instructor said, "When I start to worry, I remember Nichiren Daishonen's words: 'No one can avoid problems, not even saints or sages.' "

Write a sentence using each direct quotation. *Possible responses are given.*

12. Hope is the dream of a man awake. —French Proverb
    Mr. Barton liked to quote the French proverb "Hope is the dream of a man awake."

13. He who has imagination without learning has wings and no feet. —Joseph Joubert
    Joseph Joubert said that "he who has imagination without learning has wings and no feet."

14. A friend is one who knows you and loves you just the same. —Elbert Hubbard
    Elbert Hubbard once said, "A friend is one who knows you and loves you just the same."

15. A person who never made a mistake never tried anything new. —Albert Einstein
    "A person who never made a mistake never tried anything new," said Albert Einstein.

16. Happiness depends upon ourselves. —Aristotle
    The saying "Happiness depends upon ourselves" is attributed to Aristotle.

For additional help, review pages 464–467 in your textbook or visit www.voyagesinenglish.com.

LESSON 1

What Makes a Good Research Report?

A **research report** explores a specific idea about a topic. Facts are gathered by researching sources such as interviews, books, encyclopedias, almanacs, magazines, newspapers, maps, and documents on the Internet.

Circle the letter of the answer that correctly completes each sentence.

1. The purpose of a research report is to
   a. entertain.
   b. inform.
   c. explain how to do something.

2. The tone of a research report is
   a. formal.
   b. informal.
   c. humorous.

3. A Works Cited page lists
   a. topics.
   b. details.
   c. sources.

4. A thesis statement presents the
   a. main idea.
   b. sources used.
   c. conclusion.

5. Details that support the thesis statement are grouped into
   a. graphics.
   b. subtopics.
   c. topics.

6. Information in a research report should
   a. come from friends.
   b. be in a table of contents.
   c. have several sources.

Read each thesis statement and write two kinds of sources that may provide information for the thesis. *Possible responses are given.*

7. Zwickau, Germany, is both an ancient city and a modern one.
   atlas, online or print encyclopedia

8. Yesterday, the new library in our town was dedicated, making it easier for more people to gain free access to books and research materials.
   newspaper, interviews

9. What could be a more worthwhile way to spend your spring break than by helping build affordable housing?
   Internet news sources, magazine articles

10. The development of agriculture led to significant changes in human behavior.
    magazines, documents on the Internet

For additional help, review pages 490–493 in your textbook or visit www.voyagesinenglish.com.

Chapter 8 • 165

© Loyola Press. *Voyages in English* Grade 7

LESSON 2

Gathering and Organizing Information

Using note cards is one way to **gather and organize information.** Write on the note cards important details that relate to your topic. At the bottom of the card, write the source and page number.

Complete a note card listing at least three facts for each passage. *Possible responses are given.*

The Republic of Indonesia is a country that spans the Asian and Australian continents. It is made up of 17,508 islands, although only 6,000 of those islands are inhabited. 237 million people live in Indonesia. Only three other countries have more people: China, India, and the United States. Indonesia has an elected legislature and a president. Indonesia has a diverse collection of ethnic, linguistic, and religious groups.
— Indonesia by Heather Juno, page 115

> Indonesia
> -fourth most populous nation
> -a country made up of thousands of islands
> -many different ethnicities, languages and religions
> -government is elected
>
> *Juno p 115*

The Asian, or Asiatic, elephant is one of the three living elephant species. These are the largest living land animals in Asia and are considered endangered. Asian elephants are often domesticated for use in forestry, tourism, and special occasions and ceremonies. Asian elephants are smaller than African elephants. They can be distinguished by their smaller ears and more slightly rounded back. The tip of their trunk has only one finger-like muscle instead of two.
— Walking Thunder by Steve Smith, page 18

> Asian v. African elephant
> -Asian elephant smaller overall
> -Asian elephants have much smaller ears.
> -Asian e. have rounded backs; African e. have flatter backs.
>
> *Smith p 18*

166 • Chapter 8

For additional help, review pages 494–497 in your textbook or visit www.voyagesinenglish.com.

© Loyola Press. *Voyages in English* Grade 7

LESSON 3

Citing Sources

By **citing your sources** for the reader, you give credit to the source of each fact, idea, or quotation you find. It also tells the reader where to look for more information on the topic.

Write the type of information that is missing from each citation.

1. Book:

   Coville, Jayne. *Cooking with French Chefs.* Baton Rouge, LA: <u>name of publisher</u>, 2001.

2. Encyclopedia:

   <u>name of article</u>. *The Encyclopaedia Britannica.* 2010 edition.

3. Web site:

   Sciacca, Mark. "Antique Cars." 2 Dec. 2009 <u>Web site address</u>.

Write encyclopedia, book, or Web site to identify the source of each citation.

4. "Jane Austin." *World Book.* 2010 ed. _____ encyclopedia

5. Macaulay, David. *Castle.* New York, NY: Houghton Mifflin, 1977. _____ book

6. "Branches of Government." 25 Mar. 2009 <http://bensguide.gpo.gov/6-8/government/branches.html>. _____ Web site

7. "The Great Salt Lake." *New Book of Knowledge.* 2008 edition. _____ encyclopedia

8. Symes, Dr. R. F., Dr. R. R. Harding. *Crystal and Gem.* New York, NY: DK Publishing, 1991. _____ book

9. "Why I Am Opposed to the War in Vietnam." 16 Apr. 1967, King, Jr., Martin Luther<http://www.hpol.org/record.php?id=150>. _____ Web site

10. Porter, Robert. "Ankle Injuries." *Encyclopedia of Medicine.* 2004 ed. _____ encyclopedia

Circle the letter of the choice that best completes each statement.

11. Parenthetical notation is
    a. identifying which source a fact comes from. **c.** identifying the Web site.
    b. identifying the type of source. **d.** identifying the thesis of the report.

12. Plagiarism is
    a. listing the sources in the wrong order. **c.** using someone's ideas as your own.
    b. including facts that don't support the topic. **d.** using parenthetical notation.

LESSON 4

Varied Sentences

Variety is one key to crafting engaging writing with an original voice. Create variety by changing the length, the type, and the structure of your sentences.

Write natural or inverted to indicate the order of each sentence. Then rewrite the sentence in the opposite order.

1. Above the ocean soared several seagulls. _____ inverted
   Several seagulls soared above the ocean.

2. The angry bull paced around the circular corral. _____ natural
   Around the circular corral paced the angry bull.

3. Hovering over her young is the mother deer. _____ inverted
   The mother deer is hovering over her young.

4. On the hill overlooking the farm are packs of coyotes. _____ inverted
   Packs of coyotes are on the hill overlooking the farm.

5. Racing through the streets were throngs of runners. _____ inverted
   Throngs of runners were racing through the streets.

Rewrite each sentence as either interrogative or exclamatory. Modify the structure and add or change words if needed. *Possible responses are given.*

6. Students will begin the spring-cleanup campaign on Monday.
   Is it Monday on which students will begin the spring-cleanup campaign?

7. The fireworks finale continued for five minutes uninterrupted.
   Wow! That fireworks finale continued for five whole minutes without stopping.

Rewrite each sentence to begin with a modifier.

8. Jan lifted the boulder with the help of her brother.
   With the help of her brother, Jan lifted the boulder.

9. The city streets look like a spider web on the map.
   On the map the city streets look like a spider web.

10. The tiger crouched in its cage waiting for food.
    Waiting for food, the tiger crouched in its cage.

LESSON
5

Denotation and Connotation

A word's **denotation** is its dictionary definition. A word's **connotation** is the implied meaning of the word. Often it suggests a positive or negative value to a word.

Complete the chart by writing an appropriate word. Use a dictionary or thesaurus if you need help. *Possible responses are given.*

	POSITIVE CONNOTATION	NEGATIVE CONNOTATION	DENOTATION
1.	anticipation	*anxiety*	expectation
2.	lingers	loiters	*delays*
3.	*steed*	nag	horse
4.	moist	*dank*	damp
5.	scent	*odor*	smell
6.	converse	chatter	*talk*
7.	*timid*	cowardly	shy
8.	*bother*	pester	annoy

Rewrite each sentence using neutral words more appropriate for a research report. *Possible responses are given.*

9. The Cardinals' efforts fell short of the mark, and the Yankees won 6–3.

   The Cardinals lost to the Yankees, who won 6–3.

10. The new mall will require destroying more than 85 homes in the area.

    The new mall will be situated where there are currently 85 homes.

11. The unproven governor had to make difficult decisions only two weeks into his term.

    The new governor had to make difficult decisions only two weeks into his term.

12. Individuals who gambled in the stock market found themselves suddenly with little to no retirement funds.

    Individuals who invested in the stock market now found themselves with little to no

    retirement funds.

13. Gaunt models teetered on spindly shoes as they careened down the walkway.

    Models displayed this year's clothing and shoe fashions as they traveled back and forth

    on the walkway.

For additional help, review pages 506–509 in your textbook or visit www.voyagesinenglish.com.

Assessment Book

HOW THE ASSESSMENT BOOK WORKS

The *Voyages in English* Assessment Book provides assessment of the concepts taught and practiced in the classroom lessons. The Assessment Book is divided into two distinct parts that correspond with the grammar and writing portions of the *Voyages in English* Student Edition. These same assessments are also available for purchase separately on CD in a customizable format.

GRAMMAR ASSESSMENT

The grammar portion contains assessments for each section of grammar instruction. All Student Edition material is thoroughly assessed to determine how well students have learned the lesson's concepts. Each set of items is arranged in order of difficulty. A short passage at the end of each assessment asks students to identify features and edit text for mistakes related to the grammar section concepts.

Summative assessments follow approximately every two grammar sections. This format checks students' retention of previously learned grammar skills and has students apply these skills to a proofreading activity.

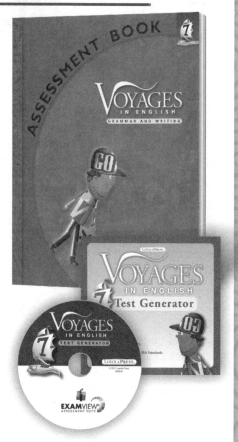

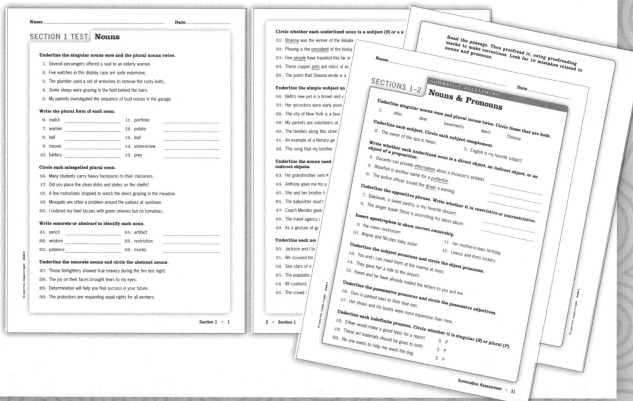

WRITING ASSESSMENT

The writing portion contains assessments for each chapter of writing instruction. Each writing skills assessment has one to three subsections related to the writing skills, word study, or study skill featured in the Student Edition writing chapters. Each writing prompt asks students to follow a set of instructions similar to those found on standardized tests.

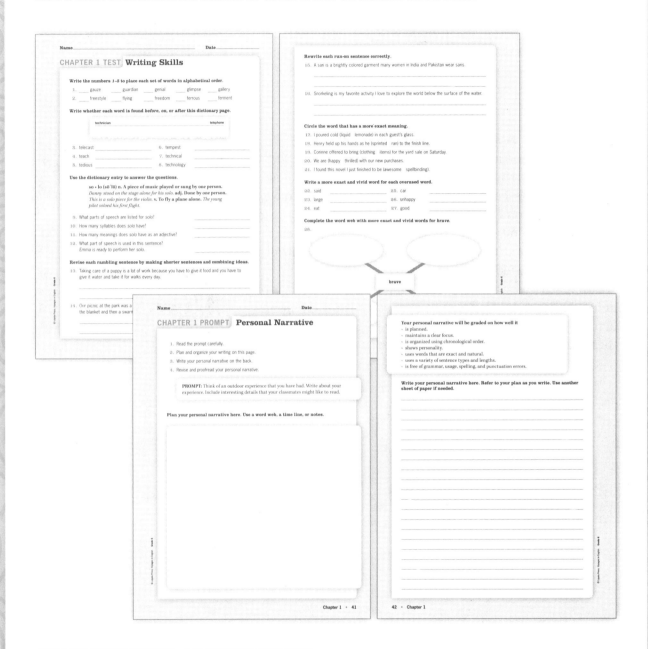

ADMINISTERING ASSESSMENTS

Teachers may choose to administer an entire grammar or writing assessment following the completion of its section or chapter, or they may choose to administer only a portion of an assessment that relates to a particular lesson or set of lessons.

SECTION 1 TEST Nouns

Underline each singular noun once and each plural noun twice.
1. A dozen mice made several holes in this wall.
2. We set up six chairs next to the couches under the window.
3. Abigail found a position working in the offices of these attorneys-at-law.
4. The man had a fireproof safe that protected his important documents.
5. My mother has a fear of all canines after she was bitten by a small pug as a child.

Write the plural form of each noun.

6. address	*addresses*	11. piano	*pianos*
7. knife	*knives*	12. handful	*handfuls*
8. roof	*roofs*	13. calf	*calves*
9. canopy	*canopies*	14. series	*series*
10. moose	*moose*	15. crisis	*crises*

Write whether each noun is *singular*, *plural*, or can be used as *both*.

16. teeth	*plural*	21. hoof	*singular*
17. burros	*plural*	22. sopranos	*plural*
18. gulf	*singular*	23. slacks	*both*
19. shelf	*singular*	24. scissors	*both*
20. salmon	*both*	25. species	*both*

Circle whether each underlined noun is a subject (*S*) or subject complement (*SC*).
26. The puppies are in the kennel. — **S** SC
27. The owner of the dog is Nicole. — S **SC**
28. Mrs. Hines was a renowned chemist for that industrial company. — S **SC**
29. After a lengthy career, the professor is an expert in her field. — **S** SC
30. These dark rain clouds are indicators of poor weather to come. — S **SC**

Circle whether each underlined noun is a direct object (*DO*), an indirect object (*IO*), an object complement (*OC*), or an object of a preposition (*OP*).
31. Dr. Black bought a bouquet for his wife. — **DO** IO OC OP
32. Owen sent his nephew a gift certificate for his birthday. — DO **IO** OC OP
33. The garden club elected Hillary president yesterday. — DO IO **OC** OP
34. Elliot gave McKenzie an extra ticket for the concert. — DO IO OC **OP**
35. Mrs. Wilkins named the new student the lead in the school play. — DO IO **OC** OP

Underline the appositive or appositive phrase. Circle whether it is restrictive (*R*) or nonrestrictive (*NR*).
36. Carrie, my sister, sings in a band. — R **NR**
37. The famous artist Pablo Picasso is buried here. — **R** NR
38. I know Larry, the president of our senior class. — R **NR**
39. Let's travel to Sea Gate, our cottage by the ocean. — R **NR**
40. Mr. Duncan, the band director, wants us to enter the contest. — R **NR**
41. Two types of grain, rice and barley, contain important amino acids. — R **NR**

Write the possessive form of each word in parentheses.
42. the (boys) soccer ball — *boys'*
43. your (kitten) bed — *kitten's*
44. several (women) vacations — *women's*
45. this (man) wallet — *man's*
46. (Mrs. Cappos) vehicle — *Mrs. Cappos's*
47. these (tomatoes) flavors — *tomatoes'*
48. the (attorneys-at-law) offices — *attorneys-at-law's*

Underline the possessive nouns in each sentence. Write whether the nouns show separate possession (*S*) or joint possession (*J*).
49. Jack's and Joe's paintings are both magnificent. — *S*
50. Miley and Sue's room is finally clean. — *J*
51. We just celebrated Mom and Dad's anniversary. — *J*
52. Janna, please take Bo's and Jarred's jackets to the closet. — *S*
53. Did you know that Ed and his family's house is new? — *J*
54. The cat and the dog's water dish is in the garage. — *J*
55. Put Harris and Kristen's project on the display table. — *J*

Read the following paragraph. Then respond to the questions.

Have you ever seen a shooting star? A shooting star, a meteor, streaks across the sky like a diamond with a tail. Last summer I was camping in the mountains with my friend's family. After we gathered two (armfuls) of wood and built a small fire, we watched the night sky. I counted 15 shooting stars that night.

56. What is the subject of the first sentence? — *you*
57. What is the appositive phrase in the second sentence? — *a meteor*
58. Add commas to indicate the nonrestrictive appositive.
59. Circle the plural compound noun and write it correctly. — *armfuls*
60. Underline the possessive noun.

SECTION 2 TEST Adjectives

Underline the descriptive adjectives. Circle the word each adjective modifies.

1. The <u>young</u> (boy) loves his <u>small</u> (dog).
2. Her friend counted <u>six</u> (cracks) in the <u>old</u> (sidewalk).
3. The <u>skillful</u> (groomer) offered to trim my <u>black</u> (poodle)'s <u>long</u> (claws).
4. That (night) was <u>cold</u> and <u>damp</u>, but Ryan searched over <u>two</u> (hours) for the <u>lost</u> (cat).
5. (Mandy) <u>nervous</u> yet <u>brave</u>, sprang forward for a <u>magnificent</u> (dive) off the <u>high</u> (board).

Underline each adjective and write whether it is _demonstrative_, _interrogative_, or _indefinite_.

6. We should see <u>this</u> play. _____ _demonstrative_
7. He wanted to consider <u>both</u> sides of the argument. _____ _indefinite_
8. <u>What</u> part of the equation did you solve? _____ _interrogative_
9. <u>Whose</u> shoes were left in the hallway? _____ _interrogative_
10. <u>Each</u> player improvised <u>several</u> parts of the composition. _____ _indefinite, indefinite_

Write the comparative form of each adjective.

11. short	_shorter_		15. pleasant	_more/less pleasant_
12. happy	_happier_		16. assertive	_more/less assertive_
13. busy	_busier_		17. little	_less_
14. strange	_stranger_		18. good	_better_

Write the superlative form of each adjective.

19. smart	_smartest_		23. little	_least_
20. cheap	_cheapest_		24. good	_best_
21. silly	_silliest_		25. unruly	_most/least unruly_
22. bad	_worst_		26. solitary	_most/least solitary_

Complete each sentence with the comparative or superlative form of the adjective in parentheses.

27. Toby is the _funniest_ person I know. (funny)
28. The house is _farther_ down this road than I thought. (far)
29. I set the lawn chair in a _sunnier_ part of the yard. (sunny)
30. This section of the path is _narrower_ than where we just came from. (narrow)
31. The steep hike up that trail was the _most difficult_ thing I ever did. (difficult)
32. This ring is _better_ because it is _more ornate_ than that one. (good, ornate)

Circle the adjective that correctly completes each sentence.

33. There were (fewer) less) dimes than nickels.
34. Our team has (fewer (less) time to practice this week than last week.
35. My mentor had (few (little) advice to offer on this particular subject.
36. Karla was disappointed that her bag held the (fewest) least) coins.
37. All of us had (few) little) ideas for how to solve the problem.
38. He applied the (fewest (least) effort, and it showed in his performance.

Underline each adjective phrase once and each adjective clause twice. Circle the noun each phrase or clause modifies.

39. We purchased those (flowers) <u>from the nursery</u>.
40. Green (apples) <u>which are sour</u>, are not his favorite fruit.
41. The small (trees) <u>in the plastic pots</u> should be planted here.
42. The (company) <u>from Milwaukee</u> opened the new hardware (store) <u>on the corner</u>.
43. That park is the (place) <u>where many children gather on bicycles</u>.
44. The (adults) <u>who volunteered to assist us</u> are wearing yellow shirts.
45. The bell (tower) <u>which no longer has any bells</u>, is still the tallest (structure) <u>in town</u>.

Underline the adjective clauses. Circle whether each clause is restrictive (_R_) or nonrestrictive (_NR_).

46. Toys <u>that contain lead</u> were recalled yesterday. (R) NR
47. She enjoys games <u>where a certain strategy is needed to win</u>. (R) NR
48. Would you like some of this tea, <u>which was just freshly brewed</u>? R (NR)
49. His composition, <u>which is on the teacher's desk</u>, seems well written. R (NR)
50. We should not choose any restaurant <u>that requires a reservation</u>. (R) NR
51. This old table, <u>which is an odd color of green</u>, is unstable. R (NR)
52. The culmination of the ceremony features a poem <u>that was written by a student</u>. (R) NR

Read the following paragraph. Then respond to the questions.

Our school is hosting a spectacular assembly about African culture. We will view traditional dances and costumes. (Some) musicians are bringing a variety of African instruments. We think our students, who come from many cultures, will learn a lot tonight.

53. What are the descriptive adjectives in the first sentence? _spectacular, African_
54. Circle the indefinite adjective. What noun does it modify? _musicians_
55. Underline the two adjective phrases once.
56. Underline the adjective clause twice.
57. Is the adjective clause restrictive or nonrestrictive? _nonrestrictive_

SECTION 3 TEST Pronouns

Write the person and number of each underlined pronoun.

1. They raked leaves all afternoon. — *third person plural*
2. Did we mention that Julie stopped by? — *first person plural*
3. After breakfast, the chores were divided among us. — *first person plural*
4. Oscar, you and I will both need a new coat. — *second person singular*
5. Robert and she offered me a ride to the game. — *third person singular*

Underline each third person pronoun and write its gender.

6. She got a new book. — *feminine*
7. What did he say about the concert? — *masculine*
8. It has not been seen since Tuesday. — *neuter*
9. You should help him complete that assignment. — *masculine*
10. I thought that he had placed it on the table. — *masculine, neuter*

Write the subject pronoun that can take the place of each word or phrase.

11. a lamp — *it*
12. Mary and I — *we*
13. John, Mike, and Les — *they*
14. the woman — *she*
15. Arthur — *he*
16. many trees — *they*

Circle the pronouns that correctly complete the sentences.

17. (They) Them) went to visit their cousins in Hawaii.
18. Only (him (he)) knew the way to the stadium.
19. Declan and (me (I)) helped Mrs. Ryan clean up her yard.
20. Could (you) him) drive me to the library after lunch?
21. The car had a dead battery, and (she (it)) wouldn't start.
22. (She) Her) already understands the directions, so (us (we)) don't need to repeat them.

Cross out each pronoun used incorrectly. Then write the correct pronoun.

23. Him blew up balloons for the party. — *He*
24. Dave and them worked together on it. — *they*
25. The people in the sailboat were Lacey, Joel, and her. — *she*
26. On Tuesday morning us left for the airport. — *we*
27. The only person with the correct answer was me. — *I*
28. After the event them and her ate lunch with Mrs. Taft. — *they, she*

Circle the pronouns that correctly complete each sentence.

29. Lisa showed (I (me)) the new book.
30. Don and Lisa were there, so I gave (they (them)) the key.
31. The teacher asked (me (I)) the most difficult question.
32. Her family gave (she (her)) a great going-away party.
33. Myron generously offered these gifts to (him) he) and (I (me)).
34. The tour guide gave (we (us)) directions, and we thanked (she (her)).

Circle the pronouns that correctly complete the sentences.

35. Lila walks faster than (she) her).
36. The large black dog barks more than (they) them).
37. Does Brad read as well as (me (you))?
38. Nate was more confused about the answer than (us (we)).
39. Mom will drive my brother to practice more often than (I (me)).
40. The math tutor must help me more often than (they (them)).
41. Ed and I borrowed more books than (he) him) and (you) them).

Underline each possessive adjective once and each possessive pronoun twice.

42. Are these your missing keys?
43. That old blue backpack is mine.
44. My art project isn't nearly as creative as his.
45. Mina hopes her experiment is chosen for our science fair.
46. Is his or your lunch box in the car, or is this yours on the kitchen counter?

Underline each possessive adjective and circle the thing owned or possessed.

47. You left your book (report) in the library.
48. Theirs is the new house down the street from our (house).
49. It may be your (wish) to see a movie, but the decision will be mine.
50. Our (dog) needs a bath because its (fur) is muddy.
51. Clark bought her coin (collection) so its rare silver (quarter) is now his.

Write the possessive pronoun that correctly completes each sentence pair.

52. This is her red jacket. The jacket is ___*hers*___.
53. Jake bought a bike over the weekend. The new bike is ___*his*___.
54. Where do the Smiths live? ___*Theirs*___ is the house on the left.
55. Ann got a good grade on her report. ___*Hers*___ was an excellent report.
56. Kay and Daniel got a beagle puppy. That new puppy is ___*theirs*___.
57. The airline tickets belong to Matt, Lisa, and me. Those tickets are ___*ours*___.

SECTION 3 TEST | Pronouns (continued)

Underline each intensive or reflexive pronoun and circle its antecedent.

58. (Rita) herself was fascinated by many animals.
59. (We) got ourselves some high-powered binoculars.
60. (Trevor) and (Ray) set themselves up for an evening of bird-watching.
61. (Maria) bought herself a bird identification manual, but (I) myself prefer Internet sources.

Underline each intensive or reflexive pronoun. Then write whether the pronoun is intensive (I) or reflexive (R).

62. This cat itself is the star of a commercial. _____ I
63. The students must prepare themselves for the upcoming quiz. _____ R
64. I can lift this box myself. _____ I
65. Leila excused herself from the table. _____ R
66. The players found themselves in an argument until the coach himself appeared. _____ R, I

Write pronouns to complete the sentences. Circle each pronoun's antecedent.

67. (Eliot) gave us this rake, and we must return it to _him_ .
68. When (Emma) and (Ray) arrive, _they_ will need to complete this form.
69. (Jill) opens her home to stray dogs, and now four dogs live with _her_ .
70. Stay off that (pile) of wood because _it_ could easily fall over.
71. The (man) in the blue shirt waved to (Susan) and then _he_ sat down next to _her_ .

Underline each interrogative pronoun and circle each demonstrative pronoun.

72. (This) is my pencil.
73. Who is your favorite teacher?
74. Which of (these) is mine?
75. What does (that) say?
76. Which match (that) best?
77. What is (that) going to cost?
78. To whom did you give (this)?
79. Whom did you mention (that) to?

Use the directions in parentheses to complete each sentence with the correct demonstrative pronoun.

80. _This_ is my coin purse. (near)
81. _That_ is the person you were looking for. (far)
82. The chef will need several of _these_ for the recipe. (near)
83. _This_ is a copy of the document that I mailed on Tuesday. (near)
84. How can we wrap _those_ so they will not be damaged? (far)
85. Can you believe that _this_ is the only one Stephanie has? (near)

Underline each relative pronoun and circle its antecedent.

86. The (squirrel) that found the seeds was fortunate.
87. Any (person) who completes the hike receives a T-shirt and an award.
88. The reference (book) that I found provides interesting facts about reptiles.
89. This jewelry was donated for an (exhibit) that opened in April.
90. Those (spectators) who were standing could see more than the (people) who were seated.

Underline each indefinite pronoun.

91. Most require a ticket.
92. My parents just think he needs something to do.
93. Has anyone looked in the closet for the missing shoe?
94. Mr. Moir's knowledge of baseball was revered by many.
95. Fluffy ate none of her treats, so Freckles ate all of them instead.

Underline each indefinite pronoun. Circle the verb that correctly completes each sentence.

96. Several (was (were)) in line to buy movie tickets.
97. Nobody ((wants) want) to eat the leftover meatloaf.
98. Carrie and Mara are cousins, and both (is (are)) coming to visit.
99. Many ((work) works) in the city, so they take the train.
100. Mosquitoes are plentiful, and some (was (were)) bothering George earlier.
101. A few (remain) behind, but most (has (have)) left by now.

Read the following paragraph. Then respond to the questions.

J.R.R. Tolkein enjoyed creating fictitious languages in his free time. He would then take these and build a mythical culture around they. His book *The Hobbit* was created in this way. Most agree that his themes of loyalty, friendship, and cooperation are as suitable for grownups as they are for children.

102. Is there a possessive pronoun or a possessive adjective in the first sentence? _possessive adjective_
103. What is the antecedent to He in the second sentence? _J.R.R. Tolkein_
104. Circle the object pronoun error. Write it correctly. _them_
105. What is the antecedent of the demonstrative pronoun in the second sentence? _fictitious languages_
106. Underline the indefinite pronoun.

SECTION 4 TEST Verbs

Underline each verb or verb phrase. Circle the auxiliary verbs.

1. The children waded in the fountain.
2. We (may) visit your town this summer.
3. Jackie played her harmonica for the talent show.
4. The two young boys (did) wash their hands before dinner.
5. (Have) you eaten your vegetables yet?
6. In case of emergency, you (should) think about each scenario and make a plan.

Complete the sentences with the past form of the verbs in parentheses.

7. The U.S. Army ___offered___ (offer) to train nurses.
8. Thousands of nurses ___served___ (serve) during World War II.
9. Many individuals ___saw___ (see) the training as a great opportunity.
10. Nurses often ___worked___ (work) and ___lived___ (live) without a source of fresh water.
11. Conditions ___were___ (be) harsh, but the job ___gave___ (give) them a sense of purpose.

Complete the sentences with the past participle form of the verbs in parentheses.

12. The art supplies were ___divided___ (divide) among the six groups.
13. By the end of the hour, I was ___done___ (do) with my sketch of a sunset.
14. Leslie had ___made___ (make) several paintings and sculptures before.
15. Their artistic talent had ___grown___ (grow) over the years.
16. Both have ___left___ (leave) early and have ___gotten___ (get) a ride home.

Circle each phrasal verb.

17. Todd and Scott (put on) their socks and shoes.
18. An old house on the corner (burned down) last weekend.
19. The suspect (handed over) the stolen property to the officer.
20. Marcie, can you (look after) your little sister while I (set up) these chairs?

Underline the verb, verb phrase, or phrasal verb in each sentence and circle whether it is transitive (T) or intransitive (I).

21. Frank practices every afternoon. — T (I)
22. Lloyd caught the ball without effort. — (T) I
23. My brothers jazzed up their room with new posters. — (T) I
24. The author has written about rare tropical snakes. — T (I)
25. Ms. Ericson, the expert on bees, has spoken at length on that topic. — T (I)

Circle the verbs that correctly complete the sentences.

26. Mel (taught) learned) us how to fish.
27. Will you (lend) borrow) your sister that board game?
28. Mr. and Mrs. Lorreli (rose (raised) thoroughbred horses.
29. Sometimes I (let (leave) my lunch box on the counter at home.
30. The very tired toddler is (laying (lying) on the sofa.
31. Marian (laid) lain) her coat on the sofa and (set (sat) down beside me.
32. Sue (lent) borrowed) Sam the leash, so he could (learn (teach) his dog the trick.

Underline each linking verb. Circle each subject complement.

33. Isaac seems (curious)
34. The warm milk quickly turned (sour)
35. Both of our pets stayed (calm) throughout the storm.
36. This music sounds (great) over the powerful speakers.
37. The dog still smelled (awful) in spite of the new shampoo.
38. Don't you think Arnold appears (tall) for his age?
39. We agreed that Kay looked (radiant) after her tennis win.

Underline each verb or verb phrase. Write whether the sentence is in the *active* or *passive* voice.

40. Andy developed his own photographs. — active
41. The old dam was tested by the heavy rain. — passive
42. Methods of water rescue were improved by this study. — passive
43. Our group finally completed its history project. — active
44. The captions for the yearbook were written by Jill. — passive
45. We dragged the sandbags and set them by the wall. — active
46. That mountain trail was often used by a group of hikers. — passive

Underline each verb or verb phrase. Write whether the verb tense is *simple*, *progressive*, or *perfect*.

47. I have read that book. — perfect
48. Wesley speaks too quickly. — simple
49. Dana danced exceptionally well. — simple
50. We will be learning about the ancient Egyptians next. — progressive
51. Eli is learning polynomial equations at school. — progressive
52. Saul has agreed with my position in the past. — perfect
53. Our youth group sang and danced for the senior center. — simple
54. Sophie and Sylvia are reading the same book. — progressive

SECTION 4 TEST Verbs (continued)

Write whether each sentence is in the indicative, imperative, or emphatic mood.

55. Read all the directions first. _____ imperative
56. Kelly did walk the dog. _____ emphatic
57. Unicycles are becoming popular again. _____ indicative
58. Jackie does win every race she enters. _____ emphatic
59. One danger would be the rocks on the path. _____ indicative
60. Did you find the best match for this sock? _____ indicative
61. Here is the best place to set those heavy crates down. _____ indicative
62. Let's tie this stack of newspapers into smaller bundles. _____ imperative

Circle the correct form of the subjunctive mood that completes each sentence.

63. I wish I (was (were)) able to record her stories.
64. Whether it (be) is) soccer or football, Maya truly loves sports.
65. If there (was (were)) more time, I could finish my homework.
66. I don't recommend that you (be) are) late for the conference.
67. Her instructors all insisted that Katie (was (be)) prepared for her audition.
68. Mom suggested that David (play) plays) outside in the fresh air.
69. Whether she (is (be)) shy or not, Olivia let us know her feelings.
70. If Jason (were) was) not a big fan, he wouldn't have been so disappointed.

Circle whether each sentence expresses a wish or desire (W), a condition contrary to fact (C), a recommendation or demand (R), or an uncertainty (U).

71. If I were taller, then I'd play basketball. W (C) R U
72. My parents and I wish we were home. (W) C R U
73. I must insist that our team be allowed to play first. W C (R) U
74. The treasurer recommended that he not spend the money yet. W C (R) U
75. If this job were easier, the workers could finish it more quickly. W (C) R U
76. Whether she be right or wrong, Alicia is always reasonable. W C R (U)
77. If there were more money, all the bills would be paid. W (C) R U
78. Some of us wish that summer vacation start earlier than it does. (W) C R U

Write a modal auxiliary to match each meaning.

79. possibility _____ might   82. necessity _____ must
80. permission _____ may   83. ability _____ can or could
81. obligation _____ should   84. intention _____ will or would

Circle each modal auxiliary and write whether whether it expresses permission, possibility, ability, necessity, obligation, or intention.

85. The performers must practice their act. _____ necessity
86. We should find out where Toby left the pick and shovel. _____ obligation
87. Susanna can purchase concert tickets for all of us. _____ ability
88. Myra might attend the festival this weekend. _____ possibility
89. Yes, Stanley may borrow my bicycle for the trip. _____ permission
90. If the meeting starts at noon, I will arrive promptly. _____ intention
91. All applicants must complete the form to be considered. _____ necessity

Circle the verb that correctly completes each sentence.

92. There (is (are)) two dogs sleeping on the couch.
93. A snack (doesn't) don't) have to taste bad to be good for you.
94. A flood of water down the driveway (happens) happen) every time it rains.
95. (Was (Were)) they at the Independence Day celebration?
96. There (has (have)) been several problems with the car's engine lately.
97. The tree with the purple flowers (is) are) my favorite one in the garden.

Underline each subject. Circle the verb that correctly completes each sentence.

98. Nobody (is) are) left in the building.
99. The audience (doesn't) don't) know whether to laugh or cry.
100. Sam and Annie (wasn't (weren't)) afraid during the movie at all.
101. Mathematics (is) are) the subject I must study for the hardest.
102. Two cups of flour (is) are) just enough.
103. Every cow and horse on the farm (grazes) graze) in the upper pasture today.

Read the following paragraph. Then respond to the questions.

Arborists are tree specialists. The health of individual trees is assessed by arborists. Some work with landowners to prune branches, remove trees, fight insects, and treat a variety of diseases. There is also those who work for county or city governments. When disease is found, private and county arborists must work together to contain it.

104. What is the linking verb in the first sentence? _____ are
105. Is the second sentence in the active or passive voice? _____ passive
106. Underline the simple present tense verbs in the third sentence.
107. Circle the error in subject-verb agreement.
108. Does the modal auxiliary express intention or necessity? _____ necessity

Underline the gerund phrase in each sentence. Write S (subject) or SC (subject complement) to identify each gerund phrase.

30. My least favorite job is cleaning the windows.	SC
31. Careening into the hedges put a stop to their antics.	S
32. Is America's favorite pastime really watching football?	SC
33. Collecting stamps was a popular activity years ago.	S
34. Understanding how to decipher complicated directions is a useful skill.	S
35. Handling snakes and lizards is her idea of a relaxing afternoon.	S

Underline the gerund phrase in each sentence. Circle DO (direct object), OP (object of a preposition) or A (appositive) to identify how the gerund phrase is used.

36. Aunt Daphne enjoys baking cakes. — (DO) OP A
37. Carla uses the calendar for remembering dates. — DO (OP) A
38. The scout troop began making paper cranes. — (DO) OP A
39. This type of quiz, recalling names and dates, is not easy for me. — DO OP (A)
40. Many people were giving credit to Perry for having the idea first. — DO (OP) A

Circle the word that correctly completes each sentence.

41. (Grandma's) Grandma) singing the lullaby put the baby to sleep.
42. (Me) (My) heaping the clothes into a pile was not helping Mom.
43. (You) (Your) deciding not to go was understandable.
44. He did not like (us) (our) inviting the others to the party.
45. I did not know what to make of (Natalie) (Natalie's) sprinting out the door.

Write whether the italicized word in each sentence is used as a gerund (G), a participial adjective (PA), or a participle in a verb phrase (VP).

46. A *bustling* crowd is a common holiday sight. — PA
47. The *dedicated* instructor turned us all into dancing fans. — PA
48. *Laughing* loudly always puts a smile on my face. — G
49. Jason was *tossing* paper balls into the trash can. — VP
50. The *climbing* monkey was attracting everyone's attention. — VP
51. He finally solved the mystery by *studying* and classifying the fingerprints. — G

Write each gerund in parentheses as an infinitive that completes the sentence.

52. _To skateboard_ to school is faster than to walk. (skateboarding)
53. _To fish_ in the morning is a wonderful way to start the day. (fishing)
54. The monkey's best hope for escape was _to pick_ the lock. (picking)
55. We considered it our good luck _to work_ with Bernardo. (working)
56. His strategy for winning was _to run_ five miles every other day. (running)

Name _____   Date _____

SECTION 5 TEST   Verbals

Circle each participle.

1. The hawks come on silent wings, (gliding) over the treetops.
2. Max, (dreaming) of warmer days, put on a second sweater.
3. In this gusty wind, the tiny dog, (anchored) by its leash, tried not to blow away.
4. Henry is an actor, (playing) to any audience who will watch him.
5. I don't like (fractured), (complicated) tales when there are so many simple ones left to tell.
6. (Twisting), (turning), but never (touching) a single leaf, the bats flew away silently.

Underline each participial phrase and circle the noun or pronoun it describes.

7. A (teenager) wearing a blue cap ran into the store.
8. That red (dress) displayed in the window is still my favorite.
9. The (deer) standing in the shady grove listened for sounds of movement.
10. That (woman) holding the leash suddenly noticed that her bag was missing.
11. Having worked his way down the steps alone, (he) was very pleased with himself.

Underline the participial adjective in each sentence.

12. Two tired children rested.
13. An annoying fly buzzed around me.
14. The tightened screw held fast.
15. The sleeping infant cooed and wriggled.
16. Katie glanced at the darkening sky.
17. We watched the traveling circus pass by.

Underline the gerund in each sentence.

18. His favorite activity in winter is skiing.
19. Writing short stories is a hobby Nathan enjoys.
20. Part of her volunteer work involves raising money for charities.
21. The worst part of this dish is peeling all those potatoes.
22. Lana's plan for exercising is walking each day.
23. During summer months camping by the lake is relaxing and inexpensive.

Use the verb in parentheses to write a gerund that completes each sentence.

24. _Relaxing_ by the pool is our goal this afternoon. (relax)
25. _Switching_ the trains' routes on the tracks was his job. (switch)
26. _Running_ after the dog was tiring and not very productive. (run)
27. Casey's favorite weekend activity is _reading_ books. (read)
28. One effective way to stay in shape is _riding_ bikes. (ride)
29. _Getting_ credit for planning this project is important. (get)

Name _____ Date _____

SECTION 5 TEST Verbals (continued)

Circle S (subject) or SC (subject complement) to identify how the infinitive is used in each sentence.

57. The man's job was to guard the gate. S (SC)
58. To counsel each student is your responsibility. (S) SC
59. To complete this project requires a great deal of patience. (S) SC
60. My plan is to retrieve the boat from the river today. S (SC)
61. Alyssa's goal remained to graduate with honors in only three years. S (SC)
62. During that year the river was to spill over its banks several times. S (SC)
63. After the bell rang, to be first in line seemed to be every student's motivation. (S) SC

Underline each infinitive used as a direct object.

64. She decided to picnic on the lawn.
65. They hoped to achieve great things very soon.
66. A judge and that lawyer wanted to resolve this conflict.
67. The police officer intended to teach his dog a new search procedure.
68. Alexa had begun to plan the trip to Montreal over a month ago.
69. Right away he politely asked the children to leave the premises.

Underline each infinitive phrase used as a noun. Write whether each phrase is used as a subject (S), a subject complement (SC), or a direct object (DO).

70. Miranda dared to dance the tango. DO
71. To feed those guinea pigs should have been Selena's first priority. S
72. The desired outcome of the project was to put a satellite in space. SC
73. Our committee decided to sell floral arrangements. DO
74. Mom and Kelly chose to stop by the post office on their way home. DO
75. The reason for that particular rule was to keep all students safe. SC

Underline each infinitive phrase used as an appositive.

76. It was his idea, to bring the flashlight, that saved the trip.
77. Franco's wish, to lengthen recess time, could not be granted.
78. Dad's mistake, to forget the flatware, caused a messy picnic.
79. Rich's action, to give the man a few dollars, sparked some controversy.
80. The goal of the mayor, to get the new convention center built, was finally realized.
81. That was Larry's misfortune, to be remembered as the cause of the trouble.
82. Did you consider my idea, to be packed the night before so we can leave early?

Underline each infinitive phrase used as an adjective. Circle the noun the phrase describes.

83. Those are the (trees) to be pruned today.
84. We are just the (people) to do the job.
85. He was not the only (student) to write a play.
86. The rocket has the (ability) to divide into separate stages.
87. Amanda was the first (person) to suggest that we leave early.
88. Our teacher did not see the student's behavior as (something) to encourage.

Underline each infinitive phrase used as an adverb. Then write the part of speech of the word the phrase describes.

89. We sang to pass the time. verb
90. Oscar and Marian were happy to play along. adjective
91. That chipmunk wasn't strong enough to carry that apple. adverb
92. The audience cheered to show their appreciation. verb
93. The Chapman family was excited to see the president. adjective
94. Sylvia ran to win but wasn't fast enough to do so. verb, adverb

Underline each hidden infinitive. Circle each split infinitive.

95. Ray was hoping (to not have) to go.
96. Matthew heard the dogs bark until well after midnight.
97. I'd rather dance on a stage than sing in front of an audience.
98. Her after-school tutor helped Carrie complete her persuasive essay.
99. The heavy silence caused Leigh (to suddenly wonder) where everyone had gone.
100. I watched the assistant gather up the books (to be immediately shelved).
101. Melanie wouldn't dare ask for a solution (to quickly solve) the puzzle.

Read the following paragraph. Then respond to the questions.

Our group, having arrived late to the first-aid fair, hurried to catch up. Training stations were set up around the room. At each one we had (to quickly assess) the situation. The goal, to earn points, was achieved by how well we assessed a problem. Later, the trainers helped us view the inside of a Life Flight helicopter.

102. Underline the participial phrase in the first sentence.
103. What is the participial adjective? _____ Training
104. Circle the split infinitive.
105. What is the hidden infinitive in the last sentence? _____ view
106. What is the infinitive phrase used as an appositive? _____ to earn points

SECTION 6 TEST Adverbs

Underline each adverb. Write whether it is an adverb of *time, place, manner, degree, affirmation,* or *negation*.

1. This king rules justly. _____ *manner*
2. The dog dug down into the dirt. _____ *place*
3. Our neighbor could be quite helpful. _____ *degree*
4. I am often late for practice if I have a lot of homework. _____ *time*
5. The team is indeed excited about the upcoming game. _____ *affirmation*
6. This particular dishwasher never needs repairs. _____ *negation*

Circle the word each italicized adverb describes. Then write the part of speech of the circled word.

7. Poppy flowers are relatively (common). _____ *adjective*
8. The team (worked) rapidly on the assignment. _____ *verb*
9. A lone black cat (moved) stealthily through the grass. _____ *verb*
10. While usually (punctual), this person has a reason to be late. _____ *adjective*
11. The ballplayer swung that bat so (incredibly) fast. _____ *adverb*
12. She was positively (jovial) about her upcoming expedition. _____ *adjective*
13. A crowd of protestors was quite (rapidly) advancing forward. _____ *adverb*

Underline each interrogative adverb.

14. Why are you late?
15. How does he spell his name?
16. When will the ferry be arriving at the dock?
17. Where are your boots, hat, and gloves?
18. Katie asked, "How do you know what the cost will be?"
19. When are you leaving for the airport, and how will you get there?

Circle each adverbial noun. Write whether it expresses *time, distance, measure, value,* or *direction*.

20. The celebration lasted two (hours). _____ *time*
21. They often traveled 20 (miles) before stopping. _____ *distance*
22. We were pleased to hear that this costs only 50 (cents). _____ *value*
23. Both children could spend (days) wandering the exhibits. _____ *time*
24. The car turned (south) onto the old dirt road. _____ *direction*
25. He spent five (dollars) on a toy that lasted five (minutes). _____ *value, time*
26. Hal traveled (west) in weather that measured 100 (degrees). _____ *direction, measure*

Write the comparative and superlative form of each adverb.

27. fast	*faster*	*fastest*
28. safely	*more/less safely*	*most/least safely*
29. late	*later*	*latest*
30. elegantly	*more/less elegantly*	*most/least elegantly*
31. well	*better*	*best*

Circle the word that correctly completes each sentence.

32. (There) (They're) walking this way.
33. Her pitching and throwing skills are very (good) (well).
34. All the musicians played (good (well)) in the competition.
35. We discussed the matter (farther (further)) before reaching a decision.
36. Tony isn't a (bad) (badly) player; he just played (bad (badly)) that day.

Underline each adverb phrase. Circle the word or words the phrase describes.

37. The drama club (meets) every Monday.
38. They (must finish) their outlines before the holidays.
39. Mr. Harper (bought) a large bouquet of lilies for his mother.
40. The carpenter (cut) the piece of plywood with a circular saw.
41. The new twins in my class just (moved in) down the street.

Underline each adverb phrase once and each adverb clause twice. Then write the word or words each describes.

42. Michael did not call her because he is shy. _____ *did call*
43. Whenever there are lilacs, I know spring has arrived. _____ *has arrived*
44. I am saving my money for my college tuition. _____ *am saving*
45. After the corn is harvested, it is shipped to the market. _____ *is shipped*

Read the following paragraph. Then respond to the questions.

Scout always digs in the flower beds. How did we get him to stop? First, my parents fenced in a large area. Then they dug a pit inside and filled it with sand and dog treats. Scout dug (most earnestly) here to find those treats than he had before and left the rest of the yard alone.

46. Does the adverb in the first sentence express place or time? _____ *time*
47. What is the interrogative adverb? _____ *How*
48. Underline the adverbial phrase in the fourth sentence.
49. Circle the comparative adverb error. Write it correctly. _____ *more earnestly*
50. What word does the adverb alone describe? _____ *left*

SECTION 7 TEST Prepositions

Underline each prepositional phrase. Circle each preposition.

1. The ball flew (over) the fence.
2. Bethany studied (throughout) the day.
3. Do not stand (in front of) the TV.
4. (According to) my mother, the plane should arrive soon.
5. A group (of) tourists crossed the river (by means of) a zip line.
6. The team decided to continue practice (in spite of) the rain.

Circle the preposition or prepositions that correctly complete each sentence.

7. Please take your papers (off) off of the table.
8. (Between) Among) you and me, I like the second choice better.
9. My mom and I differ (on) with) the need to buy me new clothes.
10. The characteristics vary (between) among) different species of penguins.
11. Michael behaves (like) as if) he never met me before.
12. The employees are angry (with) at) the decision to lower wages; consequently, they are angry (with) at the manager.

Circle whether each underlined word is used as an adverb (A) or a preposition (P).

13. The construction crew was waiting below.   A (P)
14. Let's head to the store before dark.   (A) P
15. Adrian prefers to ride his skateboard down the street.   A (P)
16. We will attend an assembly in the auditorium and then leave right after.   (A) P
17. Can you see the rising moon just above the horizon?   A (P)
18. The helicopter hovered above for twenty minutes.   (A) P
19. Below the deck is a series of small rooms.   A (P)

Circle the word each italicized adjective phrase describes.

20. The (sign) *on the post* has been taken down.
21. My dad bought (tickets) *for the movie*.
22. She is going to the (rehearsal) *for the talent show* after lunch.
23. Please hand me that (stapler) *on the desk*.
24. The soccer team will meet on the (field) *at Umberly Park*.
25. Those (plants) *in the window box* desperately need water.
26. (Everyone) *in the group* except me got an apple.
27. The (director) and the (cast) *of the musical* look forward to the opening night on Friday.

Underline each adjective phrase. Circle the word it describes.

28. The (performance) by the band was very good.
29. A (kite) with red, white, and blue streamers darted overhead.
30. The desserts for this dinner all feature fresh fruits.
31. Sue reached for the (stone) under the water.
32. He isn't familiar with the (rules) of American football.
33. Her (tickets) for the ferry ride were left on the (table) by the front door.

Underline each adverb phrase. Write the word or words the phrase describes.

34. The Jacksons traveled to the East Coast.   _traveled_
35. A polar bear slipped into the frigid sea.   _slipped_
36. Many people protested for their rights.   _protested_
37. Roger was given directions by a helpful couple.   _was given_
38. Matt helped Kim lift the boxes onto the shelves.   _lift_
39. They entered the abandoned house with caution.   _entered_

Underline each prepositional phrase used as a noun.

40. A good time to visit Grandpa is in the summer.
41. In my swimming class is where I learn the most.
42. The best hiding place from the rain is under the overhang.
43. At 7:00 p.m. sharp is when visiting hours are over.
44. The finish line for the race is just after the big oak tree.
45. By bicycle is the quickest way to get from school to the library.

Read the following paragraph. Then respond to the questions.

One evening a fox jumped (up) (on) our fence, flicked its tail, and ran (away) Our dog Brownie was like a rocket. He dodged under the fence and ran **besides** the creek. Through the field was a better route for us to take. Eventually, we caught up with Brownie. The fox, however, was long gone, most likely safe in its den.

46. Circle the prepositions used as adverbs in the first sentence.
47. How is the prepositional phrase used in the second sentence?   _subject complement_
48. Underline the prepositional phrase used as a subject.
49. Cross out the incorrectly used preposition and write it correctly.   _beside_
50. Is the prepositional phrase in the last sentence used as an adverb or an adjective?   _adverb_

Name _____ Date _____

SECTION 8 TEST | Sentences

Underline each simple subject once and each simple predicate twice.

1. Elizabeth was tired.
2. You should write a story about your adventure.
3. We sang in the choir this season.
4. Just wait until your father gets home.
5. After the celebration her parents gave her a gift.
6. My friend Robert, having little money, offered to rake the neighbor's yard.

Underline each complete subject once and each complete predicate twice.

7. The lawyer worked hard.
8. Who cleaned the dirty rug?
9. Dale and I are going to the races.
10. They had a wonderful time at the park.
11. The photographs of the bacteria helped me better understand them.
12. Besides being a full-time student, Mandy also volunteers at the animal shelter.

Write whether each sentence is declarative, interrogative, imperative, or exclamatory. Add the correct end punctuation.

13. Sit still, please. — *imperative*
14. Have we planned a picnic this weekend? — *interrogative*
15. I think you are next in line. — *declarative*
16. Please stand next to the flag pole. — *imperative*
17. What an exciting race this is! — *exclamatory*
18. We have no idea how to complete this puzzle. — *declarative*
19. Did anyone explain to you the rules of the game? — *interrogative*
20. Wow, this is not what I expected at all! — *exclamatory*

Write whether each italicized phrase is used as an *adjective* or an *adverb*.

21. Troy had never before ridden *on a horse*. — *adverb*
22. *Recalling a joyful moment*, his mother smiled. — *adjective*
23. Accustomed to herding, the small dog *tended to nip ankles*. — *adverb*
24. *Trudging up the stairs*, Jess begrudgingly went to bed. — *adjective*
25. The school year ends with a *field trip to the state capital*. — *adverb*
26. Her packages *by the front door* should be set in the car. — *adjective*

Write whether each italicized phrase is prepositional (*PREP*), participial (*PART*), or infinitive (*INF*).

27. Where has her family decided *to go today?* — INF
28. Throw any wet towels *over the rack to dry.* — PREP
29. *Rising in the sky,* the balloons could be seen for miles. — PART
30. Gypsy moths are abundant *in New England.* — PREP
31. Mike brought a video camera *to capture the event on film.* — INF

Underline each adjective clause and circle the noun it describes.

32. This is the (place) where he lost his wallet.
33. I certainly like the new (watch) that I was given.
34. Her (mother) who is from Boston, likes to vacation in Arizona.
35. The (program) which is brand new, continues to crash when I open it.
36. That (man) whose name I forgot, would like to speak to you.
37. (People) who lived in the valley had to relocate when they built the dam.

Underline each restrictive clause once and each nonrestrictive clause twice.

38. The boys are students who attend Washington Elementary.
39. Those two birds, which appear most mornings by the feeder, are cardinals.
40. Mom photographed us next to the sign that announced the elevation.
41. Please turn off the sound to the video game that plays such annoying music.
42. The caterpillars, whose diet consists only of milkweed, are not a threat to my vegetables.

Underline each adjective clause and circle if it is restrictive (*R*) or nonrestrictive (*NR*).

43. The roses that I just planted are already blooming. — (R) NR
44. That detective who solved the crime is very resourceful. — (R) NR
45. Earwigs, which are a kind of insect, care for their young. — R (NR)
46. My aunt and uncle, who arrive on Friday, will be welcome company. — R (NR)
47. The painting that was sold last week turned out to be worthless. — (R) NR
48. Jacob, whose test scores were outstanding, was just accepted into college. — R (NR)

Underline each adverb clause and circle the subordinate conjunction.

49. (When) the bell rings, we change classes.
50. Robert did the dishes (before) he went outside to play.
51. We could smell the honeysuckle (as soon as) we walked into the yard.
52. (Whenever) she sees a squirrel, my dog starts to bark.
53. Sadie covered her ears with her hands (because) she didn't like the noise.
54. Tony and his friends acted (as though) they were being forced to go along.

SECTION 8 TEST Sentences (continued)

Underline each adverb clause. Circle the word or words each clause describes.

55. If it doesn't stop raining, the coach (will cancel) our practice.
56. After I get home from school, I (hope) to play chess with my dad.
57. Justin (will see) that new movie unless he doesn't have enough money.
58. The squirrels (scurried) around the bird feeder until they saw the dog nearby.
59. In order for us to arrive on time, we (should be leaving) no later than 8:00 a.m.

Underline each noun clause used as a subject. Circle each introductory word.

60. (How) the dog got out is all we wanted to know.
61. (Why) there is a puddle of water on the floor is unclear.
62. (What) we decide to store in the attic depends on how often we use it.
63. (Who) owns this car is something for the police to find out.
64. (Where) they will stop for the night remains a topic of discussion.

Underline each noun clause. Circle whether it is used as a subject (S) or a subject complement (SC).

65. The second driveway is where they turned. S (SC)
66. That she is so honest was the reason for her employment. (S) SC
67. Whatever the doctor gave me made me feel much better. (S) SC
68. Our main concern is that the bird might have been injured. S (SC)
69. The simple truth remains that they worked much harder than we did. S (SC)

Underline the noun clause used as an appositive in each sentence.

70. Mr. Moore expressed the hope that we would not be late.
71. The knowledge that the river was too high kept us from crossing.
72. The fact that the temperature was so high was the reason the plants wilted.
73. They challenged the idea that only the adults could take on such responsibilities.
74. We accepted the fact that we needed more than the book to understand the concept.

Underline each direct object. Circle whether it is a noun (N) or a noun clause (NC).

75. The volunteers sent packages to the soldiers. (N) NC
76. I'll pick whichever cereal has less sugar. N (NC)
77. The club members discussed how we wanted to support the school. N (NC)
78. Dad asked Collin to slice the carrots and toss the salad. (N) NC
79. I understand why the park charges admission on weekends. N (NC)
80. The captain of the ship requested whoever was available to help at once. N (NC)

Circle whether the italicized clause is a noun clause (NC) or an adjective clause (AC).

81. These books that were damaged by smoke will be repaired. AC (NC)
82. That our dodgeball team was outnumbered cannot be denied. AC (NC)
83. A cat that hides under the porch tried to scratch me. (AC) NC
84. The latest rumor is that the old building will be torn down. AC (NC)
85. All the clothes that I took on vacation are now in the laundry. (AC) NC
86. The hardest choice he faced was which assignment he should complete first. AC (NC)

Underline each noun clause used as an object of a preposition.

87. My sister will sing for whoever wants to listen.
88. The class read about what was happening to the Indian elephants.
89. Mom and Dad are always interested in what I learn at school each day.
90. Afterwards we laughed about how the puppies had tumbled and played.
91. Margo looked in the paper for what the weather might be tomorrow.
92. A topic about which I know very little is statistics.
93. The problem of how to count all those butterflies was raised once again.

Write whether each sentence is simple, compound, or complex.

94. Grandpa swims every day, and I often join him. _compound_
95. After the bell rings, you may head to the door. _complex_
96. Red, white, and blue banners waved over the stadium. _simple_
97. Moths, which have huge appetites, can defoliate trees. _complex_
98. Andy voted for Edie, so he was happy when she won. _compound_
99. We noticed when they arrived and waved them over. _complex_
100. Hannah and her sisters reviewed and rewrote the list. _simple_

Read the following paragraph. Then respond to the questions.

How did you learn to ride a bike? One method *that I was told* is to wrap a towel around a child's waist and use it to correct the child's balance. Another method, which is how I learned, is to take the pedals off the bike to allow the child to learn balance. Some people just run behind the child's bike and hold onto the seat.

101. What kind of sentence is the first sentence? _interrogative_
102. How is the italicized clause used in the second sentence? _adjective clause_
103. Which word does this clause describe? _method_
104. Add the correct punctuation to the adjective clause in the third sentence.
105. Is the last sentence simple, compound, or complex? _simple_

SECTION 9 TEST Conjunctions and Interjections

Underline the coordinating conjunctions.

1. I tried to jump but tripped instead.
2. The red and brown fabric flapped in the breeze.
3. Neither Luther nor I wanted to go.
4. We had a choice of potato salad or cole slaw with our sandwiches.
5. I was very full, yet I could not resist extra servings of applesauce and bread.

Underline the coordinating conjunction in each sentence. Write whether the conjunction connects _words, phrases, or clauses._

6. Kay and Carl are leaving now. _____ words
7. Elliot sang, but the microphone didn't work. _____ clauses
8. Neither my sister nor my brother like to eat shrimp. _____ words
9. The dog jumped over the fence and onto the porch. _____ phrases
10. She wants to go, yet he's concerned about his homework. _____ clauses

Underline the correlative conjunctions in each sentence.

11. The weather is both hot and humid.
12. Neither Hadley nor Rosalie is home today.
13. Both the hamburgers and the hot dogs smell delicious.
14. I do not know whether a pen or a pencil would be better for this form.
15. Not only are they coming over, but the boys are bringing their tools to help.

Underline the words each set of italicized conjunctions connect.

16. He can ride either a bicycle or a skateboard to school.
17. These plants are both disease and drought resistant.
18. Mom had packed us not only sandwiches but also several pieces of fruit.
19. Neither the stove nor the microwave will work when the power is out.
20. Whether our team practices every day or just today, we are favored to win.

Circle the word or words that correctly complete each sentence.

21. This game sounded fun; (finally (still), I just wanted to read my book.
22. The drive was short; (later (consequently), the child did not have time to get bored.
23. It was my own phone number; (furthermore (nevertheless), I couldn't recall it.
24. There are so many dogs here; (in fact) nevertheless), I hear one barking now.
25. Evan practices every day; (moreover) however), he takes lessons twice a week.

Underline the subordinate conjunction in each sentence.

26. As the hour passed, he felt progressively worse.
27. We can be done in time for dinner if we work hard.
28. After the sun rose, everyone watched the fog rise off the damp fields.
29. The road was still wet even though the rain had stopped hours ago.
30. On some surfaces the snow was sticking, while on others it melted right away.

Underline each independent clause once and each dependent clause twice.

31. When we cleaned the basement, we found the missing tools.
32. I was thinking about the time when we all went to the beach together.
33. Although Sam told her not to, the dog jumped into the fish pond anyway.
34. If you go the laundry room, please take this basket of dirty clothes with you.
35. Molly put up signs so that everyone would know where the car wash would be held.

Circle the word or words that correctly complete each sentence.

36. The children cannot attend the party (unless (without) a parent.
37. Natalie looks (like (as if) she wants to say something.
38. Ralph remained in the house (like (as) he was asked.
39. I will not go to bed (unless) without) I brush my teeth first.
40. This hot, humid weather feels (like) as if) a suffocating blanket.

Underline each interjection.

41. Wow! We can see far more stars tonight.
42. Goodness! That was a very brisk walk.
43. Oh, the heat sure is strong coming from this campfire!
44. Great! I did better than I thought on the test.
45. Drat! I didn't win another turn on the video game.

Read the following paragraph. Then respond to the questions.

As the teams switch places, we will get a quick drink. Either water or juice would be refreshing in this heat. The blue and white team is ours. We cannot win the game without we score three more runs. Wow! Did you see how far Jamie hit the ball?

46. What is the subordinate conjunction in the first sentence? _____ As
47. What words do the correlative conjunctions connect? _____ water, juice
48. What conjunction is used in the third sentence? _____ and
49. Circle the error in the fourth sentence. Write it correctly. _____ unless
50. Underline the interjection.

Assessment Book Answer Key • 105

SECTION 10 TEST — Punctuation and Capitalization

Add periods and commas where needed.

1. The friends sat together at lunch.

2. I washed the lettuce, radishes, and sweet onions for the salad.

3. Abigail, her younger sister, was born June 5, 1992.

4. "On this problem," Ms. Green explained, "multiply before you add."

5. Our vacation to St. Louis, Missouri, will be the last one of the year.

6. "I can't imagine," said Edward, "what I was thinking when I made this choice."

Add the missing punctuation to each sentence.

7. No, I don't want any more milk.

8. Mr. Tanner, the president of our club, is absent today.

9. My dad, who has never been to the theater, is looking forward to the show.

10. "Kids, let's try this restaurant," said Mom, "since we've heard so much about it."

11. "Look, I just don't think that's a good idea, Robert," my cousin told me.

12. "My dearest Veronica," said the tall, thin, morose man. "You must go to Juneau, Alaska."

Add exclamation points, question marks, colons, and semicolons where needed.

13. What do you think the weather will be like tomorrow?

14. Yikes! That is the largest spider I've ever seen.

15. Please buy the following paint colors: green, red, blue, and brown.

16. Andy lost his hammer; consequently, he had to borrow one from Jake.

17. Where do you think the cats, who never go outside, could be hiding?

18. The Jacksons visited this morning; we were so glad to see them.

19. This year Dad traveled to Dallas, Texas; Paris, France; and Oahu, Hawaii.

20. There were five students in the musical; namely, Jake, Jen, Mark, Steve, and Heidi.

Add quotation marks and other punctuation where needed.

21. Jane said, "Let's go to the library."

22. "Where will we find that book?" asked Paul.

23. "I don't think this is a good day to go camping," Roberto remarked.

24. I read the article "Sixteen Days to Get Rich" somewhat skeptically.

25. Seth ran across the beach yelling, "Yow! This sand is so hot."

26. In the magazine *Car and Driver*, there is an article titled "Classic Automobiles."

27. I handed her the article "Patience" and said, "Return it when you have finished it."

Underline the words that should be italicized.

28. Joyce is reading the book American Sweethearts.

29. Have you seen the Academy-Award nominated film Across the Salty Sea?

30. The class went to see the art exhibit Snow Wolves at the gallery.

31. I used National Geographic to help me write my report.

32. The launching of the ship Rachel went off without a hitch.

33. My favorite television show is Deep-City Sidewalks on Thursday nights.

34. Ninety-Two was the scariest movie Carl and I have ever seen.

Write each word with hyphens to show where it would be divided into syllables.

35. haphazard	hap-haz-ard	38. fortuitous	for-tu-i-tous
36. fluctuation	fluc-tu-a-tion	39. Connecticut	Con-nect-i-cut
37. insidious	in-sid-i-ous	40. aristocracy	ar-is-toc-ra-cy

Add apostrophes, hyphens, and dashes where needed.

41. We didn't want to get up, but he couldn't wait.

42. My uncle's piano needs tuning, and Patrick's dad is just the person for the job.

43. Her great-grandfather—so I've been told—is a Korean War veteran.

44. My brother-in-law inspected the natural-gas pipeline but didn't see a problem.

45. The dock workers stacked fifty-three bags of produce—potatoes, onions, and carrots.

Underline the letters that should be capitalized in each sentence.

46. We went to visit senator hubert's office.

47. After returning from new mexico, iowa seems awfully cold.

48. Rachel cried out, "hurry up! the show is starting."

49. Did you hear that ben's brother was going to polk college in the east?

50. The crump family visited the smithsonian museums on a vacation in december.

Read the following paragraph. Then respond to the questions.

I walked into mr. todd's classroom. I didn't want to take the test. "Where is your tardy slip?" asked the substitute. I suddenly realized the following facts: there would be no test; today was Friday, and I had more time to study. Nell, my best friend, saw me sigh with relief.

51. Write the capitalization errors in the first sentence correctly. _____ Mr. Todd's

52. What is missing in the second sentence? Add it. _____ an apostrophe

53. Add the missing punctuation to the third sentence.

54. Add the missing colons and commas to the fourth sentence.

55. Punctuate the last sentence correctly. What did you add? _____ two commas, period

SECTION 11 TEST Diagramming

Underline the simple subjects once and the simple predicates twice. Diagram the sentences.

1. The <u>announcer</u> <u>declared</u> Charles the winner.

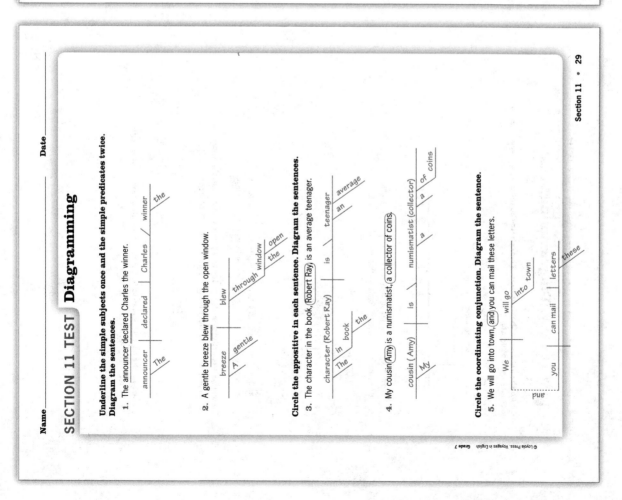

2. A gentle breeze blew through the open window.

Circle the appositive in each sentence. Diagram the sentences.

3. The character in the book, (Robert Ray) is an average teenager.

4. My cousin (Amy) is a numismatist, (a collector of coins).

Circle the coordinating conjunction. Diagram the sentence.

5. We will go into town, (and) you can mail these letters.

Circle the compound parts in the diagrams. Then circle the letter of the sentence that matches each diagram.

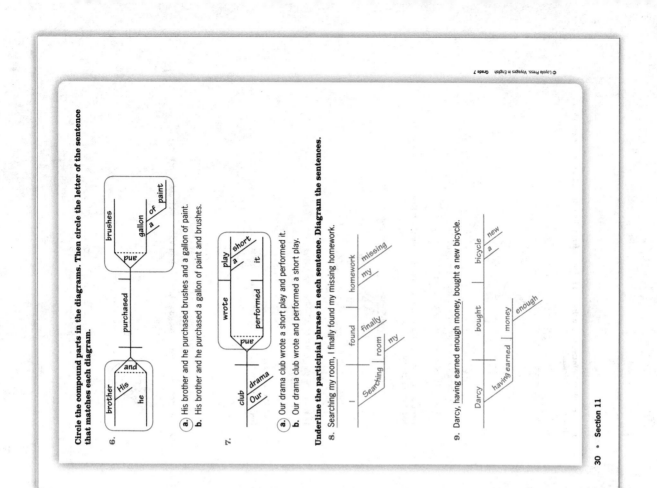

6.

a. His brother and he purchased brushes and a gallon of paint.
b. His brother and he purchased a gallon of paint and brushes.

7.

a. Our drama club wrote a short play and performed it.
b. Our drama club wrote and performed a short play.

Underline the participial phrase in each sentence. Diagram the sentences.

8. Searching my room, I finally found my missing homework.

9. Darcy, having earned enough money, bought a new bicycle.

SECTION 11 TEST Diagramming continued

Circle the gerund in the diagrams. Then circle the letter of the sentence that matches each diagram.

10.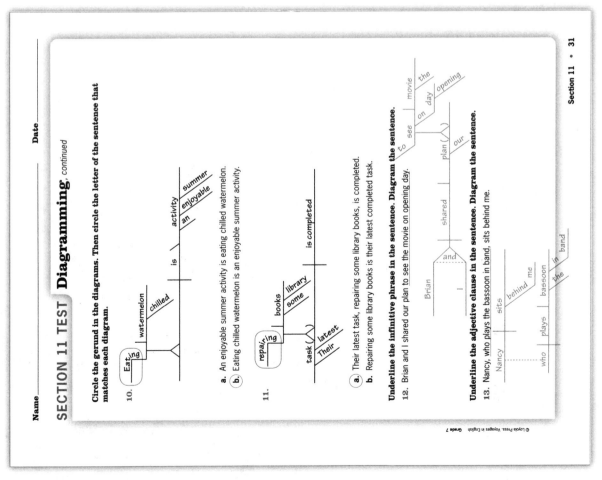

a. An enjoyable summer activity is eating chilled watermelon.
b. Eating chilled watermelon is an enjoyable summer activity.

11.

a. Their latest task, repairing some library books, is completed.
b. Repairing some library books is their latest completed task.

Underline the infinitive phrase in the sentence. Diagram the sentence.
12. Brian and I shared our plan to see the movie on opening day.

Underline the adjective clause in the sentence. Diagram the sentence.
13. Nancy, who plays the bassoon in band, sits behind me.

Circle the adverb clause in the diagram. Then circle the letter of the sentence that matches the diagram.

14.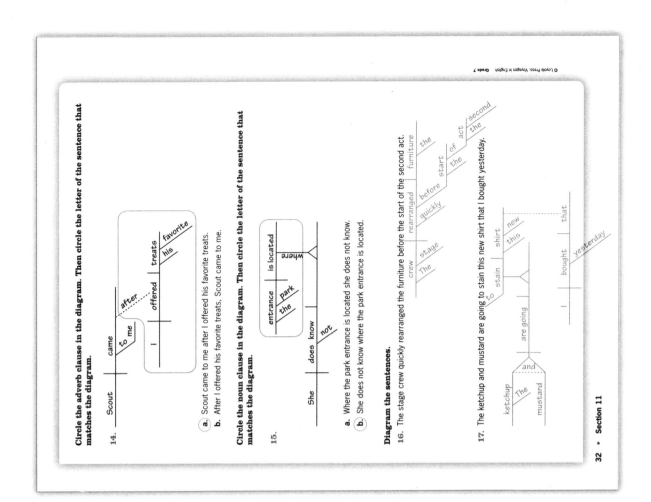

a. Scout came to me after I offered his favorite treats.
b. After I offered his favorite treats, Scout came to me.

Circle the noun clause in the diagram. Then circle the letter of the sentence that matches the diagram.

15.

a. Where the park entrance is located she does not know.
b. She does not know where the park entrance is located.

Diagram the sentences.
16. The stage crew quickly rearranged the furniture before the start of the second act.

17. The ketchup and mustard are going to stain this new shirt that I bought yesterday.

SECTIONS 1-2 SUMMATIVE ASSESSMENT

Nouns & Adjectives

Underline singular nouns once and plural nouns twice. Circle those that are both.

1. wolf   birds   (bison)   ring   (pants)

Underline the subjects once. Circle the subject complement if there is one.

2. Richmond is a (town) in Illinois.   3. The village has many antique shops.

Write whether the underlined noun is a *direct object*, an *indirect object*, an *object complement*, or an *object of a preposition*.

4. The actors in the play wore elaborate costumes.   _____ object of a preposition

5. The new restaurant on the block serves fajitas.   _____ direct object

Underline each appositive. Circle whether it is restrictive (R) or nonrestrictive (NR).

6. His father, Michael Garcia, will be performing tonight.   R   (NR)

7. The musician will be appearing with his sister Margaret.   (R)   NR

Insert apostrophes to show correct ownership.

8. a commander-in-chief's uniform   10. both cowboys' hats

9. Jesse's and Shane's card collections   11. Bess and Jim's house

Write whether each underlined adjective is *demonstrative*, *interrogative*, or *indefinite*.

12. That dollar just fell from his pocket.   _____ demonstrative

13. Mia gave every child a slice of apple.   _____ indefinite

14. Which stack of books belongs to you?   _____ interrogative

Write the comparative and superlative forms of each adjective.

15. lucky	luckier	luckiest
16. dependable	more/less dependable	most/least dependable
17. practical	more/less practical	most/least practical

Underline each adjective phrase once and each adjective clause twice.

18. Mason and I borrowed several books from the library.

19. Brown University, which is in Rhode Island, is a prestigious university.

20. Dancers from Germany were participants in this year's festival.

21. We will celebrate with a dinner that features corn on the cob and apple pie.

Read the passage. Then proofread it, using proofreading marks to make corrections. Look for 10 mistakes related to nouns and adjectives.

Why did the Honus wagner baseball card sell for so much
money yesterday? The demand for an item goes up when more
people ^people^ want to buy it. The seller can request more money.

Generally, if the supply of items goes up, then the price goes
down. The less ^fewer^ items that are available, the higher the price.

When an item is sold at auction, its condition is important.
An item in its original condition has a high value. Ironically, a
damaged item that has been restored may be worth lesser ^less^ than
an item that shows slight damage but has never been altered.

Only one honus Wagner baseball card was up for auction
yesterday. There are very fewer ^few^ of these cards in circulation.
Furthermore, there were many buyers. The price rose beyond
expectations. In the end the Honus Wagner card proved to
be the popularest ^most popular^ card of all. Wagner's card, a hot commodity,
commanded $520,000 from the thrilled man who won the auction.

SUMMATIVE ASSESSMENT
SECTIONS 3–4 Pronouns & Verbs

Circle the correct subject or object pronoun and write its person and number.

1. May was late, but ((she) her) couldn't explain why. — third person singular
2. Tara, Joe and ((you) us) should be done by now. — second person singular
3. At last ((they) them) found where the car was parked. — third person plural
4. David read the passage much faster than ((I) me). — first person singular

Circle the word that correctly completes each sentence.

5. The blue jacket on the hook is (her (hers)).
6. ((Their) Theirs) vacation was cut short by the sudden storm.

Underline the antecedent of each italicized pronoun.

7. Raul was *himself* an excellent candidate for class president.
8. The pilot invited us into the plane's cockpit, and *she* explained its controls.

Underline each verb and write whether it is *transitive* or *intransitive*.

9. Renee writes for three hours every day. — intransitive
10. The clerk stacked the sales items on the center table. — transitive

Write whether each sentence is in the *active* or *passive* voice.

11. Ricardo placed the suitcase by the dresser. — active
12. This experimental rocket was launched by the flight crew. — passive

Write whether each sentence is in the *indicative, imperative, emphatic,* or *subjunctive* mood.

13. Mr. Wise requested that we be ready at noon. — subjunctive
14. Please put the boxes on the table. — imperative
15. Which would you prefer for a snack? — indicative
16. I do indeed care about my effect on the environment. — emphatic

Underline each subject. Circle the verb that correctly completes each sentence.

17. Something ((is) are) out there by the trash cans.
18. Several (was (were)) waiting by the backstage door.
19. You may ((sit) set) in any of those chairs while you wait.
20. There (is (are)) a dozen people waiting in line already.
21. Noah and Logan (doesn't (don't)) want to be late for class.

Read the passage. Then proofread it, using proofreading marks to make corrections. Look for 10 mistakes related to pronouns and verbs.

Whom would want to be known throughout history as
Ethelred the Unready? This English king were still a child [was]
when the death of his half-brother put him on the throne. Most
accepted him in spite of her young age. Unfortunately, Ethelred [his]
didn't enjoy much peace as king.

When King Ethelred was 14, Danish Vikings sended parties [sent]
of raiders to attack seaside towns in England. After these raiders
attacked, them would take shelter in nearby Normandy. As King [they]
Ethelred grew into his twenties, the Danish attacks increased and
growed larger. The English grew tired of the attacks and just [grew]
wanted to be let alone. King Ethelred actually paid the Danes to [left]
go away, and these worked at first. However, all that gold gave the [this]
Danes another reason to conquer England.

Most historians would agree that Ethelred was unprepared to
rule England. At the time of his death, him was merely the king [he]
of London and parts of the south. It should be a long time before [would]
England was unified again by William the Conqueror.

SUMMATIVE ASSESSMENT

SECTIONS 5-6 Verbals & Adverbs

Underline the participle in each sentence. Circle the noun the participle describes.

1. (Norman), speaking on the condition of anonymity, confirmed the story.
2. Harassed constantly by the cat, the (mice) vacated the old stone house.

Write whether the italicized word in each sentence is used as a gerund (G), a participial adjective (PA), or a participle in a verb phrase (VP).

3. The group of children played happily in the *wading* pool.   PA
4. *Stepping* quickly and lightly is how we ran across the hot pavement.   G
5. He was *steadying* the model with one hand as he glued on the part.   VP
6. The *thriving* gorillas were a favorite attraction.   PA

Underline each infinitive phrase. Write whether it is used as a *subject, subject complement,* or *direct object.*

7. John planned to serve chili with beans.   *direct object*
8. Rich's hope was to see a real lion.   *subject complement*
9. To understand algebra well is my goal for this year.   *subject*

Circle each infinitive phrase. Write whether it is used as an *adjective* or *adverb*.

10. Those are the dishes (to be cleaned).   *adjective*
11. The participants were eager (to begin the contest).   *adverb*
12. (To be perfectly clear), she repeated the directions again.   *adverb*

Underline each adverb. Circle the word or words the adverb describes.

13. Everyone agreed that the other table was obnoxiously (loud).
14. The bus with the group of tourists (will arrive) soon.
15. A volunteer (read) the story aloud to the class.

Circle each adverbial noun. Write whether it expresses *time, direction,* or *value*.

16. Once we headed (east), the sun wasn't in our eyes.   *direction*
17. Marla and her children are leaving (Tuesday).   *time*
18. The box of pencils costs eight (cents) more than I have.   *value*

Underline each adverb phrase once and each adverb clause twice.

19. I will deposit my money in the bank.
20. After we hear the lecture, a test will be given.
21. Within the crowd, Ryan sang loudly until he was tired.

Read the passage. Then proofread it, using proofreading marks to make corrections. Look for 10 mistakes related to verbals and adverbs.

Our school, located in Lukachukai, Arizona, has a fantastic track team. We run races three kilometers long, who [which] is a little less than two miles. This year our dedicated team was real [really] fast. As a result we were invited to running [run] in a meet in Chicago, Illinois. Raising funds for the trip went good [well] and the day for our departure was here before we knew it.

For many of us, this track meet was the furthest [farthest] we had ever traveled. On the first day, we were able to do some sightseeing. The next day we noticed the temperature had dropped really bad [badly] overnight. Soon it started to (lightly snow).

There were so many runners that when we registered, we were given a group number. Our start time was based on the number we had. The race sponsors determine the winners by finding which [who] had the shortest overall time. Everyone enthusiastic [enthusiastically] cheered one another on. Our school did very good [well].

The next day we headed back to Arizona. We were glad that our love of running had given us such an exciting opportunity.

SUMMATIVE ASSESSMENT

SECTIONS 7-8 Prepositions & Sentences

Underline each prepositional phrase. Write the object of the preposition.

1. The pitcher threw the ball over the plate. _____ *plate*
2. Do not walk under the ladder. _____ *ladder*

Write whether each underlined word is used as an adverb (A) or a preposition (P).

3. Head straight out past the mailbox and make a left. _____ *A*
4. <u>Below</u> the cereal boxes you will find the canned goods. _____ *P*

Underline each prepositional phrase. Write whether it is an adjective or adverb phrase.

5. The huge flag on that ship has blue stripes. _____ *adjective*
6. Lola and her sister rode the escalator to the upper floor. _____ *adverb*
7. Tara's new tree house is popular with all the kids. _____ *adverb*

Underline each prepositional phrase used as a noun.

8. Above the trees is the place my kite should be flying.
9. A great time of year to see New England is in the fall.

Write whether each sentence is declarative, interrogative, imperative, or exclamatory.

10. Please do not park on the grass. _____ *imperative*
11. Have they picked up all the trash on the field? _____ *interrogative*
12. Several hungry rabbits were spotted in the garden. _____ *declarative*

Underline each adjective clause and circle the word the clause describes.

13. I really appreciate this gift that I was given.
14. Joe's jacket, which is from the store on the corner, has lasted three years.

Underline each adverb clause. Circle the subordinate conjunction.

15. Although it was almost midnight, we were not the least bit tired.
16. The class was canceled because too few students signed up for it.

Underline each noun clause used as an appositive once and each noun clause used as an object of a preposition twice.

17. Mr. Wilkins was shocked by what he read in the paper.
18. Amos's belief that there should be two winners was not held by everyone.

Read the passage. Then proofread it, using proofreading marks to make corrections. Look for eight mistakes related to prepositions and sentences.

The Ramblin' Wreck from Georgia Tech is the official mascot of Georgia Tech University. Unlike other college mascots, this is not a person inside an animal suit doing gymnastics? The Ramblin' Wreck, which was restored for the college, is a 1930 Ford Model A sports coupe.

The original Ramblin' Wrecks were vehicles made by Georgia Tech engineers that *[who]* were stationed in South America. Working in the jungle, they used parts from old automobiles, tractors, and other machinery to assembling *[assemble]* these vehicles. These contraptions were called rambling wrecks by the other workers.

Onto a playing field is where you'll see a Ramblin' Wreck today. Beside *[Besides]* home games, the mascot often travels with the football team to away games. It also appears at rallies, sporting events, and other college festivities. The mascot is so popular that other alumni have similar cars. However, there are subtle differences between *[among]* all the cars.

SUMMATIVE ASSESSMENT

SECTIONS 9–10 Conjunctions and Interjections & Punctuation and Capitalization

Underline the coordinating conjunction in each sentence. Write whether the conjunction connects words, phrases, or clauses.

clauses
words
phrases

1. Ted wanted to apologize, but he didn't know what to say.
2. Yellow and blue are her favorite colors.
3. Do you prefer to swim in a lake or in the ocean?

Underline the correlative conjunctions in each sentence.
4. Stacey is both a musician and a vocalist.
5. Neither Gustav nor Robert brought their bikes with them.

Underline the subordinate conjunction in each sentence.
6. As I thought about the problem, I began to form a plan.
7. The crops will be ruined if it keeps raining.

Underline the interjection in each sentence.
8. Oh no! I forgot my lunch again.
9. Terrific! That log is just what we need for the fire.

Add question marks, colons, and semicolons to each sentence where needed.
10. When do you think the rain will end?
11. Will we travel to these places: Chicago, IL; Boston, MA; and Philadelphia, PA?
12. From the island we could do the following: swim, snorkel, or parasail.

Add periods, commas, and quotation marks to each sentence where needed.
13. Its descriptions of people, places, and things make "Summer Breezes" my favorite poem.
14. "I wish that we could still leave on our trip tomorrow."

Add apostrophes, hyphens, and dashes to each sentence where needed.
15. The vacation—if I'll have the money—is to celebrate my twenty-seventh birthday.
16. Because Andy doesn't cross his t's, the letters look like ls.

Circle the letters that should be capitalized.
17. The tour took the Smyths to Mount Vernon, President Washington's former home.
18. Randy and Jacob are both from Portland, Oregon.

Read the passage. Then proofread it, using proofreading marks to make corrections. Look for nine mistakes related to conjunctions, interjections, punctuation, and capitalization.

Kyle squeezed his eyes shut as the spaceship touched down.

No matter how many times he flew back and forth between Earth and home, he never got used to the landing. At least he no longer needed the air sickness bags. Kyle felt his sister's wary eyes on him, so as soon as he was sure the landing was complete, he opened his eyes and smiled reassuringly at her. She watched the color come back to his cheeks and nodded approvingly.

Then everything seemed to go into hyperdrive. People hopped up and grabbed their belongings from storage compartments, suitcases, spare air tanks, pet carriers, and a thousand other artifacts of human life. Kyle and his sister didn't have much. Their grandparents had a full set of clothes for them back on Earth so they could travel light. The doors opened; the passengers spilled out onto the ramp that led to the spaceport. Walking much faster now, both Kyle and his sister were eager to see their parents again and to be home at last.

SUMMATIVE ASSESSMENT

SECTION 11 Diagramming

Circle the subject. Underline the subject complement. Diagram the sentence.

1. The last activity will always be painting model cars.

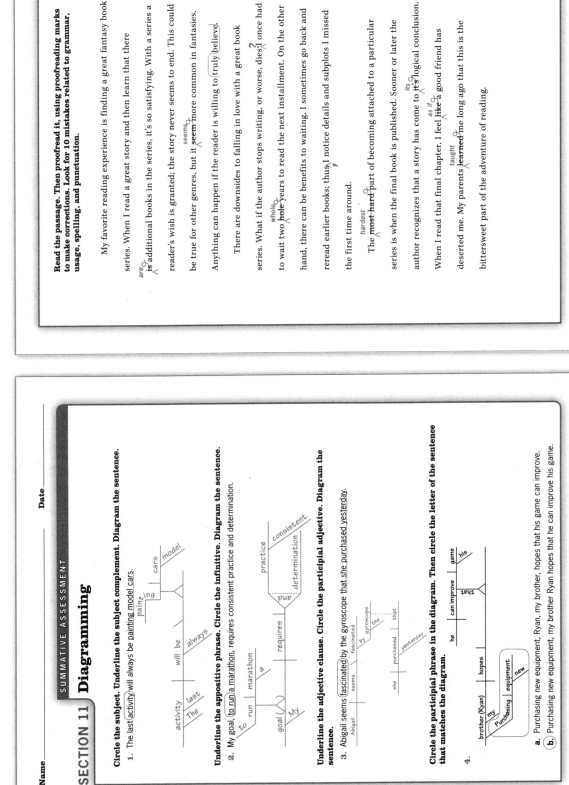

Underline the appositive phrase. Circle the infinitive. Diagram the sentence.

2. My goal, to run a marathon, requires consistent practice and determination.

Underline the adjective clause. Circle the participial adjective. Diagram the sentence.

3. Abigail seems fascinated by the gyroscope that she purchased yesterday.

Circle the participial phrase in the diagram. Then circle the letter of the sentence that matches the diagram.

4.

a. Purchasing new equipment, Ryan, my brother, hopes that his game can improve.

b. Purchasing new equipment, my brother Ryan hopes that he can improve his game.

Read the passage. Then proofread it, using proofreading marks to make corrections. Look for 10 mistakes related to grammar, usage, spelling, and punctuation.

My favorite reading experience is finding a great fantasy book series. When I read a great story and then learn that there are is additional books in the series, it's so satisfying. With a series a reader's wish is granted; the story never seems to end. This could be true for other genres, but it seems seem more common in fantasies.

Anything can happen if the reader is willing to truly believe.

There are downsides to falling in love with a great book series. What if the author stops writing, or worse, dies once had to wait two whole hole years to read the next installment. On the other hand, there can be benefits to waiting. I sometimes go back and reread earlier books; thus, I notice details and subplots I missed the first time around.

The hardest most hard part of becoming attached to a particular series is when the final book is published. Sooner or later the author recognizes that a story has come to its it's logical conclusion. When I read that final chapter, I feel as if like a good friend has taught learned me long ago that this is the deserted me. My parents learned me long ago that this is the bittersweet part of the adventure of reading.

CHAPTER 1 TEST Writing Skills

Revise each rambling sentence. *Possible responses are given.*

1. After Michelle left work, she went to the store and bought some milk, but then she realized she had forgotten something and she had to go back.

   After Michelle left work, she bought milk at the store. Later, she realized she had forgotten
   something and had to go back.

2. I wrote a short story called "Polishing Pennies" which I really hope is published in our school journal and maybe will even win the school writing award in the spring.

   I wrote a short story called "Polishing Pennies." I really hope it is published in our school journal.
   Maybe I will even win the school writing award this spring.

Rewrite the run-on sentence correctly.

3. Melons are fruits grown on vines during the summer season they have juicy flesh and are filled with many seeds my favorite type of melon is the cantaloupe.

   Melons are fruits grown on vines during the summer season. They have juicy flesh and
   are filled with many seeds. My favorite type of melon is the cantaloupe.

Draw a line through the redundant word or words in each sentence.

4. I think sea stars are the most amazing, ~~fascinating~~ creatures.
5. The debate team has won three consecutive contests ~~in a row~~.
6. Lynnette has the tiniest, ~~smallest~~ handwriting.
7. Our punctual principal, ~~who is always on time,~~ rang the bell.

Circle the word in parentheses that has the more exact meaning.

8. Please put that (book) thing) back where you found it.
9. Ricardo placed his famous (meal (lasagna) in the oven.
10. The cat (walked (crept) around the corner.
11. We hesitated when we entered the (musty) smelly) attic.
12. Finding my misplaced homework made me so (happy (ecstatic).

Circle the homophone that correctly completes each sentence.

13. The actor took his (cue) queue) from the others and strode onstage.
14. Another name for corn is (maze (maize).
15. Yesterday the student council met the new (principle (principal).
16. Do you know (whose) who's) jacket this is?
17. I know that (its (it's) important to get enough sleep each night.

Write each event in the correct order on the time line.

18.
- aced the test
- teacher announced upcoming test
- listened to test instructions

- checked my answers
- studied with friends
- answered all questions

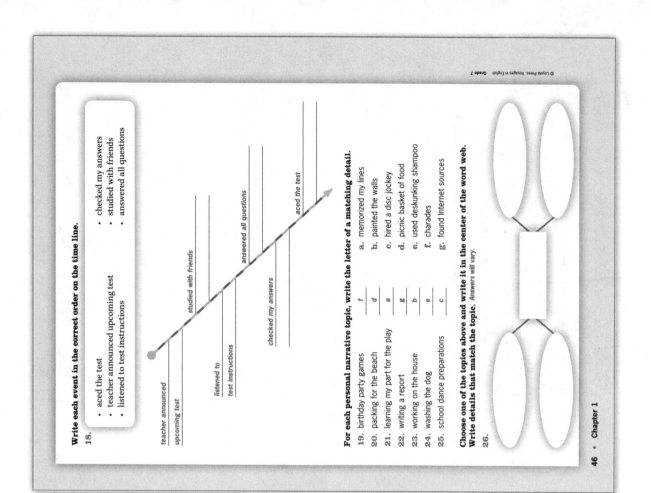

teacher announced
upcoming test

listened to
test instructions

studied with friends

checked my answers

answered all questions

aced the test

For each personal narrative topic, write the letter of a matching detail.

19. birthday party games _f_   a. memorized my lines
20. packing for the beach _d_   b. painted the walls
21. learning my part for the play _a_   c. hired a disc jockey
22. writing a report _g_   d. picnic basket of food
23. working on the house _b_   e. used deskunking shampoo
24. washing the dog _e_   f. charades
25. school dance preparations _c_   g. found Internet sources

Choose one of the topics above and write it in the center of the word web.
Write details that match the topic. *Answers will vary.*

26.

Your personal narrative will be graded on how well it

- is planned.
- maintains a clear focus on the chosen topic.
- uses chronological order.
- uses an appropriate tone and conveys a sense of authenticity.
- uses exact words and natural language.
- avoids run-on and rambling sentences.
- uses correct grammar, punctuation, spelling, and capitalization.

Write your personal narrative here. Refer to your plan as you write. Use another sheet of paper if needed.

Name _____   Date _____

CHAPTER 1 PROMPT   Personal Narrative

1. Read the prompt carefully.
2. Plan and organize your writing on this page.
3. Write your personal narrative on the back.
4. Revise and proofread your personal narrative.

PROMPT: Think about an outdoor experience you have had. Write about your experience, including details that might interest readers.

Plan your personal narrative here. Use a word web, a time line, or notes.

CHAPTER 2 TEST Writing Skills

Underline each adjective clause.

1. My teacher, who is from Morocco, does not speak with an accent.

2. The Waffle House, which is our town's most popular restaurant, is on College Avenue.

3. The results that were all on the first page of the report were mistyped.

4. That movie, which was nominated for an Oscar, was showing at the local theater.

5. One bird that was red with a yellow beak was hogging the bird feeder.

6. The store was closed for the holiday, which falls on a Monday this year.

7. The chicken, which was frozen, was going to take over an hour to cook.

8. Maggie, who performs in Alice in Wonderland, made her own costume.

9. The couch, which is falling apart, will go to the dump tomorrow.

10. This author's new book, which comes out tomorrow, is predicted to be a best seller.

Rewrite each sentence to change the emphasis. *Possible responses are given.*

11. Their plan, which will be expensive, requires several costly materials.
Their plan, which requires several costly materials, will be expensive.

12. That man who is setting up the stage is my uncle.
That man, who is my uncle, is setting up the stage.

13. The kitchen, which was clean an hour ago, is filled with dirty dishes.
The kitchen, which is filled with dirty dishes, was clean an hour ago.

14. Our dog, which was adopted from the animal shelter, is affectionate and intelligent.
Our dog, which is affectionate and intelligent, was adopted from the animal shelter.

15. St. Louis, which is in Missouri, was the site of the 1904 World's Fair.
St. Louis, which was the site of the 1904 World's Fair, is in Missouri.

16. That old tugboat, which is tilting badly, has been neglected for years.
That old tugboat, which has been neglected for years, is tilting badly.

For each underlined root, write the letter of the matching word meaning.

17. demographic   c   a. see or watch
18. precisely   d   b. follow
19. telescope   a   c. people
20. interdiction   e   d. cut
21. sequential   b   e. say or speak
22. vocational   f   f. call

Complete each sentence, using a word with the root shown in parentheses.

23. An ___inspection___ of the cargo revealed many smuggled items. (spec)

24. Since this table and chairs are ___portable___, we'll take them to the beach. (port)

25. She speaks so softly that her words are often ___inaudible___. (aud)

26. Since the electronic ignition isn't working, we'll start the engine ___manually___. (man)

27. Several ___aquatic___ species of plants grow at the pond's edge. (aqu)

Write *true* or *false* for each statement about writing tools.

28. A summary is a condensed version of a text written in your own words.   true

29. To summarize a story, you restate only important elements.   true

30. A summary must be as long as one-third the length of the original.   false

31. Paraphrasing is restating individual passages of a work in your own words.   true

32. A paraphrased passage is less detailed than a summary.   false

33. A direct quotation contains words that are similar to the original text.   false

34. Taking someone else's research, words, or ideas and presenting them as your own is plagiarism.   true

Read each passage. Then write a *summary* or *paraphrasing* to identify the italicized text that follows the passage.

35. Morocco is a country along the northwestern coast of Africa. An ally of the United States, it is not a member of the African Union; it is a member of the Arab League. The country has a long history, with evidence of human habitation going back to 8000 BC. Islam was introduced around the seventh century and is the dominant religion today. The country's relationship with the United States goes back to 1777, when it was the first nation to recognize the newly formed United States as an independent nation.

Morocco is an Arab country along the coast of Africa. It is an Islamic country with a long history of friendship with the United States, going back to 1777.

This is an example of _a summary_.

36. The "Star-Spangled Banner" is the national anthem of the United States of America. The lyrics were written by Francis Scott Key as a poem titled "Defense of Fort McHenry." He wrote the words in 1814 as he watched the unsuccessful British attack on Baltimore's Fort McHenry. Later set to music, the song achieved immediate popularity. However, it was not named the national anthem until 1931.

America's national anthem is the "Star-Spangled Banner," written by Francis Scott Key. He wrote the lyrics after watching the failed British attack on Baltimore in 1814. Although the poem was set to music and became immediately popular, it did not become the national anthem until 1931.

This is an example of _paraphrasing_.

CHAPTER 2 PROMPT Business Letter

1. Read the prompt carefully.
2. Plan and organize your writing on this page.
3. Write your business letter on the back.
4. Revise and proofread your business letter.

PROMPT: Imagine a job you would like to do for a company named Cerberus Game Systems. Write a letter to the company president explaining why you would be the best person for the job. Use an imaginary inside address.

Plan your business letter here. Use an idea web, a list, or notes.

Your business letter will be graded on how well it

- is planned.
- states its purpose and summarizes relevant accomplishments.
- includes all parts of a business letter.
- uses an appropriately professional and enthusiastic tone.
- includes a variety of clear, concise sentences.
- avoids unnecessary details.
- uses correct grammar, spelling, punctuation, and capitalization.

Write your business letter here. Refer to your plan as you write. Use another sheet of paper if needed.

CHAPTER 3 TEST Writing Skills

Underline the transition word or phrase in each sentence. Write whether the word or phrase shows *chronological* or *spatial* order.

1. Meanwhile, coat the bottom of the pan with olive oil. *chronological*
2. Be sure to clean the tray well after you are done. *chronological*
3. Above the box you should hang the bucket of water. *spatial*
4. Now praise your dog at the exact moment it sits. *chronological*
5. Attach the clamp on the side opposite to the hinge. *spatial*
6. Make three quick turns to the left and stop at zero. *spatial*

Underline the best transition word or phrase to complete each sentence.

7. The substance is light, (finally   yet) it acts as a strong bonding agent.
8. (In conclusion   Because), all you need is a little patience to complete these steps.
9. Use deck screws (instead   then) if you are concerned that nails will not hold.
10. Remove any loose tiles first (because   likewise) they can cause someone to trip.
11. Select a hard wood, (additionally   namely), oak, mahogany, or teak.
12. The traffic is expected to be heavy; (for this reason   nevertheless), many stayed home.

Circle the word or words each underlined adverb clause modifies.

13. The jelly leaked everywhere because the cold jar had cracked in the hot water.
14. If you do the laundry now, the clothes will be clean in the morning.
15. Skippy has been working as a guide dog since he completed his training.
16. After the old barn's roof caved in, the park committee determined it a hazard.
17. All of us can go to the show if Scott gets enough tickets.
18. Unless the sky clears soon, we should change our plans.
19. Whisk the egg whites briskly until they form stiff peaks.

Underline the adverb clause in each sentence. Circle the word the clause modifies.

20. Lydia stirred the bubbling sauce until her arms ached.
21. The kids bolted for the door once they heard Dad's car in the driveway.
22. Because she was running late for school, Jillian made toast for breakfast.
23. Close the tent flap before it starts to rain.
24. You start the engine while I figure out what is making that noise.
25. Trudy will most likely mail this package when she goes to the bank.
26. Before you use the hammer, put on your safety goggles.
27. So that we sing the final note in unison, watch the conductor closely.

Circle the letter of the definition that matches the meaning of the underlined word in each sentence.

28. We knew it was Frisky by the gray markings on his muzzle.
    a. the end of a firearm
    b. the part of the head of an animal that includes the mouth, nose, and jaws
    c. to restrain from speech

29. Ted's trick seemed to confound the audience.
    a. to perplex or amaze
    b. to contradict or refute
    c. to mistake as identical

30. The nest of tables at the garage sale caught Mom's eye.
    a. a pocketlike structure formed by birds
    b. a snug retreat or refuge
    c. a set of things lying or set close together or within one another

31. It was considered bad form to refuse to play backgammon with my father.
    a. a dummy used for fitting or displaying clothing
    b. the shape of a thing or person
    c. a way of behaving, as judged by social standards

32. He got a bigger coat when the old one started to bind in the shoulders.
    a. to join together by legal means
    b. to chafe or restrict
    c. to fasten within a cover

Use the dictionary entry to answer the questions.

form • u • late (fôr′ myə lāt′) *tr. v.*, 1. to express in precise form; state definitely or systematically. 2. to devise or develop. 3. to reduce to or express in a formula. **-lat•ed, -lat•ing**

33. How many syllables are in the word formulate? ___3___
34. What is the past tense form of formulate? *formulated*
35. Write the number of the definition that best fits the context of this sentence: ___2___
    We decided to formulate a plan to get the stolen statue back.

Circle *P* (print dictionary), *O* (online dictionary), or *B* (both) to identify a source for each item.

36. allows you to hear how a word is pronounced P **O** B
37. gives information about the origin of a word P **O** B
38. uses guide words at the top of each page **P** O B

Your how-to article will be graded on how well it

- is planned.
- maintains a clear focus for a specific audience.
- presents steps in chronological order.
- uses clear, precise language and avoids unnecessary information.
- includes transition words.
- uses imperative sentences and adverb clauses.
- is free of grammar, punctuation, spelling, and capitalization errors.

Write your how-to article here. Refer to your plan as you write. Use another sheet of paper if needed.

Name _____   Date _____

CHAPTER 3 PROMPT How-to Article

1. Read the prompt carefully.
2. Plan and organize your writing on this page.
3. Write your how-to article on the back.
4. Revise and proofread your how-to article.

PROMPT: Think of a project you completed with your family or at school. Use this experience to write a how-to article so others can complete a similar project. List any needed materials. Be sure your instructions are written clearly.

Plan your how-to article here. Use a sequence chart, an idea web, or notes.

CHAPTER 4 TEST Writing Skills

Underline the noun clause in each sentence.

1. I do not know where the library book has been misplaced.
2. What the library needs is new funds for the children's section.
3. I prefer how this thermal blanket keeps me warm in winter.
4. Whichever topic you choose will make a great report.
5. Mr. Degliomini is who you should ask to help you fix the lamp.

Write whether each underlined noun clause is a subject (S), a subject complement (SC), a direct object (DO), an object of a preposition (OP), or an appositive (A).

6. I cannot find where the house is located. — DO
7. Look up the information for how to change the oil. — OP
8. Whoever uses the brush last is the one who should clean it. — S
9. The idea that he will attempt to fix the leak in the rain is concerning. — A
10. Mr. and Mrs. Hopkins are who you should interview next. — SC
11. He doesn't understand how his account can be so overdrawn. — DO

Rewrite each sentence, using a noun clause. *Possible responses are given.*

12. The idea was practical and inexpensive.
That the idea was practical and inexpensive was not in question.
13. We look forward to our upcoming vacation.
Wherever our upcoming vacation may take us, we look forward to it.
14. Our committee needs a clear plan and new ideas.
What our committee could really use is a clear plan and new ideas.
15. The topic for Richard's report is unknown.
What Richard will choose for the topic of his report is unknown.

Write a new word by adding an adjective suffix (-ible, -al, -ent, -less, -ous) to each base word.

16. divide — *divisible*
17. courtesy — *courteous*
18. obey — *obedient*
19. emotion — *emotional*
20. relent — *relentless*
21. terror — *terrible*
22. sense — *sensible*
23. care — *careless*
24. fiction — *fictional*
25. excel — *excellent*
26. luxury — *luxurious*
27. motion — *motionless*

Pair a suffix from the chart with the word in parentheses to write a word that completes each sentence.

RELATING TO	STATE OR QUALITY OF	RESEMBLING	MANNER OR DIRECTION
-ative	-ate	-like	-ways
-an	-ese	-ly	-wise
-ary	-ive	-oid	

28. My sister has a *childlike* curiosity that keeps her constantly learning. (child)
29. Mike turned the key in a *counterclockwise* direction. (counterclock)
30. The Meyer twins have *American* citizenship, so they will not require a passport. (America)
31. That desk will fit through the door if we carry it *sideways*. (side)
32. Mr. Fielding is *passionate* about baseball and mathematics. (passion)
33. Their *Japanese* exchange student will be here in two more weeks. (Japan)
34. The robot stood on two legs, and its familiar features seemed vaguely *humanoid*. (human)
35. The college gave Mr. Tolafson an *honorary* degree in physics. (honor)
36. Linda is *talkative* today, but usually she is quite shy. (talk)

Write true or false for each statement about using a thesaurus.

37. A thesaurus is a reference tool for finding synonyms for words. — *true*
38. A thesaurus only gives words with exactly the same meaning. — *false*
39. A dictionary thesaurus lists the words in alphabetical order, using guide words. — *true*
40. An index thesaurus groups words into categories and assigns a number. — *true*
41. Thesauruses never give the definitions of the synonyms they list. — *false*
42. A thesaurus is useful to find a replacement for an overused word. — *true*
43. If you are unsure of the meaning of a synonym, you may need to look it up in a dictionary. — *true*

Use the thesaurus entry to write a replacement for the word make. *Possible responses are given.*

make 1. *verb:* manufacture, fashion, build, form, invent
2. *verb:* force, coerce
3. *verb:* earn
4. *noun:* brand, model, brand name, type

44. I don't want to finish this, and no one can make me. — *force or coerce*
45. Daniel works hard because he wants to make money. — *earn*
46. Li can make the most amazing things out of toothpicks. — *build*

Page 60 (top panel, rotated)

Your description will be graded on how well it

- is planned.
- promotes a clear focus on a particular possession.
- uses a logical order with an introduction, a body, and and a conclusion.
- features an appropriate voice.
- uses vivid adjectives and verbs and rich sensory details.
- maintains a variety of sentence types and natural transitions.
- is free of grammar, spelling, punctuation, and capitalization errors.

Write your description here. Refer to your plan as you write. Use another sheet of paper if needed.

Page 59 (bottom panel, rotated)

Name _____   Date _____

CHAPTER 4 PROMPT   **Description**

1. Read the prompt carefully.
2. Plan and organize your writing on this page.
3. Write your description on the back.
4. Revise and proofread your description.

PROMPT: Think about a family heirloom or a favorite possession. Describe this possession for your classmates. Be sure to include sensory details and vivid adjectives and verbs.

Plan your description here. Use a word web, a Venn diagram, or a list.

CHAPTER 5 TEST Writing Skills

Combine each pair of sentences, using an appropriate conjunction. *Possible responses are given.*

1. The dog whimpered. The back door stood open.
The dog whimpered, yet the back door stood open.

2. Several canoes glided in the water. Mine was one of them.
Several canoes glided in the water, and mine was one of them.

3. I want a snack. We have nothing to eat in the refrigerator.
I want a snack, but we have nothing to eat in the refrigerator.

4. Their vacation will take them to the Grand Canyon. They might go to Yosemite instead.
Their vacation will take them to the Grand Canyon, or they might go to Yosemite instead.

5. The boat sprang a leak. It was immediately pulled from the water.
The boat sprang a leak, so it was immediately pulled from the water.

Expand each sentence, using the words in parentheses. *Possible responses are given.*

6. The bird landed. (exotic, on the uppermost branch, unsteadily)
The exotic bird landed unsteadily on the uppermost branch.

7. The tree crashed. (rotten, onto the forest floor)
The rotten tree crashed onto the forest floor.

8. His car started. (vintage, with a roar)
His vintage car started with a roar.

9. Breakfast is ready. (finally, after two dropped eggs, in spite of many delays)
After two dropped eggs and in spite of many delays, breakfast is finally ready.

10. A peacock strutted. (around the enclosure, elegant, noble)
A peacock, elegant and noble, strutted around the enclosure.

Write true or false for each statement about outlines.

11. An outline is a tool that helps you organize ideas for writing.   true
12. Outlines follow a specific format.   true
13. An outline divides ideas into four categories: main ideas, topics, subtopics, and details.   false
14. Label each main idea with a Roman numeral followed by a period.   true
15. Each subtopic is indented and labeled with a capital letter followed by a period.   true
16. Once an outline is created, it should never be revised.   false

---

Use this section of an outline to answer the questions.

II. Body
  A. Andrew finds a way to get to the school in the next town.
    1. He finds spare parts and fixes an old bicycle.
    2. He convinces his brother to do chores for him by promising to teach his brother everything he learns at school.
    3. He gets his mother's blessing to attend school.
    4. When the other boys ride the 15 miles to school, Andrew goes with them.

17. What would you expect to come before this part of the outline?
(introduction)   conclusion   title

18. What is the subtopic?
Andrew finds a way to get to the school in the next town.

19. From reading the outline, what problem does the main character face?
Andrew wants to go to school but doesn't have a way to get there.

20. What other characters do you learn about in the supporting details?
his brother, his mother, other boys

Write a word from the box that matches each definition.

misunderstand	submarine	postmodern	prepay
superimpose	antibiotic	antitheft	subway
postscript	extraordinary	transcontinental	supersonic

21. a substance that kills or inactivates bacteria   *antibiotic*
22. beyond average   *extraordinary*
23. a short message added after a letter's signature   *postscript*
24. a boat that can go under water   *submarine*
25. pay in advance   *prepay*
26. to understand in the wrong way   *misunderstand*
27. moving faster than the speed of sound   *supersonic*
28. an underground railroad   *subway*
29. across a continent   *transcontinental*
30. to place or lay over something   *superimpose*
31. something that prevents theft   *antitheft*
32. relating to an era after a modern one   *postmodern*

CHAPTER 5 PROMPT **Book Review**

1. Read the prompt carefully.
2. Plan and organize your writing on this page.
3. Write your book review on the back.
4. Revise and proofread your book review.

PROMPT: Review a book you have read recently and about which you have a strong opinion. Be sure to include information that will help readers understand your conclusions and motivate them to follow your recommendation.

Plan your book review here. Use a chart, a story map, a word web, or notes.

Your book review will be graded on how well it

- is planned.
- conveys key information about characters, setting, plot, and theme.
- uses a logical order to summarize and recommend the book.
- provides a sense of conviction and uses an appropriate tone.
- uses precise and persuasive words.
- features a variety of sentence types.
- is free of grammar, spelling, punctuation, and capitalization errors.

Write your book review here. Refer to your plan as you write. Use another sheet of paper if needed.

CHAPTER 6 TEST Writing Skills

Write true or false for each statement about dialogue.

1. Using dialogue can add interest to a story and help develop the characters.   _true_
2. There is no need to start a new paragraph each time the speaker changes.   _false_
3. Use dialogue that shows the personality of the characters.   _true_
4. Short spoken lines can convey strong emotions in a character.   _true_
5. Dialogue can reveal conflict between characters and advance the plot.   _true_
6. Good writers repeatedly use the dialogue tag said in conversations.   _false_

Circle a synonym for the dialogue tag said that best completes each sentence.

7. The snake (laughed (hissed)) at us, "Be careful where you step, children."
8. "No!" ((gasped) sighed) Colin, "Don't go in there! It's haunted!"
9. "Well," she (cooed (hesitated)), holding the money firmly, "we're going to stay right here."
10. Mr. Gray ((chuckled) screamed) as he handed us each a card. "Anyone can do the trick."
11. The prisoner (giggled (muttered)), "I'd have escaped if it weren't for those kids."
12. Looking shyly at her feet, she ((murmured) gushed), "Thank you."
13. The workers (whispered (shouted)), "Watch out for the bus!"
14. I ((giggled) roared), "Ha! I think Mr. Chesney has played another trick on us."

Write yes or no to identify if each line of dialogue is punctuated correctly.

15. "Stop! shouted Harry. "You have the wrong keys."   _no_
16. "When are we going to get the map, asked Charlie."   _no_
17. "I think we should follow the trail on the left," announced Jenna.   _yes_
18. "Look at that shooting star," exclaimed Charlotte, "next to the moon."   _yes_
19. "Derrick asked," When does the show start?   _no_

Write whether the italicized words in each sentence are an example of personification, metaphor, simile, cliché, or hyperbole.

20. We sat around in the waiting room _for a week_.   _hyperbole_
21. The tall grass _stood at attention_.   _personification_
22. Her diamond necklace was _a string of sparkling ice_.   _metaphor_
23. Mike was _a wall_ that our team's offense could not topple.   _metaphor_
24. We all figured _what goes around comes around_ and felt no sympathy for her situation.   _cliché_
25. The cat's tongue is _like wet, rough sandpaper_.   _simile_
26. I wanted our vacation _to last forever_.   _hyperbole_

Write an example of each kind of figurative language for the topic. _Possible responses are given._

27.

clouds

Simile: _Clouds covered the sun like a thick blanket._

Metaphor: _The clouds were tall peaks of fluffy whipped cream._

Hyperbole: _A million clouds scuttled across the sky._

Personification: _A lone cloud wandered across the sun._

Cliché: _Every cloud has a silver lining._

Write true or false for each statement about limericks.

28. Limericks are short, fun, and easy to remember.   _true_
29. Real people are always the subject of limericks.   _false_
30. Limericks feature an ababa rhyme scheme.   _false_
31. The rhyme scheme often helps a limerick tell a story.   _true_
32. All the syllables in a limerick are unstressed.   _false_
33. The rhythm in a limerick is anapestic rhythm.   _true_
34. To determine a poem's rhythm, read it aloud and listen for words with greater stress.   _true_

Write a word to complete each pair of lines from a limerick. _Possible responses are given._

35. A flea and a fly in a flue, / Were caught, so what could they _do_ ?
36. There once was a bird in the sand, / Who agreed to eat out of my _hand_ .
37. There sat a small boy on the floor, / Unwilling to do one more _chore_ .
38. She found a screwdriver, / And freed the _survivor_ .
39. There once was a puppy named Sprite, / Whose bark was much worse than his _bite_ .
40. He snarled and he growled, / He hissed and he _howled_ .

Name _____ Date _____

CHAPTER 6 PROMPT Creative Writing: Fantasy Fiction

1. Read the prompt carefully.
2. Plan and organize your writing on this page.
3. Write your fantasy story on the back.
4. Revise and proofread your fantasy story.

PROMPT: Imagine that two friends are able to travel through time to a different era. Write a fantasy story that tells about their adventure. Be sure to include the features of fantasy fiction in your story.

Plan your fantasy story here. Use a story map, a time line, a word web, or notes.

Your fantasy story will be graded on how well it

· is planned.
· includes characters, a setting, and other characteristics of fantasy fiction.
· uses a good plot structure with a clear beginning, middle, and ending.
· features a lively, suspenseful voice.
· uses original word choice.
· uses literary techniques such as flashback, foreshadowing, and dialogue.
· is free of grammar, usage, punctuation, capitalization, and spelling errors.

Write your fantasy story here. Refer to your plan as you write. Use another sheet of paper if needed.

CHAPTER 7 TEST Writing Skills

Use the information in parentheses to write a noun suffix word that completes each sentence.

1. The crowd winced as the _____skater_____ fell to the ice. (one who skates)
2. Being on the team is a big _____commitment_____ of time. (state of being committed)
3. The _____florist_____ arranged a lovely bouquet of tulips. (one who arranges flowers)
4. My grandfather enjoys his _____retirement_____. (state of being retired)
5. Dan is celebrating his recent job _____promotion_____. (state of being promoted)
6. There is no excuse for their level of _____tardiness_____. (state of being tardy)

Write the word made by adding a verb suffix (-ate, -en, -ify, -ize) to each word.

7. active   _activate_
8. hard   _harden_
9. identity   _identify_
10. simple   _simplify_
11. less   _lessen_
12. motor   _motorize_
13. motive   _motivate_
14. idol   _idolize_

Underline the suffix in each word and write whether it is a noun or verb suffix.

15. vigilance   _noun_
16. accentuate   _verb_
17. curiosity   _noun_
18. conviction   _noun_
19. clarify   _verb_
20. citizenship   _noun_
21. cellist   _noun_
22. familiarize   _verb_

Circle the letter of the choice that best completes each sentence.

23. Direct quotations are
   a. only the exact words a person speaks.
   b. only the exact words a person writes.
   c. the exact words a person speaks or writes.
24. A direct quotation may
   a. reinforce an important point in an expository essay.
   b. leave a strong impact on the reader.
   c. do both of the above.
25. The person who said or wrote the words in a direct quotation is called
   a. the source.
   b. the impact.
   c. the celebrity.
26. Usually, quotations are punctuated just like
   a. dialogue.
   b. declarative sentences.
   c. both of the above.

Write yes or no to identify whether each quotation is written correctly.

27. Plato once said, "Ignorance is the root and stem of all evil."   _yes_
28. "Marie Curie said, Be less curious about people and more curious about ideas."   _no_
29. The poet Euripides claimed that "Cleverness is not wisdom."   _yes_
30. Mark asked, "Was it Plato who said, Necessity . . . the mother of invention?"   _no_
31. "Action speaks louder than words," said Mark Twain, but not nearly as often.   _no_

Use the reference sources from the box to complete the outline.

almanac/yearbook   atlas   periodical   encyclopedia

32. I. Library Reference Sources
   A. _almanac/yearbook_
      1. annual facts
      2. statistics
      3. news articles
   B. _atlas_
      1. maps
      2. other geographic data
   C. _encyclopedia_
      1. articles on specific topics
      2. alphabetically arranged topics
   D. _periodical_
      1. up-to-date articles
      2. information published periodically

Write the letter of the source from the box that is best used to research each topic.

a. almanac   b. atlas   c. encyclopedia   d. catalog

33. the annual rainfall of Japan for the last decade   _a_
34. a detailed biography of Thomas Jefferson   _d_
35. a list of accomplishments of Louis Pasteur   _c_
36. books about Impressionism   _d_
37. major mountain ranges in Asia   _b_
38. maps of North America   _b_
39. a brief history of the California Gold Rush   _c_
40. major metropolitan areas in Germany   _b_

Your expository article will be graded on how well it

• is planned.
• has a clear focus and provides factual information.
• includes an interesting introduction, a body, and a summarizing conclusion.
• expresses a confident voice.
• uses formal language.
• features concise sentences and presents information in a variety of ways.
• is free of grammar, usage, punctuation, capitalization, and spelling errors.

Write your expository article here. Refer to your plan as you write. Use another sheet of paper if needed.

CHAPTER 7 PROMPT Expository Article

1. Read the prompt carefully.
2. Plan and organize your writing on this page.
3. Write your expository article on the back.
4. Revise and proofread your expository article.

PROMPT: Think of a hobby or sport that you know something about. Write an expository article that tells readers more about this topic.

Plan your expository article here. Use an outline, an idea web, or notes.

CHAPTER 8 TEST Writing Skills

Write the letter of the description that matches each term.

1. Works Cited page — **c** — a. each source listed on a Works Cited page
2. parenthetical notation — **d** — b. where most source information is found
3. citing sources — **f** — c. a complete list of sources used in a report
4. plagiarism — **e** — d. citing a source at the end of a sentence
5. title and copyright pages — **b** — e. claiming someone's writing as your own
6. entry — **a** — f. showing your writing is credible

Write book, periodical, Web site, or encyclopedia to identify each source.

7. "Locomotives." Encyclopedia Britannica. 2010 edition. — **encyclopedia**

8. Markum, Michael. Raising Homing Pigeons.
   Los Angeles, CA: Streeter Books, 2005. — **book**

9. Suchala, Anthony. "Deciphering Hieroglyphics."
   3 August 2011 <www.ancientegypt.edu>. — **Web site**

10. Jensen, Benjamin. Battles of the American Civil War.
    Philadelphia, PA: Freedom Press, 2010. — **book**

11. Davidson, Sally. "Visiting Rome." Vacation Times
    15 September 2008: 110–115. — **periodical**

12. "American Standard Poodles." New Book of Knowledge.
    2011 edition. — **encyclopedia**

Write whether each sentence is in natural or inverted order.

13. Behind the red door waits the final clue. — **inverted**
14. On the river during the summer are many boats. — **inverted**
15. The monument is open every night this summer. — **natural**
16. At the top of the dead tree is an eagle's nest. — **inverted**
17. That sweater is going on sale tomorrow. — **natural**
18. Over the heads of the crowd flew the hawk. — **inverted**

Write whether each sentence is declarative, interrogative, or exclamatory.

19. The traffic was heavy all the way to the coast. — **declarative**
20. Can anybody see the ocean yet? — **interrogative**
21. Hey, the waves crashing on the beach are enormous! — **exclamatory**
22. Sandpipers and seagulls patrolled the water's edge. — **declarative**
23. We watched the waves crash and roll out to sea again. — **declarative**
24. What an amazing day this has been! — **exclamatory**

Rewrite each sentence as indicated in parentheses. *Possible responses are given.*

25. Crows are intelligent creatures. (exclamatory)
    What intelligent creatures crows are!

26. Oleander shrubs are poisonous. (interrogative)
    Did you know that oleander shrubs are poisonous?

Write a modifier from the box to complete each sentence.

| Suddenly | After the rainstorm | Because he was afraid |
| Unfortunately | Along the beach | Once the sun had set |

27. *Because he was afraid* , Ian called out to locate the others.
28. *Suddenly* , the audience burst into applause.
29. *After the rainstorm* , the flowers in the garden grew tall.
30. *Along the beach* , we examined each tide pool.
31. *Unfortunately* , I did not have the winning ticket.
32. *Once the sun had set* , the temperature dropped considerably.

Underline the word with the incorrect connotation in each sentence. Then write the word from the box that has the correct connotation.

| cautious | famous | intelligent | melody | odor | ordeal |

33. Albert Einstein is a notorious scientist. — **famous**
34. His whistling was a pleasant racket as we worked. — **melody**
35. The plane crash was an adventure he didn't want to relive. — **ordeal**
36. Chimpanzees seem nearly as brilliant as humans. — **intelligent**
37. His paranoid actions show that he is aware of the dangers. — **cautious**
38. The aroma of rotting garbage came from the alley. — **odor**

Circle the word in each pair that has a positive connotation.

39. smirking (smiling)
40. (fragrant) smelly
41. (weeping) sniveling
42. stingy (thrifty)
43. rot (decompose)
44. (persistent) stubborn
45. fanatic (enthusiast)
46. (relaxed) lazy
47. conceited (proud)
48. (curious) nosy

CHAPTER 8 PROMPT Research Report

1. Read the prompt carefully.
2. Choose a topic and conduct research.
3. Plan and organize your writing on this page.
4. Write your research report on the back.
5. Revise and proofread your research report.

PROMPT: What aspect of ancient Rome interests you most? Write a research report to show what you have learned about this topic. Be sure to include a thesis statement.

Use your notes to plan your research report here. Use an outline or a KWL chart.

Your research report will be graded on how well it

- is planned.
- clearly focuses on one topic.
- presents logically ordered paragraphs with main ideas supported by details.
- projects a confident voice.
- expresses ideas using formal language.
- includes different sentence styles and varied ways of providing information.
- is free of grammar, usage, punctuation, capitalization, and spelling errors.

Write your research report here. Refer to your plan as you write. Use another sheet of paper if needed.

Grade 6

VIE Section	EIE Lesson
NOUNS	
1.1	1
1.2	2
1.3	4
1.4	5–6
1.5	7–9
1.6	7–9
1.7	10–11
1.8	12
1.9	13–14
1.10	15
1.11	16
Noun Review	17
Noun Challenge	17
PRONOUNS	
2.1	18–19
2.2	20
2.3	21
2.4	22–23
2.5	24–26
2.6	27–29
2.7	29–30
2.8	31
2.9	32
2.10	33–34
2.11	35
Pronoun Review	36
Pronoun Challenge	36
ADJECTIVES	
3.1	37–38
3.2	39
3.3	40
3.4	41–42
3.5	43
3.6	44
3.7	45
3.8	46–47
3.9	48
3.10	49
3.11	50
Adjective Review	51
Adjective Challenge	51

VIE Section	EIE Lesson
VERBS	
4.1	52–53
4.2	54
4.3	55–56
4.4	57, 59, 61
4.5	58–59, 61
4.6	60–61
4.7	62, 66
4.8	63, 66
4.9	64–66
4.10	67–73
4.11	74
4.12	75
4.13	76
4.14	77
4.15	78
4.16	79
Verb Review	80
Verb Challenge	80
ADVERBS	
5.1	81–83
5.2	84–85
5.3	86–87
5.4	88
5.5	89
5.6	90
Adverb Review	91
Adverb Challenge	91
SENTENCES	
6.1	92–94
6.2	95–96
6.3	97–99
6.4	100–101
6.5	102–103
6.6	104–105
6.7	106–107
6.8	108
6.9	109–110
6.10	111–112
6.11	113
Sentence Review	114
Sentence Challenge	114

VIE Section	EIE Lesson
CONJUNCTIONS, INTERJECTIONS, PUNCTUATION, AND CAPITALIZATION	
7.1	115–118
7.2	119
7.3	122
7.4	123–127
7.5	128
7.6	129
7.7	130
7.8	131
7.9	132
7.10	133
7.11	134
Section 7 Review	135
Section 7 Challenge	135
DIAGRAMMING	
8.1	136
8.2	137
8.3	138
8.4	139
8.5	140
8.6	141
8.7	142
8.8	143
8.9	144
8.10	145
8.11	146
Diagramming Review	146
Diagramming Challenge	146

Grade 7

VIE Section	EIE Lesson
NOUNS	
1.1	1
1.2	2
1.3	3
1.4	4–7
1.5	8–9
1.6	10–12
Noun Review	13
Noun Challenge	13
ADJECTIVES	
2.1	14–15
2.2	16–17
2.3	18–19
2.4	20–21
2.5	22–23
Adjective Review	24
Adjective Challenge	24
PRONOUNS	
3.1	25–26
3.2	27–28
3.3	29–31
3.4	32
3.5	33
3.6	34
3.7	35
3.8	36–37
3.9	38
3.10	39
3.11	40
Pronoun Review	41
Pronoun Challenge	41
VERBS	
4.1	42–44
4.2	45–46
4.3	47
4.4	48–49
4.5	50
4.6	51–53
4.7	54–55
4.8	56
4.9	57
4.10	58–61
4.11	62–66
Verb Review	67
Verb Challenge	67

VIE Section	EIE Lesson
VERBALS	
5.1	68
5.2	69–70
5.3	71–72
5.4	73–74
5.5	75
5.6	76
5.7	77
5.8	78
5.9	79
5.10	80
5.11	81
Verbal Review	82
Verbal Challenge	82
ADVERBS	
6.1	83
6.2	84–85
6.3	86
6.4	87–90
6.5	91–92
Adverb Review	93
Adverb Challenge	93
PREPOSITIONS	
7.1	94–95
7.2	96–97
7.3	98
7.4	99
7.5	100
7.6	101
Preposition Review	102
Preposition Challenge	102
SENTENCES	
8.1	103–106
8.2	107
8.3	108, 110
8.4	109–110
8.5	111–112
8.6	113
8.7	114
8.8	115
8.9	116
8.10	117
8.11	118–122
Sentence Review	123
Sentence Challenge	123

VIE Section	EIE Lesson
CONJUNCTIONS AND INTERJECTIONS	
9.1	124
9.2	125
9.3	126
9.4	127
9.5	128
9.6	129
Section 9 Review	130
Section 9 Challenge	130
PUNCTUATION AND CAPITALIZATION	
10.1	131–135
10.2	136–137
10.3	138
10.4	139
10.5	140
Section 10 Review	141
Section 10 Challenge	141
DIAGRAMMING	
11.1	142
11.2	143
11.3	144
11.4	145
11.5	146
11.6	147
11.7	148
11.8	149
11.9	150
11.10	151
11.11	152
Diagramming Review	152
Diagramming Challenge	152

VIE sections refer to 2011 edition; EIE lessons refer to 2008 edition.